The Autumn House
of Contemporary
American Poetry

The Autumn House Anthology of Contemporary American Poetry

edited by
Sue Ellen Thompson

PITTSBURGH

Autumn House Press Staff
Executive Director: Michael Simms
Community Outreach Director: Michael Wurster
Minority Outreach Coordinator: Eva Simms
Website and Newsletter Editor: Matthew Hamman
Editorial Consultant: Ziggy Edwards
Media Consultant: Jan Beatty
Contributing Editor: Susan Hutton

ISBN: 1-932870-06-7
Library of Congress Control Number: 2005926056

Landscape with Onlooker

One night shy of full, the moon
looks not lonesome shining through the trees, but replete

with the thoughtless sensuality of well-being.
A chill in the air? No, under the air, like water

under a swimmer. The unsteadfast leaves grow crisp
and brittle, the better to fall away. Some nights

fear, like rising water in a well, fills these hours—
the dead of night, as the phrase goes, when you quicken

and the dank metallic sweat beads like a vile dew.
But tonight you stand at your window, framed and calm,

and the air's as sweet as a freshly peeled orange.
There's a moon on the lake, and another in the sky.

William Matthews

The Autumn House Poetry Series

Michael Simms, editor

OneOnOne by Jack Myers
Snow White Horses: Selected Poems 1973-1988 by Ed Ochester
The Leaving: New and Selected Poems by Sue Ellen Thompson
Dirt by Jo McDougall
Fire in the Orchard by Gary Margolis
Just Once: New and Previous Poems by Samuel Hazo
The White Calf Kicks by Deborah Slicer
  Winner of the 2003 Autumn House Poetry Prize,
  selected by Naomi Shihab Nye

The Divine Salt by Peter Blair
The Dark Takes Aim by Julie Suk
Satisfied with Havoc by Jo McDougall
Half Lives by Richard Jackson
Not God After All by Gerald Stern (with drawings by Sheba Sharrow)
Dear Good Naked Morning by Ruth L. Schwartz
  Winner of the 2004 Autumn House Poetry Prize,
  selected by Alicia Ostriker

A Flight to Elsewhere by Samuel Hazo
Collected Poems by Patricia Dobler
The Autumn House Anthology of Contemporary American Poetry
  edited by Sue Ellen Thompson

Contents

Introduction: A Poetry of Clarity and Depth

I have always preferred poems that, like the deep green pools in a mountain stream, combine surface clarity with depths whose mysteries are revealed only upon sustained or repeated visits. It has also been my experience as a teacher that students are more willing to work at understanding and appreciating a poem when something about it—a compelling narrative, the inventive use of language, an arresting image, or its ability to trigger a profound emotional response—immediately focuses their attention.

This was my primary criterion in selecting the poems for this anthology. I also looked for poems that would provoke lively discussions in the classroom, perhaps because of their unusual approach to a familiar subject or for their dazzling technique, whether carefully crafted or heedless and headlong. Not surprisingly, I found that love and desire, family relationships, and death remain American poets' most enduring subjects. But that's where the similarities end.

While I couldn't help being drawn first to those poets whose work has sustained and inspired me over the years—William Matthews, Sharon Olds, Philip Levine, Robert Hass, Stephen Dunn, and Jane Kenyon, to name a few—I was determined to discover younger and/or less established voices as well. I was delighted when the recommendations of friends and the editors at Autumn House Press led me to read the work of Catherine Barnett, Nick Flynn, Terrance Hayes, Joy Katz, Maurice Kilwein Guevara, G.E. Patterson, Tracy K. Smith, and Mark Wunderlich for the first time. As someone who spent 14 summers at the Bread Loaf Writers' Conference, I wanted to revisit some of the poets whose work I'd first heard there in the 1980s and early 90s: Andrea Budy, John Canaday, Judith Ortiz Cofer, Steven Cramer, Frank X. Gaspar, Andrew Hudgins, David Huddle, Sydney Lea, Judson Mitcham, Robert Pack, Lawrence Raab, Sherod Santos, and Sidney Wade.

I welcomed the opportunity to re-enter the lyric hush of Jane Hirshfield, the wild inventiveness of Mary Ruefle, and

Baron Wormser's quirky, moving narratives. I also made a point of reading poets whose names I kept hearing without knowing what all the fuss was about—were they really that good? I can tell you without reservation that in the case of Bob Hicok, Campbell McGrath, and Tony Hoagland, yes, they're really that good. As a faithful attendee at the famed Sunken Garden Poetry Festival in Farmington, Connecticut, for many years, I asked myself which poets had read poems that remained with me to this day, and the names of Tom Lux, Billy Collins, Linda McCarriston, Marie Howe, Maxine Kumin, and Hayden Carruth immediately came to mind. I was, of course, honored to include the poets whose work has been published over the last six years by Autumn House Press, a list that now includes Peter Blair, Patricia Dobler, Samuel Hazo, Richard Jackson, Gary Margolis, Jo McDougall, Jack Myers, Ed Ochester, Ruth L. Schwartz, Deborah Slicer, Gerald Stern, and Julie Suk.

When I think back over the more than 250 books of poetry I've read in the last 10 months, a few things stand out. One is that free verse continues to reign, although I have included a number of poems exhibiting American poets' continuing fascination with rhyme and form. I've never felt completely comfortable with prose poems and have included relatively few of these, although Robert Hass's stunning "A Story About the Body" and Joy Katz's "The Lettuce Bag" are among my favorites. Something else that struck me in my reading was the extent to which ethnic and minority voices have changed the language traditionally associated with poetry. One need only read Tim Seibles' "Four Takes of a Similar Situation" or Maurice Kilwein Guevara's "Doña Josefina Counsels Doña Concepción Before Entering Sears" to see what I'm talking about. Love has extended its arms beyond romance—read Doug Anderson's "New Woman Blues" or Jan Beatty's "Modern Love." And that 50s film known as "The American Childhood" is now more likely to be laced with danger and violence (Dorianne Laux's "Family Stories," Terrance Hayes's "Pine").

The majority of the poems in this volume are short, a page or less in length. This is partly due to the restrictions of space in an anthology where almost a hundred American poets are represented. But I also made my selections with the classroom in mind. The challenge of plumbing a poem's emotional depths or untangling its metaphorical complexities can often be too overwhelming when the poem itself runs on for pages. One of the few exceptions here is B. H. Fairchild's "Rave On"—a longer poem that, when I heard the poet read it in the barn at The Frost Place in Franconia, New Hampshire, last summer, conveyed its tale of teenage recklessness with such intensity that I could not bear to leave it out.

What seemed at first like an overwhelming task received a significant boost from a few well-known poets who signed on to the project early: Wendell Berry, who went out of his way to help despite never having met or heard of me; Phil Levine, who provided me with the new and exciting work represented here; Sebastian Matthews, who made sure that I was able to include four of my favorite poems by his father, the late William Matthews; and Gerald Stern, a new friend whose phone calls were always welcome. Their support gave me the confidence I needed to approach the many publishers whose authors are represented here, and who were generous enough to waive their fees for a relatively new, nonprofit press. I would like to thank Melanie Greenhouse, Susan Hutton, and Leslie McGrath for sharing their poetry libraries, and Mike Simms, my editor at Autumn House, for his ongoing faith in me. Finally, I would like to beg forgiveness from the poets—many of them my friends—whom I was unable to include. May they and all the readers of this book find here the kind of poetry that confirms, consoles, surprises, and illuminates—poems that, in the words of Stephen Dunn, provide us with "a better way to be alone."

Sue Ellen Thompson
January 2005

Doug Anderson

Doug Anderson has written three books of poems, of which *The Moon Reflected Fire* won the Kate Tufts Discovery Award, and *Blues for Unemployed Secret Police* a production grant from the Eric Matthieu King Fund of the Academy of American Poets. He teaches at the University of Connecticut and is the recent recipient of a Pushcart Prize.

Blues

Love won't behave. I've tried
all my life to keep it chained up.
Especially after I gave up pleading.
I don't mean the woman,
but the love itself. Truth is,
I don't know where it comes from,
why it comes, or where it goes.
It either leaves me feeling the knife
of my first breath
or hangdog and sick
at someone else's unstoppable
and as the blues song says,
can't sit down, stand up, lay down pain.

Right now I want it.
I'm like a country who can't remember the last war.
Well, that's not strictly true.
It's just been too long.
Too long and my heart is like
a house for sale in a lot full of high weeds.
I want to go down to New Orleans
and find the Santeria woman
who will light a whole table full of candles
and moan things, place a cigar
and a shot of whiskey in front of Chango's picture
and kiss the blue dead Jesus on the wall.
I want something.
Used to be I'd get a bottle
and drink until the lights went out
but now I carry my pain around everywhere I go
because I'm afraid
I might put it down somewhere and lose it.
I've grown tender about my mileage.
My teeth are like Stonehenge and my tongue
is like an old druid fallen in a ditch.
A soul is like a shrimper's net they never haul up
and it's full of everything:
A tire. A shark. An old harpoon.
A kid's plastic bucket.
An empty half-pint.
A broken guitar string.
A pair of ballerina's shoes with the ribbons tangled
in an anchor chain.
And the net gets heavier until the boat
starts to go down with it and you say,
God, what is going on.
In this condition I say love is a good thing.
I'm ready to capsize.
I can't even see the shoreline.
I haven't seen a seagull in three days.
I'm ready to drink salt water,
go overboard and start swimming.
Suffice it to say I want to get into the bathtub
with the Santeria woman and steam myself pure again.
The priest that blesses the water may be bored.

Hung over. He may not even bless it,
just tell people he did. It doesn't matter.
What the Santeria woman puts on it with her mind
makes it like a holy mirror.
You can float a shrimp boat on it.
The spark that jumps between her mind
and the priest's empty act
is what makes the whole thing light up
like an oilslick on fire against a sunset over Oaxaca.
So if I just step out into it.
If I just step off the high dive over a pool
that may or may not have water in it,
that act is enough
to connect the two poles of something
and make a long blue arc.
I don't have a clue about any of this.
Come on over here and love me.
I used to say that drunk.
Now I'm stark raving sober
and I say, *Come on over here and love me.*

Xin Loi

The man and woman, Vietnamese,
come up the hill,
carry something slung between them on a bamboo mat,
unroll it at my feet:
the child, iron gray, long dead,
flies have made him home.
His wounds are from artillery shrapnel.
The man and the woman look as if they are cast
from the same iron as their dead son,
so rooted are they in the mud.
There is nothing to say,
nothing in my medical bag, nothing in my mind.
A monsoon cloud hangs above,
its belly torn open on a mountain.

Itinerary

In Arizona coming across the border with dope in my tires
and for a month tasting the rubber in what I smoked.
With a college degree and a trunk full of the war.
Working in one place long enough to get the money
to stay high for a month and then moving on. Drinking a quart
of whiskey, then getting up, going to work the next day.
A little speed to burn off the hangover. In the afternoon
a few reds to take the edge off the speed and then to the bar.
At the bar, the madonna in the red mirror. My arm around her
waist and the shared look that said: The World Is Coming Apart,
Let Us Hold One Another Against The Great Noise of It All.
Waking with her the next morning and seeing her older,
her three-year-old wandering in and staring with a little worm
of confusion in his forehead. The banner on the bedroom wall
that read ACCEPTANCE in large block letters.
At night going out to unpack the war from my trunk.
A seabag full of jungle utilities that stank of rice-paddy silt
and blood. To remind myself it happened. Lost them somewhere
between Tucson and Chicago. Days up on a scaffold
working gable-end trim with Mexicans who came through
a hole in the fence the night before. Rednecks who paid
me better than them. Laughing at jokes that weren't funny
to keep the job. At a New Braunfels Oktoberfest getting in a fight
with a black army private who wore a button that read,
Kiss me I'm German. Don't remember what the fight was about.
Back in Tucson. Up against the patrol car being cuffed
for something I don't remember doing. Leaving the state.
Back with Jill in San Antonio. Finding her in the same bar,
driving her home in her car because she was too drunk.
The flashers on behind me and the flashlight in my face.
In those gentle days, they drove you home. Stealing Jill's car
out of the impound lot next morning to avoid the fee.
Later sitting buck-naked across from one another at the breakfast
table wondering who we were. This woman who wanted to live
with a man who had dreams so bad he would stay awake for days
until the dreams started to bleed through into real time
and he had to go back the other way into sleep to escape them.
Who woke with the shakes before dawn
and went to the kitchen for beer. Later walking down
to the barrio slowly, without talking, our hips touching.

The Mexican restaurant, a pink adobe strung with chili pepper
Christmas lights the year round. Inside, the bullfight calendar
with the matador's corpse laid out on a slab, naked and blue
with a red cloth across his loins and the inevitable grieving virgin
kneeling at his side. The wound in the same place the centurion
euthanized Christ with his spear. Our laughing then not laughing
because laughter and grief are born joined at the hip.
An old Mexican woman fanning herself at the cash register,
her wattles trembling. *Recordar*: to remember, to pass again
through the heart. Corazón. Coraggio. Core.

New Woman Blues

Inside my white armor I am covered with hair and lice.
I haven't bathed for so long I no longer stink
but give off the odor of perfumed catacombs.
When I open my mouth to say I love you
spiders run over my lower lip and down into my beard.
There is a mouse tail hanging out of the corner of my mouth.
I want our first moments alone to be messy.
I want you to feel all the terror of me you will ever feel, now.
If you take me as I am I will never disappoint you.
I wake at night and cut my dreams into paste-ups;
the snack snack snack of the scissors will test you.
I am violent and unpredictable.
I eat snake heads.
I have invited my beast to come live in my skin,
look out through my eyes.
I deny nothing.
I have no secrets.
I will give you more truth than you ever wanted.
I fuck like the last day on earth.
When your parents come to visit
I will lead them into the room which is always in darkness
and there under the black light
show them my collection of missionaries
from all over the world.

When I say I love you
great greased cogs begin to turn
down below the sewers.
With me you have always more than you wanted.
Your leprosy is nothing to me.
Your psychotic episodes,
your collection of Filipino war knives,
nothing; your vibrating bras
ringed with Italian Christmas lights,
nothing compared to the vise-grip I'll put on your heart.
Your legs will shake so badly waiting for me to come home
you'll scarcely notice they get worse when I'm there.
I drink a glass of blood every morning.
The Jehovah's Witnesses will not knock on my door.
Now I've told you everything.
No surprises down the road, no disappointments.
I'm sorry I've done all the talking.
That's the hardest thing of all you'll have to bear.

Catherine Barnett

Catherine Barnett's *Into Perfect Spheres Such Holes Are Pierced* won the 2003 Beatrice Hawley Award and the 2004 Glasgow Prize for Emerging Writers. Her poems have appeared in *The Iowa Review, The Massachusetts Review, The Washington Post, Barrow Street, Interim, The Hat,* and *Pleiades*, among other publications. She won a 2005 Pushcart Prize and teaches creative writing at New York University.

photo by Emily Barnett Highleyman

Evening in the Garden

At the edge of the field where rare species
had overgrown a corner of the school playground,
some kind souls built a garden.

They made a spiral path with sea glass
the children separated by color,
one boy sorting each kind of green

from every other. I looked hard for something
to like because I thought my sister,
leaning against the marble wall where her daughters' names

were carved, might want me to find beauty there.
I saw her youngest daughter was named first
and I thought oh!

I never noticed there were two B's in her name,
that must be why the marble looks so strange—
alliteration—

or the lettering, or the stone itself,
or the ledge against which
lay the small shiny whisk broom

I admired, too,
until my sister began sweeping the path,
until my son took the broom from her

and began sweeping things not meant to be swept,
the edge of the flower beds raised up in a row,
the benches, all made out of the same enormous stone.

Refusal

The god of footprints accepts no prayers, he's
a cheap and sweaty god who must have lost his mind.
It's dark with my back turned but what else is there to do?
Fine, fine, yes, yes, she's surviving,
don't ask me again.
We only hummed with the rabbi
but my son heard us sing *die, die, die, die.*
He's just turned four and on his face
there's a strange pleasure when he says *died,*
as if he'd seen a door in a mountain—
but there's only my sister's house
and the string of profanity
I tie to the empty chairs we drag behind us.
And every window is a curse,
something to break that shatters.
The two birds we saw on our usual walk
were blue and gold, they flew
too close to the ground.
Upstairs the girls' room does not change
and I sleep there now, when I come to visit.
I prefer the high bed, but I can't say why.

Family Reunion

My father scolded us all for refusing his liquor.
He kept buying tequila, and steak for the grill,
until finally we joined him, making margaritas,
cutting the fat off the bone.

When he saw how we drank, my sister
shredding the black labels into her glass
while his remaining grandchildren
dragged their thin bunk bed mattresses

first out to the lawn to play
then farther up the field to sleep next to her,
I think it was then he changed,
something in him died. He's gentler now,

quiet, losing weight though every night
he eats the same ice cream he always ate
only now he's not drinking,
he doesn't fall asleep with the spoon in his hand,

he waits for my mother to come lie down with him.

Jan Beatty

Jan Beatty's new collection of poems, *Boneshaker,* was published in Spring 2002 by the University of Pittsburgh Press. Her first book, *Mad River,* won the Agnes Lynch Starrett Prize from the University of Pittsburgh Press, and her chapbook, *Ravenous,* won the 1995 State Street Chapbook Prize.

My Father Teaches Me Light

7 AM I get the call you have died.
To get to the hospital before my mother &
sister & their arsenal of sorrows:
I rush to your bedside, nothing
has ever been this important.
I'm standing in the shaft of morning,
the light through the window splitting
the room in half: the dead body of you/
the living me. I talk to the air, tell you
it will be alright, look to the ceiling
for floating bodies: there is no you there.
The part of me in your heart, where is it?
And what is the body now, old empty house?
You said you'd come to haunt me,
pound your cane on the floorboards,
I'd hear you say, *Pay your bills!*
I hang your cane on my bedroom door,

I wear your VFW jacket & sometimes
old men stop me to make sure I'm not
mocking the War. I want to tell them: You
were the one who spun me into the fire
of myself; I am the one you left behind,
the one you saved while you were here.

My Father Teaches Me Desire

Once it starts you can't stop it:
My father leans into it like a hunchback
at the particle-board table in the light
of our kitchen, arranging his little world:
Vidalia with paring knife; Iron City next
to French's; open sardine tin/no plate.

His left hand grabs the onion/the right
slashes a fat slice/the right dips into
the briny swamp of sardine/lifts one
by the tail/down to the French's/then
plunges it headfirst into his cavernous mouth.

Crunch of Vidalia, then pump an Iron, and
we are livin now, baby, we are home—
me watching my Dad from the dining room,
the grunt and slosh of it all, thinking,
*My god, he's eating the head—where
are its eyes?*

What world is this? He's god and brute,
half quake/half precision, what kind of man
can stare down the milky eye of the sardine
sans flinch, then sever its head with
those same incisors he grew in his mother's belly?

Now he's starting again, reaching
for the onion, two-fisted and ravenous,
king of kings in this 6X6 tabernacle,
he's the holy spirit of torque and focus,
and this is more action than
I've ever seen in church.

I'm standing here at age 12, learning
that sweet seduction of revulsion/desire,
I'm learning real good that the guy I want
to marry is the one who can do the worst
thing without blinking, a man who eats life
raw, the heads of things—and what else
won't scare him?

Oh Father, oh terrible primate, I am one of you.
Together we can skin the rabbit, stuff
the apple in the pig's mouth, in this kitchen
there is so much I don't know yet:
That I can write this poem.
That I will want to die many times in this life.
That in ten years I will drive back to this house,
to this kitchen, looking for your glasses.
I'll drive back to you at the funeral home
and gently place them on your face
in the casket, with no flash
or fanfare, just the music
of my heart playing:
too soon,
too soon.

My Father Teaches Me Longing

Empty eye of your onyx ring where
the diamond used to be; iron tack-hammer,
wooden cane, hat, hat—things I
dream on to conjure you back: thick

knuckles of your freckled hands, quick
laugh, Old Spice & Beeman's gum, your
life of work, work—everywhere, *love*—
over me, through, a wash of bloom, I'm
crossing Morewood, I'm the flood
of students, rolling buses, I pass
a tulip path and there you are:
Yellow tulip, singular, brutal fire,
is it here I find my foothold?
Pin of light that curses & saves.

Modern Love

Early evening, five minutes before
you're due home, I slam the dishes
in the dishwasher, squeeze rivers
of 409 onto the kitchen floor and
counters, smear it white with too many
paper towels, check the clock, listen
for the doorbell of your arriving—
Love, this is not my dreamscape,
my answer to romance's longing—but Love,
still I grab old food from the refrigerator
and sail it into the trash, call for
take-out with the breathy voice of
a woman in want—burritos again,
with enough jalapeño to make our eyes
water; Strange new world this shape
of our love: the details of our lives
stacked in piles of tabloids, month-
old pretzels in their lonely bag, and yes,
the paint peeling off the porch since spring,
no time now to wash the clothes. I do
the only thing a woman in love can:
clear papers off the bed with a wide sweep,
slide in the video, pour the soft drinks,
so we can eat in our element, our little city;

so we can tear open time to find the heart,
heart enough for us to fill our bellies and
fill our bodies with each other until
we surface to ourselves again, until we're
the only ones here tonight, and the look
in your eyes looking at me is the beautiful
sight, and my only complaints are two:
that I didn't make myself ready
for you sooner in life, that
I can't give better,
love you more.

Wendell Berry

Wendell Berry, the author of more than 30 books of poetry, fiction, and essays, lives and farms with his wife, Tanya Berry, in Kentucky.

The Current

Having once put his hand into the ground,
seeding there what he hopes will outlast him,
a man has made a marriage with his place,
and if he leaves it his flesh will ache to go back.
His hand has given up its birdlife in the air.
It has reached into the dark like a root
and begun to wake, quick and mortal, in timelessness,
a flickering sap coursing upward into his head
so that he sees the old tribespeople bend
in the sun, digging with sticks, the forest opening
to receive their hills of corn, squash, and beans,
their lodges and graves, and closing again.
He is made their descendant, what they left
in the earth rising into him like a seasonal juice.

And he sees the bearers of his own blood arriving,
the forest burrowing into the earth as they come,
their hands gathering the stones up into walls,
and relaxing, the stones crawling back into the ground
to lie still under the black wheels of machines.
The current flowing to him through the earth
flows past him, and he sees one descended from him,
a young man who has reached into the ground,
his hand held in the dark as by a hand.

Creation Myth

This is a story handed down.
It is about the old days when Bill
and Florence and a lot of their kin
lived in the little tin-roofed house
beside the woods, below the hill.
Mornings, they went up the hill
to work, Florence to the house,
the men and boys to the field.
Evenings, they all came home again.
There would be talk then and laughter
and taking of ease around the porch
while the summer night closed.
But one night, McKinley, Bill's young brother,
stayed away late, and it was dark
when he started down the hill.
Not a star shone, not a window.
What he was going down into was
the dark, only his footsteps sounding
to prove he trod the ground. And Bill
who had got up to cool himself,
thinking and smoking, leaning on
the jamb of the open front door,
heard McKinley coming down,
and heard his steps beat faster

as he came, for McKinley felt the pasture's
darkness joined to all the rest
of darkness everywhere. It touched
the depths of woods and sky and grave.
In that huge dark, things that usually
stayed put might get around, as fish
in pond or slue get loose in flood.
Oh, things could be coming close
that never had come close before.
He missed the house and went on down
and crossed the draw and pounded on
where the pasture widened on the other side,
lost then for sure. Propped in the door,
Bill heard him circling, a dark star
in the dark, breathing hard, his feet
blind on the little reality
that was left. Amused, Bill smoked
his smoke, and listened. He knew where
McKinley was, though McKinley didn't.
Bill smiled in the darkness to himself,
and let McKinley run until his steps
approached something really to fear:
the quarry pool. Bill quit his pipe
then, opened the screen, and stepped out,
barefoot, on the warm boards. "McKinley!"
he said, and laid the field out clear
under McKinley's feet, and placed
the map of it in his head.

They Sit Together on the Porch

They sit together on the porch, the dark
Almost fallen, the house behind them dark.
Their supper done with, they have washed and dried
The dishes—only two plates now, two glasses,
Two knives, two forks, two spoons—small work for two.

She sits with her hands folded in her lap,
At rest. He smokes his pipe. They do not speak,
And when they speak at last it is to say
What each one knows the other knows. They have
One mind between them, now, that finally
For all its knowing will not exactly know
Which one goes first through the dark doorway, bidding
Goodnight, and which sits on a while alone.

The Sky Bright after Summer-Ending Rain

The sky bright after summer-ending rain,
I sat against an oak half up the climb.
The sun was low; the woods was hushed in shadow;
Now the long shimmer of the crickets' song
Had stopped. I looked up to the westward ridge
And saw the ripe October light again,
Shining through leaves still green yet turning gold.
Those glowing leaves made of the light a place
That time and leaf would leave. The wind came cool,
And then I knew that I was present in
The long age of the passing world, in which
I once was not, now am, and will not be,
And in that time, beneath the changing tree,
I rested in a keeping not my own.

The Old Man Climbs a Tree

He had a tall cedar he wanted to cut for posts,
but it leaned backward toward the fence,
and there's no gain in tearing down one
fence to build another. To preserve the fence
already built, he needed to fasten a rope

high up in the cedar, and draw it tight
to the trunk of another tree, so that as he sawed
the cedar free of its stance it would sway
away from the fence as it fell. To bring
a ladder would require too long a carry
up through the woods. Besides, you can't
climb into a cedar tree by means of a ladder—
too bristly. He would need first to cut off
all the branches, and for that would need a ladder.

And so, he thought, he would need to climb
the tree itself. He'd climbed trees many times
in play when he was a boy, and many times
since, when he'd had a reason. He'd loved
always his reasons for climbing trees.
But he'd come now to the age of remembering,
and he remembered his boyhood fall from an apple tree,
and being brought in to his mother, his wits
dispersed, not knowing where he was,
though where he was was this world still.
If that should happen now, he thought,
the world he waked up in would not be this one.
The other world is nearer to him now.
But trailing his rope untied as yet to anything
but himself, he climbed up once again and stood
where only birds and the wind had been before,
and knew it was another world, after all,
that he had climbed up into. There are
no worlds but other worlds: the world
of the field mouse, the world of the hawk,
the world of the beetle, the world of the oak,
the worlds of the unborn, the dead, and all
the heavenly host, and he is alive
in those worlds while living in his own.
Known or unknown, every world exists
because the others do.

               The treetops
are another world, smelling of bark,
a stratum of freer air and larger views,

from which he saw the world he'd lived in
all day until now, its intimate geography changed
by his absence and by the height he saw it from.
The sky was a little larger, and all around
the aerial topography of treetops, green and gray,
the ground almost invisible beneath.
He perched there, ungravitied as a bird,
knotting his rope and looking about, worlded
in worlds on worlds, pleased, and unafraid.

There are no other worlds but other worlds
and all the other worlds are here,
reached or almost reachable by the same
outstretching hand, as he, perched upon
his high branch, almost imagined flight.
And yet when he descended into this other
other world, he climbed down all the way.
He did not swing out from a lower limb
and drop, as once he would have done.

George Bilgere

George Bilgere has published three books of poetry: *The Good Kiss* (University of Akron Press, 2002), *Big Bang* (Copper Beech Press, 1999), and *The Going* (University of Missouri Press, 1995). His poems have appeared in *Poetry, Ploughshares, The Sewanee Review, The Southern Review, Best American Poetry,* and elsewhere. A Fulbright Scholar, a Witter Bynner Fellow, and winner of the 2003 Cleveland Arts Prize in Literature, he teaches at John Carroll University in Cleveland, Ohio.

Magellan

When a beautiful woman lies down
On her brown belly, on her pink beach towel,
And reaches back and behind to perform
That curious legerdemain whereby
Her dazzling white
Bikini top is undone
And she stretches out under the sun,

I continue watching the breakers
Stagger to their knees, and listen
To the gulls work through
Their chronic desolation,

Thinking, for some reason,
Of my mother, struggling
Into the cross-stitched straitjacket
Of her girdle
Before a night out with my father,

And I think of the boundless
Surge and heave of the ocean,
Swollen and unfettered
Before any man, crazed
By indifferent beauty, raised
White sails to cup
The wind's breasts
And girdle the globe.

The Garage

On these summer nights, I play
Ping-Pong with my brother-in-law,
A couple of beers sweating
On the tool shelf, the Giants game
Coming in loud and clear
On the paint-spattered shop radio,
And tonight I'm working very seriously
On my troublesome forehand,
Giving more concentration than usual
To the problem of topspin.

Today a woman on our street,
Running late for work, backed up
Her SUV and rolled over
Her three-year-old son. All day
I've thought of her as she goes
Through the hours, living in that remote,
Astonishing place she has discovered,
Someplace wholly new

Where few of us have ever ventured,
And as I trot down the driveway
To retrieve an errant smash,
I realize that the sheer speed and pressure
Of her passage out of the world
I'm living in tonight, and into the blazing
Spaces where she is traveling
Far beyond me, like the blue fleck
Of a satellite, utterly alone,
Is what makes the lighted mouth
Of the garage, with its beer and ball game,
Its smell of oil and gas, its cardboard boxes
Of family history, seem like a sweet
Refuge, a cave I return to gratefully,

Holding the white moon of the ball—
A fragile, weightless thing.

Pain

Animals in the wild are perfect and know nothing
About pain. Also perfect
Is an Olympic sprinter pulling off
His jersey after a race; the body, flexing
For TV, blinds you; Oh, you say,
That's what it's supposed to look like.
But all wild animals are like this because they live
In a perpetual Olympics. There's no
Margin for error out there,
And any ragged flock of gulls
Surfing a wind current, any rag
Of a jackrabbit poised by the roadside
Dwells in the lean, perfected moment; one
Busted bone, one gray hair, one
Moment's inattention, and he's a goner,
Crunched in the maw of a larger, wilder
Perfection. That's why

They're wild; pain
Never has a chance to teach them
A thing. The parakeet in his cage
Of pain, the ferret on his sexy chain,
Nosing the nipple ring
Of a tattooed punker, the cocker
Spaniel tied by the neck
To the railing outside Starbuck's, waiting
For the slim blonde in the pale,
Translucent blouse to finish her latte
With a pale unshaven man she's enjoying
Breaking up with—they're not wild
But bewildered, like us, having learned
From us what pain is, and thus
What it is to be tame, and human.

Peter Blair

Peter Blair's most recent full-length collection of poems, *The Divine Salt,* was published in 2003 by Autumn House Press. His first book, *Last Heat,* won the 1999 Washington Prize and was published by Word Works Press. He lives in Charlotte, NC, with his wife and son.

Litany For Edwin

Eyes open, the 18-year-old boy lies stiff
and still on the bed. I whisper, *Edwin,*
it's not so bad. He stares at the ceiling,
as if into a deep sky looking for lost stars
among paint cracks and a beige void.
The world, I mean. I touch a wet cloth
to his sad, pimply face. *Consciousness*
is pleasing, Edwin. Adam says that
in Paradise. He's in the last room at the end
of the unit. If he doesn't wake up soon
they'll ship him to the chronic ward. *Edwin, most*
madness is divinest sense. Like the grief-stricken
friend of a coma patient in a soap opera,
I keep talking: *the best wisdom is only a sublime*
misery. But his sleep is conscious, open-eyed.
The words I throw against a dark window
on lonely nights mean nothing here.

His parents arrive with their own words.
My, my, Edwin dear, my, my, his mother
murmurs. Thin, shrugging, apologetic,
she tucks and smoothes the sheet. I leave him
to his wide-eyed sleep, wondering where he goes
in dreams: to the elf forest of Rivendell,
or to the moon where Jung's patient fled
for years to escape her incestuous brother,
or any world, free of bare walls and the pure
white sheet stretched over his motionless body.

Death For Breakfast

I'm feeding Stash in his wheelchair.
Fish-like he opens his mouth
around the spoon, flecks of corn flakes
spackling his chin: *Cardiac arrest,*
eight east. His hands strain against
the wristlets belted to the steel arms
of the chair. The head nurse runs.
An orderly shoves furniture into the hallway.

Stethoscope swinging like the tail
of a lizard, a doctor enters
from a stairwell door. *Bang-bang,*
the double wheels of the crash cart
lurch off the elevator. The cart speeds by us
with a cadre of nurses, the *swish, swish*
of nyloned thighs down the hall. *Who?*
Stash asks. *822?* The pool players in the lounge
lower their cue sticks like rifles at ease.

Patients, nurses, aides, the janitor
unclogging a toilet—we all watch
the glowing light of the doorway.

Out the window the sun bleeds pale
light like a round wound in clouds,
the white stigmata above the city.

Head down, the doctor emerges,
his stethoscope slung lifeless
over the back of his neck.
The crash cart's wires dangle
like useless hands as a nurse switches off
the heart monitor. Its screen goes gray,
a blank round eye. Stash gazes
down into his soggy cereal.
For a moment, none of us is crazy.

Freight Train

There's always the freight train,
the black and white steel-tube tank cars
and flat-faced boxcars ramming through it all.
There's always the freight train
along the bank, dividing the mountain
from the waves, while a woman vomits
on the levee and a boater pours a fifth
of whiskey overboard when the police boat
gurgles around the bend. There are always
the snub-nosed diesels, back to back,
pulling straggling empty coal cars
into the vanishing point under the bridge.
Someone always looks up at the freight train,
says, *That's a long one.* The red speed boat
guns its motor, races the train, beats it.
You can always beat it to some arbitrary point,
but it keeps going when you tire
of its loaded, lumbering daily body of rust
and cracked paint. And there's always

another one, not too soon or too late,
plain as the molecules on your face
and you turn away to the young lovers in jeans
rolling on the lawn. She gets up.
He throws a blanket at her.
She swings her bag at him in a slow, hard arc,
walks away. He catches her. She throws
a half-hearted fist that ends in a kiss
that's always too soon, and long.
And then they're on the grass again.
He's between her legs, dry-humping,
before he lets her throw him off
and the freight train bears down on them
from a distant notch between the hills.

Andrea Hollander Budy

Andrea Hollander Budy is the writer-in-residence at Lyon College. Her most recent poetry collections are *The Other Life* and *House Without a Dreamer,* which won the Nicholas Roerich Poetry Prize. She is also the winner of a Pushcart Prize and fellowships from the NEA and the Arkansas Arts Council. Recent work appears in *The Georgia Review, Poetry, Shenandoah, FIELD,* and *Creative Nonfiction.*

The Hunters

Dressed in their green spotted drabs to blend in
with trees, my brother and his new friends, then
nineteen, erected their dark tents and dug
a latrine, then gathered twigs from the edge

of their camp and the driest leaves, and at
twilight all of them assembled, then bent
their heads for a moment over their Tang
or their coffee or tea, and one boy sang

a little prayer in the unarmed quiet
(at night sometimes my brother still sings it),

and even the air began to settle
except for the occasional rattle

of insects and in the nearby distance
mortar fire from Da Nang, insistent.

History

What if there hadn't been that one
moment when a man came home
and said to his wife, "No,
we will not leave that way, made to go
off someplace to work. I heard some talk. I know."

And what if there hadn't been that one
word, *know*, that his wife knew
to be the truth, the way the heart knows when blue
is really black disguised as blue, a bruise
cruelly thicker than it seems, news
that the dead were her own blood, and she knew
when they said they'd be safe that something truly
dark was speeding through.

And what if there hadn't been that one
night when even making love wasn't
safe enough, when, though the depot was crowded with cousins
and friends, the man and woman lied, said "visitors," said "Russian"
to the right smileless face, walked instead of running
to the other waiting train, watched as the landscape ran out, then
the sea, then all that was ahead of them, nearly crushing
each other with love, but never speaking it.

Thank God, thank love, thank even terror—that one
seed already in place, my mother.

A Tree Like This One

Once, when my mother was alive
and the Russian olive tree in the backyard not yet
blown over by the storm, and we lay awhile

under it on a blanket, feeling lazy, looking
up into the gray of its leaves,
teasing one another

not at all like mother and daughter
but two friends who had poked
pins into their index fingers and had sworn

by the blood, we decided to pretend
that, like her grandparents, we had walked
all night through a forest to get there

and taken everything important
with us, everything
we could carry, that is,

having buried the copper pots
and taken the Seder dish,
but thinking, too,

that her grandparents would have walked
out under a tree just like this one, pretending
they had already arrived

in the New World, that this
was only a picnic, after all,
here on the uneven grass

that a little way off they could hear
my mother and me
already alive and giggling.

Poem in October

After Dylan Thomas

It was my twenty-third year and heaven
broke away from my reach as I stood

at her grave. Rain carved
the morning's stone face into the earth,

and the sky grayed and lowered
until they were one. Back by the trees

men smoked, as if they had nothing
better to do. But I knew as soon as I left

they would cover even
the roses my father, brother and I

had tossed upon her as if our wishing
could do what prayer had not.

When I finally left, I thought her
gone. I am fifty-four. I was wrong.

John Canaday

photo by Jan Mazur

John Canaday's first book of poems, *The Invisible World*, won the 2001 Walt Whitman Award from the Academy of American Poets. His poems have appeared in *Poetry*, *Raritan*, *Slate*, *The Paris Review*, and other journals and anthologies. His is also the author of a critical study, *The Nuclear Muse: Literature, Physics, and the First Atomic Bombs*.

[from "Major John Dudley"]

By then I'd had it up to here
with stuck-up, smart-ass scientists.
For months I'd asked to join the war
and been mañanaed by the Corps
with lines a moron wouldn't buy:
"Your work here just might win the war."
So when Lebow turned my request
for transfer down again and said
instead I'd have to baby-sit
these prima donnas while they played
at building bombs, I really blew
my stack. "Six months," he promised me.
Alright, I thought, I'll give it that.
But three months nearly did me in.
These men were children—smart as hell,
of course, with all their theories and
the laws of atoms and all that,
but when it came to common sense,
the Lord had clearly passed them by.
Somehow they couldn't understand
that requisitioning supplies

took time. They wanted everything
the day before they asked for it.
They didn't seem to understand
what safes were for. How many times
did I find classified reports
left lying on their desks, their safes
wide open a few feet away?
And then they'd clam up when I asked
for stats to help me build a shed
to house their precious cyclotron.
Later, I'd find them in the bar
at the La Fonda, arguing
top secret information with
a dozen locals listening.
I've had some physics in my day
and chemistry: it doesn't take
an Einstein or an Edison
to figure out that something's up
when words like "fission," "nucleus,"
and "bomb" are thrown around for free.
I tried to tell them even I
was not supposed to know these things.
I couldn't get them to shut up.
Some days my biggest job was just
to keep their secrets from myself.

[from "Major John Dudley"]

And then the longhairs did it, damn
them. I was in the shower when
the news hit—Truman's voice broadcast
on the PA—"A rain of fire
the like of which was never seen"—
and everyone out of their tents
shouting and laughing—"Take that, you

son-of-a-bitch, you Hirohito!"—
banging on trash can lids, singing,
dancing, and breaking out the booze.
The camp was one big festival,
and wilder than on VE day.
I wandered here and there and had
a beer or two. Eventually
I walked down to the beach and found
a young kid puking in the sand.
At first I thought that he was drunk.
But he was crying, and he looked
embarrassed, so I tried a joke:
"What's wrong, boy? You gone soft on Japs?"
"No, sir," he said. "It's...well,
I just can't help imagining
if it had been Los Angeles.
My family's in..." and then he stopped.
I knew what he was saying, but
it wasn't New York or Des Moines
because our boys had got there first.
I never thought they would, and yet
those sorry bastards pulled it off.
God damn you, boys. You saved my life.

[from "Major John Dudley"]

I thought I'd seen destruction. And
I had—whole islands beaten flat.
We'd lay like bugs trapped in cocoons,
our hammocks by the hundred slung
in the huge hold of a troop transport,
with nothing to relieve the ache
of cramped limbs or the itch of boredom
but talk and sleep and listening
as the big guns of our battleships

roared night and day along the shores
of some poor former paradise,
pitching ten thousand tons of hell
down on the goddamned Japs' doomed heads.
The sweaty steel walls seemed to ring
with the call and response of gun
and silent arc and bursting shell.
My ears still rang weeks later as
I picked my way among palm stumps
and mango groves reduced to drifts
of ash, past concrete bunkers cracked
open like skulls that seeped pulped flesh.
But when my company arrived
in Nagasaki to repair
the water mains, the sewers, and
the hospital, I saw that this
was something new. A single plane.
One bomb. A city crushed the way
you'd swat a fly. An effortless
annihilation. In Dresden
or Tokyo, B-29s
swarmed by the thousand; yet they left
more standing. Here survivors walked
like ghosts, searching for a place
to haunt. Though nothing marked where doors
or walls once stood. Rubble and filth,
charred bodies they had cherished once.
God knows they had it coming, but
I wish I'd never had a part
in bringing it to them. I knew
we had our work cut out for us.

Hayden Carruth

Hayden Carruth is the author of 31 books, chiefly of poetry but including also a novel, four books of criticism, and two anthologies. He has been editor of *Poetry*, poetry editor of *Harper's,* and a recipient of fellowships from the Bollingen Foundation, the Guggenheim Foundation, the Lannan Foundation, and the National Endowment for the Arts. Among his many awards are the National Book Critics' Circle Award for Poetry, the National Book Award, The Lenore Marshall Award, and the Ruth Lilly Prize.

Pittsburgh

And my beautiful daughter
had her liver cut open in Pittsburgh.
My god, my god! I rubbed
her back over the swollen and wounded
essentiality, I massaged
her legs, and we talked of death.
At the luckiest patients with liver cancer have
a 20% chance. We might have talked
of my death, not long to come. But no,
the falling into death of a beautiful
young woman is so much more important.
A wonderful hospital. If I must die
away from my cat Smudge and my Vermont Castings stove
let it be at Allegheny General.

I read to her, a novella by Allan Gurganus,
a Russian serious flimsiness by Voinovich,
and we talked. We laughed. We actually
laughed. I bought her a lipstick
which she wore though she disliked the color.
Helicopters took off and landed on the hospital pad,
bringing hearts and kidneys and maybe livers
from other places to be transplanted
into people in the shining household of technology
by shining technologists, wise and kindly.
The chances are so slight. Oh, my daughter,
my love for you has burgeoned—
an excess of singularity ever increasing—
you are my soul—for forty years. You
still beautiful and young. In my hotel
I could not sleep. In my woods, on my
little farm, in the blizzard on the mountain,
I could not sleep either, but scribbled
fast verses, very fast and
wet with my heartsblood and brainjuice
all my life, as now
in Pittsburgh. I don't know which of
us will live the longer, it's all a flick
of the wrist of the god mankind invented
and then had to deinvent, such a failure, like all
our failures, and the worst and best
is sentimentality after all. Let us go out together.
Here in brutal Pittsburgh. Let us
be together in the same room,
the old poet and the young painter,
holding hands, a calm touch, a whisper,
as the thumping helicopters go out and come in,
we in the crisis of forever inadequately medicated
pain, in the love of daughter and father.

I, I, I

First, the self. Then, the observing self.
The self that acts and the self that watches. This
The starting point, the place where the mind begins,
Whether the mind of an individual or
The mind of a species. When I was a boy
I struggled to understand. For if I know
The self that watches, another watching self
Must see the watcher, then another seeing that,
Another and another, and where does it end?
And my mother sent me to the barber shop,
My first time, to get my hair "cut for a part"
(Instead of the dutch boy she'd always given me),
As I was instructed to tell the barber. She
Dispatched me on my own because the shop,
Which had a pool table in the back, in that
Small town was the men's club, and no woman
Would venture there. Was it my first excursion
On my own into the world? Perhaps. I sat
In the big chair. The wall behind me held
A huge mirror, and so did the one in front,
So that I saw my own small strange blond head
With its oriental eyes and turned up nose repeated
In ever diminishing images, one behind
Another behind another, and I tried
To peer farther and farther into the succession
To see the farthest one, diminutive in
The shadows. I could not. I sat rigid
And said no word. The fat barber snipped
My hair and blew his brusque breath on my nape
And finally whisked away his sheet, and I
Climbed down. I ran from that cave of mirrors
A mile and a half to home, to my own room
Up under the eaves, which was another cave.
It had no mirrors. I no longer needed mirrors.

Testament

So often has it been displayed to us, the hourglass
with its grains of sand drifting down,
not as an object in our world
but as a sign, a symbol, our lives
drifting down grain by grain,
sifting away—I'm sure everyone must
see this emblem somewhere in the mind.
Yet not only our lives drift down. The stuff
of ego with which we began, the mass
in the upper chamber, filters away
as love accumulates below. Now
I am almost entirely love. I have been
to the banker, the broker, those strange
people, to talk about unit trusts,
annuities, CDs, IRAs, trying
to leave you whatever I can after
I die. I've made my will, written
you a long letter of instructions.
I think about this continually.
What will you do? How
will you live? You can't go back
to cocktail waitressing in the casino.
And your poetry? It will bring you
at best a pittance in our civilization,
a widow's mite, as mine has
for forty-five years. Which is why
I leave you so little. Brokers?
Unit trusts? I'm no financier doing
the world's great business. And the sands
in the upper glass grow few. Can I leave
you the vale of ten thousand trilliums
where we buried our good cat Pokey
across the lane to the quarry?
Maybe the tulips I planted under
the lilac tree? Or our red-bellied
woodpeckers who have given us so
much pleasure, and the rabbits

and the deer? And kisses? And
love-makings? All our embracings?
I know millions of these will be still
unspent when the last grain of sand
falls with its whisper, its inconsequence,
on the mountain of my love below.

Judith Ortiz Cofer

Judith Ortiz Cofer is the author of several books in various genres. Her work has appeared in *The Georgia Review, The Kenyon Review, The Southern Review,* and other journals. Her latest novel, *The Meaning of Consuelo,* was published by Farrar, Straus, & Giroux in 2003. A native of Puerto Rico, she now resides in Georgia, where she is the Franklin Professor of English and Creative Writing at the University of Georgia.

The Gift of a Knife

When I was very young,
she let me shower with her once,
and I saw it, the scar that divided her body
in half like a sardonic smile. Eye level
to me, it was a preface to my life
as a woman. When will I have one?
I asked her, imagining the silver knife
that had exposed the mystery
of my mother's body, opening a door
for her children; she had survived
the good agony of birth, payment for the gift
of a baby in your arms. It was not an entrance,
she said, but an exit; *la operación*, given her
for free at eighteen, a gift from the government,
to make sure she did not let any more
babies enter a small island already crowded
as the stall we were in, the cubicle

where I was having trouble breathing
through the steam, hearing her words, *no más hijos,*
through the water. I felt our bodies were separated
by oceans. And my mother's wound—those pale hieroglyphs
over a crescent—it was the writing on the wall
of a dead queen's tomb, a message
in an ancient language
I had yet to decipher.

Lessons of the Past

I was born the year my father learned to march in step
with other men, to hit bull's eyes, to pose for sepia photos
in dress uniform outside Panamanian nightspots—pictures
he would send home to his pregnant teen-age bride inscribed:
To my best girl.

My birth made her *La Madona,* a husbandless young woman
with a legitimate child, envied by all the tired women
of the pueblo as she strolled my carriage down dirt roads,
both of us dressed in fine clothes bought with army checks
                                When he came home,
he bore gifts: silk pajamas from the Orient for her; a pink
iron crib for me. People filled our house to welcome him.
He played Elvis loud and sang along in his new English.
She sat on his lap and laughed at everything.
They roasted a suckling pig out on the patio. Later,
no one could explain how I had climbed over the iron bars
and into the fire. Hands lifted me up quickly, but not before
the tongues had licked my curls.

                        There is a picture of me
taken soon after: my hair clipped close to my head,
my eyes enormous—about to overflow with fear.
I look like a miniature of one of those women
in Paris after World War II, hair shorn,

being paraded down the streets in shame,
for having loved the enemy.

                    But then things changed,
and some nights he did not come home, I remember
hearing her cry in the kitchen. I sat on the rocking chair
waiting for my cocoa, learning how to count, *uno, dos, tres,*
cuatro, cinco, on my toes. So that when he came in,
smelling strong and sweet as sugarcane syrup,
I could surprise my *papasito*—
who liked his girls smart, who did not like crybabies—
with a new lesson, learned well.

Siempre

Tomorrow I will be with my mother
in a different world, only three hours
flight time away, yet foreign as Venus.
Tomorrow I will be facing the mirror
that reflects my future. Soon
I will feel a need
to step into it, growing smaller
to fit into her tiny kingdom
of two-by-four-inch memories.
She, whose beauty she can now recall
as her fondest memory, she and I
will turn the pages of the family album,
and gradually I will become
a child again. Again, I will follow
her laughter through the unfamiliar
apartments and houses in new cities
she now calls *sitios*, empty places
she had to transform into homes.

She, whose nervous energy was a presence
I felt hovering near me like a phantom sibling
even when she left the room.
She, who is still vibrant with her other selves:

the timidly exultant teenage bride, the anxiety-driven
young mother in a strange country, and always
the battle to keep loving life in spite of exile,
loneliness, and the early death
of her husband's spirit. She and I
will turn the pages of the album together.
All is perfectly preserved: the posed smiles,
the Sunday clothes, the handsome man at attention
next to his pretty wife, the radiance
of his crisp Navy uniform and me,
reflective in my communion dress.

I can count on this: All is always well
in the past. *Siempre.*

Tomorrow I will be with my mother,
but today I remember my father.
My father gone so long
he is now a decade younger than I.
My father of the luminous brown eyes
trained to see in the dark, scanning the horizon
for signs of storm, who brought his despair to us
along with gifts: dolls dressed in the costumes
of countries he took no pleasure in exploring,
silk from far-off places where he practiced
his *soledad,* his *tristeza*: Madrid, Palermo,
Pompeii, Tripoli, Guantanamo Bay.

Father of the vigilant gaze,
forever expecting to be called away.
Father of elegant sadness.
Father of the crisp white *guayaberas*
and the razor's-edge-creased pants,
of the military-issue black-as-coffins shoes,
shined every morning before coffee.
Father of darkness.
Father of pain without end.
Father, today I remember
the terrible beauty of your yearning,
I carry it with me *siempre,*
the gift you did not intend to give me.

Billy Collins

Billy Collins' latest collection is *Nine Horses*. He served as U.S. Poet Laureate 2001-2003.

Consolation

How agreeable it is not to be touring Italy this summer,
wandering her cities and ascending her torrid hill towns.
How much better to cruise these local, familiar streets,
fully grasping the meaning of every road sign and billboard
and all the sudden hand gestures of my compatriots.

There are no abbeys here, no crumbling frescoes or famous
domes and there is no need to memorize a succession
of kings or tour the dripping corners of a dungeon.
No need to stand around a sarcophagus, see Napoleon's
little bed on Elba, or view the bones of a saint under glass.

How much better to command the simple precinct of home
than be dwarfed by pillar, arch, and basilica.
Why hide my head in phrase books and wrinkled maps?

Why feed scenery into a hungry, one-eyed camera
eager to eat the world one monument at a time?

Instead of slouching in a café ignorant of the word for ice,
I will head down to the coffee shop and the waitress
known as Dot. I will slide into the flow of the morning
paper, all language barriers down,
rivers of idiom running freely, eggs over easy on the way.

And after breakfast, I will not have to find someone
willing to photograph me with my arm around the owner.
I will not puzzle over the bill or record in a journal
what I had to eat and how the sun came in the window.
It is enough to climb back into the car

as if it were the great car of English itself
and sounding my loud vernacular horn, speed off
down a road that will never lead to Rome, not even Bologna.

Taking Off Emily Dickinson's Clothes

First, her tippet made of tulle,
easily lifted off her shoulders and laid
on the back of a wooden chair.

And her bonnet,
the bow undone with a light forward pull.

Then the long white dress, a more
complicated matter with mother-of-pearl
buttons down the back,
so tiny and numerous that it takes forever
before my hands can part the fabric,
like a swimmer's dividing water,
and slip inside.

You will want to know
that she was standing
by an open window in an upstairs bedroom,
motionless, a little wide-eyed,
looking out at the orchard below,
the white dress puddled at her feet
on the wide-board, hardwood floor.

The complexity of women's undergarments
in nineteenth-century America
is not to be waved off,
and I proceeded like a polar explorer
through clips, clasps, and moorings,
catches, straps, and whalebone stays,
sailing toward the iceberg of her nakedness.

Later, I wrote in a notebook
it was like riding a swan into the night,
but, of course, I cannot tell you everything—
the way she closed her eyes to the orchard,
how her hair tumbled free of its pins,
how there were sudden dashes
whenever we spoke.

What I can tell you is
it was terribly quiet in Amherst
that Sabbath afternoon,
nothing but a carriage passing the house,
a fly buzzing in a windowpane.

So I could plainly hear her inhale
when I undid the very top
hook-and-eye fastener of her corset

and I could hear her sigh when finally it was unloosed,
the way some readers sigh when they realize
that Hope has feathers,
that Reason is a plank,
that Life is a loaded gun
that looks right at you with a yellow eye.

Workshop

I might as well begin by saying how much I like the title.
It gets me right away because I'm in a workshop now
so immediately the poem has my attention,
like the Ancient Mariner grabbing me by the sleeve.

And I like the first couple of stanzas,
the way they establish this mode of self-pointing
that runs through the whole poem
and tells us that words are food thrown down
on the ground for other words to eat.
I can almost taste the tail of the snake
in its own mouth,
if you know what I mean.

But what I'm not sure about is the voice,
which sounds in places very casual, very blue jeans,
but other times seems standoffish,
professorial in the worst sense of the word
like the poem is blowing pipe smoke in my face.
But maybe that's just what it wants to do.

What I did find engaging were the middle stanzas,
especially the fourth one.
I like the image of clouds flying like lozenges
which gives me a very clear picture.
and I really like how this drawbridge operator
just appears out of the blue
with his feet up on the iron railing
and his fishing pole jigging—I like jigging—
a hook in the slow industrial canal below.
I love slow industrial canal below. All those l's.

Maybe it's just me,
but the next stanza is where I start to have a problem.
I mean how can the evening bump into the stars?
And what's an obbligato of snow?
Also, I roam the decaffeinated streets.
At that point I'm lost. I need help.

The other thing that throws me off,
and maybe this is just me,

is the way the scene keeps shifting around.
First, we're in this big aerodrome
and the speaker is inspecting a row of dirigibles,
which makes me think this could be a dream.
Then he takes us into his garden,
the part with the dahlias and the coiling hose
though that's nice, the coiling hose,
but then I'm not sure where we're supposed to be.
The rain and the mint green light,
that makes it feel outdoors, but what about this wallpaper?
Or is it a kind of indoor cemetery?
There's something about death going on here.

In fact, I start to wonder if what we have here
is really two poems, or three, or four,
or possibly none.

But then there's that last stanza, my favorite.
This is where the poem wins me back,
especially the lines spoken in the voice of the mouse.
I mean we've all seen these images in cartoons before,
but I still love the details he uses
when he's describing where he lives.
The perfect little arch of an entrance in the baseboard,
the bed made out of a curled-back sardine can,
the spool of thread for a table.
I start thinking about how hard the mouse had to work
night after night collecting all these things
while the people in the house were fast asleep,
and that gives me a very strong feeling,
a very powerful sense of something.
But I don't know if anyone else was feeling that.
Maybe that was just me.
Maybe that's just the way I read it.

Robert Cording

Robert Cording teaches English and creative writing at Holy Cross College in Worcester, MA. He has published four collections of poems: *Life-list*, which won the Ohio State University Press/Journal award; *What Binds Us To This World* (Copper Beech Press, 1991), *Heavy Grace*, (Alice James, 1996), and *Against Consolation* (CavanKerry Press, 2002). He lives in Woodstock, CT, with his wife and three children.

The Weeper

The name his followers gave Ignatius, who wept
while saying mass, or while listening to the coos
of a common dove. Ignatius never knew
when his throat would tighten, a wave of sobs
breaking him open as he stood watching clouds
move in the wide gaze of the sky, or passed a boy
climbing a pine, lost in the play of his body.
It wasn't the reverie of blue sky and clouds,
nor even the boy's self-forgetful happiness
that brought on those tears beyond his control.
These days, when passion is cooled by irony,
when we try to live as if each day were
predictable and self-determined, when God
and the soul are off-limits, how can we understand

such abandonment in a man who wept
almost daily—not because of the time he'd wasted
or would waste, not because of his weak stomach
or his leg's old war injury, or because he'd given up
the feel of trembling flesh along the inner curve
of a woman's thigh or the full, idle hours
in his father's castle; and not even because of
the wearied and hopeless poor whom he met
on every road and went among in cities.
He wept, they say, because he'd suddenly feel
entirely empty, and utterly grateful, all the doors
of his heart, which was and was not his
at these moments, and which we know
only as metaphor, swung wide open, able now
to receive and find room for all the world's
orphaned outpourings and astonishments.

Against Consolation

The lecturer is talking
about Weil's essay on "Detachment."
          The scent of lilacs
intoxicates the air inside the room,

          cut branches brought in
to represent the flowering outside,
          spring flaring up
again like those beliefs, I imagine,

          Weil warns against—
beliefs which fill up voids and sweeten
          what is bitter. A thousand
miles from here, you have given up

          belief in the providential
ordering of events. No proverb sweetens
          your suffering. What endures
is your bewilderment—the freakish

wheel of that truck
breaking off and hurtling through
        the sunlit air, not enough
time to say *Look out* or even *Shit*,

        before it struck
your car, one of hundreds lined up
        in rush-hour traffic
on the other side of the highway.

        You told me, the more
you think, the less you understand.
        You can't explain
the roof caved in all around you,

        your two friends buried
under metal, and you, who sat alongside
        them, untouched.
Home from the hospital, your friends

        dead, you went to
the kitchen, and everything, you said,
        was just as you left it,
as if the accident were only an interruption

        in daily life, a tornado
that leaves a kitchen table set for dinner.
        *The contradictions the mind
comes up against—these are the only realities:*

        *they are the criterion
of the real.* Weil again, who believes
        we come to know
our radical contingency only through

        such contradictions.
We must suffer them unconsoled.
        "Let the accident go,"
your friends tell you, "Don't hold on"—

what we say, I fear,
to rid ourselves of the pain we feel
          when your pain closes
in on us. It's late in the afternoon

          and the rustling
of feet and papers has begun. I look out
          the window—a gusty wind
polishes the morning's rain-washed glass

          of air, and the late sun
lavishes each new green with its shine.
          I'd like to dismiss Weil's
haunted, unnerving life as my colleague

          quickly does, the lecture
ended: "Brilliant, but crazy." Anorexic,
          psychotic, suicidal. Labels
that fit, I suppose, and yet I cannot deny

          the stark attraction
of her words. *Stay with your suffering,*
          I've heard her say
over and over today, always the extremist.

          The last time I saw you,
I knew you lived at the border of what is
          bearable, that you'd seen
the skeleton underneath all your thought,

          everything stripped
of sense or summation; you knew
          your friend's deaths
would make no more sense in time

          and you would have
to live in that knowledge—no, not
          knowledge, the word
itself a kind of consolation, but the void

Weil speaks of,
where you cannot escape the skewed
          wheel of a truck, the blood
on your hands, the voice you still have

          that calls out, *O God, no,*
the scent of lilacs that pierce the air
          each spring for no cause,
beautifully innocent of meaning.

Fashion Shoot, Frijoles Canyon

Where did they come from?—suddenly, among the Anasazi
ruins: two models, a photographer, two hair stylists,
a smiling entourage. Racks of dresses and skirts,
of blouses and vests and accessories. Across the canyon,
in the emptied rooms of a pueblo, I had been pretending
to piece together dusty traces of the past. I couldn't
imagine the effort required to cut dwellings out of cliffs.
I watched them through binoculars: flutter of hands,
sweep of skirts, a loose blouse luffing in hot breezes—
and the faces, changing expressions as the photographer
moved right then left, as he kneeled and lay down,
the rest following, as if wherever the models were going,
desire would be satisfied. He waved his arm
and the wind covered or revealed a face, the sun imparted
its fashionable radiance and shadings, and soon enough
I imagined the pages of the magazine taking shape,
its glossy attractions like a vague desire enlarging itself,
each new item turning into a necessity, its cost
and possession always larger and more elusive,
and always promising a greater satisfaction, the glory
of a different future alive in those clothes, in those two
models who went on posing long into the afternoon
in a world where the Anasazi scratched deer and running
men into the million-year-old-canyon walls and then
vanished, leaving us to ask all these years, where did they go?

·
·
·
·
·
·
·

Moths

I woke to the flutter of all
their wings over the screen
as, slowly, they assembled
themselves out of the dusty
half-light of morning—
thirty-four moths,
their small grey-brown bodies
covering the screen like lichen.
At noon, they basked
in what little sun there was,
the pale September light
resting briefly on wings
that moved hardly at all
yet never stopped moving
until the moths began
to die. Even then they
seemed more composed
than exhausted, taking
the time they needed,
as if they were dreaming
their death into being.
They simply became their end,
death so naturally wrought,
I needed to touch each one
to be certain. Where
I placed my finger, they broke
out of their bodies
in little puffs of dust, leaving
behind an imprint
on the screen. By then
evening had entered
the day, and the sky, dense
with saturated colors,
collapsed in on itself,
the low clouds igniting
in a bonfire of last light.
And I felt suddenly
the slow, irreversible moment-
to-moment urgency

of every thing to keep
moving—and I leaned close
to the screen and blew
my breath on what remained
until nothing was there,
then stood a while listening
to the wind in the leaves
while the plush dark freed
a scattering of stars and the moon
broke clear of the trees.

Mark Cox

Mark Cox teaches in the Department of Creative Writing at UNC-Wilmington. His honors include a Whiting Writers' Award, a Pushcart Prize, the Oklahoma Book Award, The Society of Midland Authors Poetry Prize, and numerous fellowships. His latest books are *Thirty-Seven Years from the Stone* (Pitt Poetry Series, 1998) and *Natural Causes* (Pitt Poetry Series, 2004).

Finish This

When Gram died, her last act
was to hand back a Dixie cup
half-trembling with water
as if to say, "here, finish this."
My mother took it, separating the fingers,
thin and glossy with illness,
then guiding the whole arm down
to its place across her chest.
I was on the other side,
the hospital bed rail
pushing one cool shirt button into me
as if I were a doorbell. "I'm out here,"
Death was saying, "You don't have a lot of time,
you coming or not?"
The railing gave a little, sideways,

and since there was nothing left
but those most accidental of sounds—
the involuntary frictions of left/right,
up/down, in/out,
the sound of a loose tire iron
in the back of a pick-up,
of two emaciated swords
meeting farther and farther away—
that final letting go of the guard
by which all week she had pulled herself up toward me,
was a release into silence, a recognition
of the true completeness of every gesture.
And having relayed to me that dry, barely tangible kiss,
she could stop now, thereby seeming calmly to recede.
Outside, the cold white ashes of eons
piled high against the curbs
and Death leaned on his shovel
near a narrow, heavily salted path into underground parking,
and the car stalled,
and it seemed for a moment,
the past so completely with me, so heavy and sodden,
I'd never turn the key again.
That was when I remembered the Dixie cup,
the pale purple lilacs ringing its lip,
and how my mother raised it like a shot glass to her own mouth
then chose merely to sip.

The Lion's Share

They are gathered as if to be told a story.
Three kids, perhaps seventeen, facing
the headstone, a pastel bedsheet beneath them.
That bottle of wine on its side in the grass?
Safe to assume it is empty, safe to assume
the center girl being comforted, leaning
forward as if speaking, drank the lion's share;

her hair now mussed, her posture so clearly
deflated and spent. The other girl and boy,
they are here because they promised to be.
One year to the day, perhaps, since the death
they have in common. A toast, an awkward
eulogy, a token gift, all of it more difficult
than they'd bargained for.

And you and I, reader, we are parked in the cemetery, why?
Because I thought it a shortcut to a parallel road?
Because I needed to feel for a moment the fact of my own life?
A sparse flock of starlings is feeding in the short grass.
The wind flutters in memorial flowers, even the artificial ones.
Whatever the reason, I am grateful you've come.
So much that needs saying. In such little time.

Sonata

At ninety, the piano plays him.
He's like a man by the sea
the wind knows it must wear down,
sculpt to a profile,
then fill out again,
billowing his sleeves and trouser legs
into a younger musculature.
Over and again, the music grays
then reddens, the part
in its hair shifting left to center
until those few blades of sea grass
are all that's left to be
combed over the rocks,
and the thin fingers skitter,
leaving impressions in the keyboard
that waves wash level,
cleansing its audience of shell halves,
now glistening, now scoured dry.

And the house, the house just outside
this sonata's frame,
begs him to turn around
to pick his way back
along the stony runner,
his hands stopping his ears.
But, at ninety, the music plays the piano,
which plays the man, who finally, fearlessly,
plays himself, which is the landscape,
which is everything that ends.

Steven Cramer

Steven Cramer is the author of four poetry collections: *The Eye That Desires to Look Upward* (1987), *The World Book* (1992), *Dialogue for the Left and Right Hand* (1997), and *Goodbye to the Orchard* (2004). Recipient of fellowships from the Massachusetts Artists Foundation and the National Endowment for the Arts, he directs the low-residency MFA program in creative writing at Lesley University in Cambridge, MA.

Goodbye to the Orchard

Beautiful from the get-go, we were
incarnations of the new, and pure sex.
I'll miss that, along with the unicorns.
The organic bower of our garden grew
into anybody's memory of a bed
or a mattress, in a shack near a lake.
"Mistakes, like love, are to be *made*,"
you said. I hadn't thought of that.

That first autumn was easy, the liquor
of decay headiest at noon. And the orchard,
let's face it, had begun to resemble a casino,
all its tables rigged in our favor. The yoke
of being cared for is what cast us out,

not that immense, bearded librarian,
our curator, and not our having learned
how to get on one another's nerves.

Goodbye to the orchard: green
one day, the next day blood. We know
to stiffen at a voice; how to tell the truth
from an untruth; what's sweet, what stinks.
Behind each sleeping dog, another to let lie.
Who knew an innocence taking ages to perfect
could fall so short when time came to live?
You knew, and then you let me know.

The Dread Museum

Another plane, flames inside, gone down—
fundamentalist genius for terror, or just
an apolitical mechanical malfunction,
no one knows. Not the aeronautics
or explosive experts; not the anchors
paid too much to tell us; and most
terribly, not the relatives who watch
On Time switch to *Canceled* on the monitors.

Maybe it was too much picturing—
the sheared wing thrust from the sea,
torsos afloat like hand puppets in a tub,
the grim business of the divers, nosing through
the ribs of Business and Coach—that brought on
this nosebleed hampering me all morning.
Can't bend, can't yawn, can't make a face
without my nostril-wad of Kleenex reddening.

Amazing—isn't it?—how one swerves
from pity for bodies and body parts to hordes
of corpuscles and antibodies surging.
Should I be ashamed? I'm not. And I'm not

that I'm relieved I'm not, once again,
the relative reaching over the butcherblock
for the telephone, and in that lurch
having the notion common to us all—
now's my time to pay for pleasure—
prove true.
                    Oh, I could weep
out of frustration for my nose, and may.
I'll put my head back, daub a few last drops
on another bloody lucky day, and dwell
on the wheels, on the spokes of the wheels,
of my daughter's tricycle, while someone
whom I'll never meet and care about
as much as care imagined can, tears out
the front-page photo of a size-4 Nike
washed ashore, because he knows
he knows the shoe.

Bipolar

Just after the downpour moves on, and it's
still a swamp of viridian and emerald
indoors and out; and the central power grid,
iffy at best, still sputters and spits;

and the citizens, alert, still hunch
by their wavering flames, tensed for the flinch
between each white shock and its thunderclap
(relaxing, a bit, as quiet widens the gap)—

it's then this German-folktale kind of calm
seeps in: brown of the briar rose, a bone-
meal wariness, the green tone of *once upon
a time, a woodman and his wife wanted children*—

and soon children came. That's the time
to pray whoever loves you escaped harm.

Patricia Dobler

photo by Mark Perrott

Patricia Dobler was born in Middletown, Ohio, in 1939. Her books include *UXB* (Mill Hunk Books, 1991) and *Talking to Strangers* (University of Wisconsin Press, 1986), which won the Brittingham Prize. Her *Collected Poems* is available from Autumn House Press. She lived in Pittsburgh, PA, where she taught at Carlow College and directed the Women's Creative Writing Center. She died July 24, 2004.

Ghazal: For the Out-of-Work Man

I crossed by foot on the cold mornings, saw
icy tusks hanging from each bronze panther's jaw,

the white disk of pond below the bridge refractive,
self-contained; air like mother-of-pearl and raw

cracked opal, color spread on spires and nets of branches.
I knew he was back in the house chained to a snarl

of wire, acid, oil, deep in the coils of his anger.
Still I wanted for nothing on the bridge, drawn

on by another day, the outlined tasks, and happy
to be there, a piece of the morning, a part

of the landscape, blessed dailiness of walking
past the four poised panthers, mist withdrawn

from offices, joggers, dogs, kids sliding to school.
The habit of joy: my willed amnesia to ignore

the afternoons, the slow walk back, the pause
before fumbling the key at the front door, the inward

suck of heated air, then having to share the small
meal which had simmered all day on the stove.

Bound Hands

When he ordered me to untie his hands
and hide the restraints in my bag
I obeyed him instantly, though I knew
it was wrong. He was still strong,
he had already scared the nurses
by wandering into some woman's room
and refusing to leave, saying he'd wait
till Mass started—but when we entered
his room, he lifted his bound hands
and said to Mother, "Look here, Betty,
I would never let them do this to you!"
and to me, "Hide these damned things!"—
so I obeyed him, fast as I'd have flinched
from his soldering iron, and not because
I knew he was dying or that I hated to see
this proud man humbled—I did what he said
without thinking and in fearful haste
(after decades of flaunting my uncurbed will,
as if his poor tongue still could blister me)
like the good German girl I was raised to be.

Jazz

Chicago how I loved you
my release my out of jail my joy
the sweet heat of the drinks in those clubs
under the city, southern comfort on the rocks
always late at night smoky horns
underground underneath the city streets and rain
falling from far away, another world, always dripping
down there from the arms of the El around midnight.

I was so blonde I stuck out like a flare
so tall I had to bend just to get down there
where the music was succulent like honey
oh it was before the 60s I could go to those clubs
sticking out like I did because I loved that jazz
and it didn't matter how corn-fed
and blank I was, I felt the sweetness,
I was indulged even in my whiteness,
even I could hear the intricate unwinding
of the riffs careening from the alto sax.
I knew nothing at all, not what the music
cost, nor what would break loose or how soon.

Rita Dove

Rita Dove's eighth book of poetry, *American Smooth,* was published by W.W. Norton in 2004. She is a former Poet Laureate of the United States and the current Poet Laureate of Virginia. Her many honors also include the 1987 Pulitzer Prize in Poetry. She is Common-wealth Professor of English at the University of Virginia.

Hattie McDaniel Arrives at the Coconut Grove

late, in aqua and ermine, gardenias
scaling her left sleeve in a spasm of scent,
her gloves white, her smile chastened, purse giddy
with stars and rhinestones clipped to her brilliantined hair,
on her free arm that fine Negro,
Mr. Wonderful Smith.

It's the day that isn't, February 29th,
at the end of the shortest month of the year—
and the shittiest, too, everywhere
except Hollywood, California,
where the maid can wear mink and still be a maid,
bobbing her bandaged head and cursing
the white folks under her breath as she smiles
and shoos their silly daughters
in from the night dew... what can she be
thinking of, striding into the ballroom
where no black face has ever showed itself
except above a serving tray?

Hi-Hat Hattie, Mama Mac, Her Haughtiness,
the "little lady" from *Showboat* whose name
Bing forgot, Beulah & Bertha & Malena
& Carrie & Violet & Cynthia & Fidelia,
one half of the Dark Barrymores—
dear Mammy we can't help but hug you crawl into
your generous lap tease you
with arch innuendo so we can feel that
much more wicked and youthful
and sleek but oh what

we forgot: the four husbands, the phantom
pregnancy, your famous parties, your celebrated
ice box cake. Your giggle above the red petticoat's rustle,
black girl and white girl walking hand in hand
down the railroad tracks
in Kansas City, six years old.
The man who advised you, now
that you were famous, to "begin eliminating"
your more "common" acquaintances
and your reply (catching him square
in the eye): "That's a good idea.
I'll start right now by eliminating you."

Is she or isn't she? Three million dishes,
a truckload of aprons and headrags later, and here
you are: poised, between husbands
and factions, no corset wide enough
to hold you in, your huge face a dark moon split
by that spontaneous smile—your trademark,
your curse. No matter, Hattie: it's a long, beautiful walk
into that flower-smothered standing ovation,
so go on
and make them wait.

Daystar

She wanted a little room for thinking:
but she saw diapers steaming on the line,
a doll slumped behind the door.

So she lugged a chair behind the garage
to sit out the children's naps.

Sometimes there were things to watch—
the pinched armor of a vanished cricket,
a floating maple leaf. Other days
she stared until she was assured
when she closed her eyes
she'd see only her own vivid blood.

She had an hour, at best, before Liza appeared
pouting from the top of the stairs.
And just *what* was mother doing
out back with the field mice? Why,

building a palace. Later
that night when Thomas rolled over and
lurched into her, she would open her eyes
and think of the place that was hers
for an hour—where
she was nothing,
pure nothing, in the middle of the day.

Aircraft

Too frail for combat, he stands
before an interrupted wing,
playing with an idea, nothing serious.
Afternoons, the hall gaped with aluminum
glaring, flying toward the sun; now
though, first thing in the morning, there is only
gray sheen and chatter

from the robust women around him
and the bolt waiting for his riveter's
five second blast.

The night before in the dark
of the peanut gallery, he listened to blouses shifting
and sniffed magnolias, white
tongues of remorse
sinking into the earth. Then
the newsreel leapt forward
into war.

Why *frail*? Why not simply
family man? Why wings, when
women with fingers no smaller than his
dabble in the gnarled intelligence of an engine?

And if he gave just a four second blast,
or three? Reflection is such

a bloodless light.
After lunch, they would bathe in fire.

Straw Hat

In the city, under the saw-toothed leaves of an oak
overlooking the tracks, he sits out
the last minutes before dawn, lucky
to sleep third shift. Years before
he was anything, he lay on
so many kinds of grass, under stars,
the moon's bald eye opposing.

He used to sleep like a glass of water
held up in the hand of a very young girl.
Then he learned he wasn't perfect, that

no one was perfect. So he made his way
North under the bland roof of a tent
too small for even his lean body.

The mattress ticking he shares in the work barracks
is brown and smells
from the sweat of two other men.
One of them chews snuff:
he's never met either.
To him, work is a narrow grief
and the music afterwards
is like a woman
reaching into his chest
to spread it around. When he sings

he closes his eyes.
He never knows when she'll be coming
but when she leaves, he always
tips his hat.

Roast Possum

The possum's a greasy critter
that lives on persimmons and what
the Bible calls carrion.
So much from the 1909 Werner
Encyclopedia, three rows of deep green
along the wall. A granddaughter
propped on each knee,
Thomas went on with his tale—

but it was for Malcolm, little
Red Delicious, that he invented
embellishments: *We shined that possum*
with a torch and I shinnied up,
being the smallest,

to shake him down. He glared at me,
teeth bared like a shark's
in that torpedo snout.
Man he was tough but no match
for old-time know-how.

Malcolm hung back, studying them
with his gold hawk eyes. When the girls
got restless, Thomas talked horses:
Strolling Jim, who could balance
a glass of water on his back
and trot the village square
without spilling a drop. Who put
Wartrace on the map and was buried
under a stone, like a man.

They liked that part.
He could have gone on to tell them
that the Werner admitted Negro children
to be intelligent, though briskness
clouded over at puberty, bringing
indirection and laziness. Instead,
he added: *You got to be careful*
with a possum when he's on the ground;
he'll turn on his back and play dead
till you give up looking. That's
what you'd call sullin'.

Malcolm interrupted to ask
who owned Strolling Jim,
and who paid for the tombstone.
They stared each other down
man to man, before Thomas,
as a grandfather, replied:
                              Yessir,
we enjoyed that possum. We ate him
real slow, with sweet potatoes.

Denise Duhamel

Denise Duhamel's most recent books are *Two and Two* (University of Pittsburgh Press, 2005) and *Queen for a Day: Selected and New Poems* (University of Pittsburgh Press, 2001). *Mille et un sentiments* was published in a limited edition by Firewheel in 2004. She teaches creative writing at Florida International University in Miami.

Blue Beard's One-Hundredth Wife

This was before battered women's shelters,
before serial killers were called serial killers,
before divorce, even before handguns.
Blue Beard's one-hundredth wife found his dead ninety-nine others
stored in a forbidden room. Some said he tired of a woman
once her mystery faded. Others thought
he was too quick to temper. He went on
long business trips before there were business trips,
trying perhaps to curb his domestic violence.
His beard was blue before punk rock was fashionable
which manipulated some women into feeling bad for him.
They stroked his speckled mustache—his navy bristles
and his soft gray hairs which grew in aqua.
He curled into their breasts, playing sensitive,
his big rough hands stroking the backs of their necks.
In a week or two a wedding, in another month
she'd drop a dish or smell up the outhouse
and it was all over. No one ever found his weapon.
Certain forensics guess he used his bare hands,
pulling his wives apart as though they were roasted chickens.
Luckily for them, this was before magic was obsolete
and Blue Beard's one-hundredth wife knew how to sew.
When she found that pile of dead wife parts
she pieced them together like Butterick patterns

and took to arms and heads with a needle and thread.
After two afternoons of non-stop work,
the women breathed again, all perfectly proportioned.
Some said, "Thank you, I've always wanted red hair."
Or, "Wow! I wondered what it was like to have big breasts!"
Blue Beard's one-hundredth wife sewed the light eyes
to the light skin, the small ankles on the small legs.
This was before plastic surgery, this was before women's magazines,
before body doubles were used in movies. Yet here were ninety-nine
untouchable pin-ups, their creator a Plain Jane
with a good eye for detail. When Blue Beard came home
his grief shook the stained glass windows of his castle.
He tried to kill his one-hundredth wife,
using the excuse of her entrance into the forbidden room,
but his ninety-nine exes pushed him out his heavy oak front door.
This was before lawyers, but the one hundred wives still got the house.

Oriental Barbie

She could be from Japan, Hong Kong, China,
the Philippines, Vietnam, Thailand, or Korea.
The little girl who plays with her can decide.
The south, the north, a nebulous
province. It's all the same, according to Mattel, who says
this Barbie still has "round eyes,"
but "a smaller mouth and a smaller bust"
than her U.S. sister. Girls, like some grown men,
like variety, as long as it's pretty, as long
as there's long hair to play with.
On a late-night Manhattan Cable commercial,
one escort service sells *Geishas to Go,*
girls from "the Orient, where men are kings..."
White Ken lies on his stomach
while an Oriental Barbie walks on his back.
Or is it a real woman stepping on Ken?
Or Oriental Barbie stepping on a real man?
You have to travel to Japan

to buy this particular Barbie doll. A geisha girl
can be at the door of your New York apartment
in less than an hour. Of course,
there is no Oriental Ken.
Those who study the delicate balance
of American commerce and trade understand.

Ego

I just didn't get it—
even with the teacher holding an orange (the earth) in one hand
and a lemon (the moon) in the other,
her favorite student (the sun) standing behind her with a flashlight.
I just couldn't grasp it—
this whole citrus universe, these bumpy planets revolving so slowly
no one could even see themselves moving.
I used to think if I could only concentrate hard enough
I could be the one person to feel what no one else could,
sense a small tug from the ground, a sky shift, the earth changing gears.
Even though I was only one mini-speck on a speck,
even though I was merely a pinprick in one goosebump on the orange,
I was sure then I was the most specially perceptive, perceptively sensitive.
I was sure then my mother was the only mother to snap—
"The world doesn't revolve around you!"
The earth was fragile and mostly water
just the way the orange was mostly water if you peeled it
just the way I was mostly water if you peeled me.
Looking back on that third-grade science demonstration,
I can understand why some people gave up on fame or religion or cures—
especially people who have an understanding
of the excruciating crawl of the world,
who have a well-developed sense of spatial reasoning
and the tininess that it is to be one of us.
But not me—even now I wouldn't mind being god, the force
who spins the planets the way I spin a globe, a basketball, a yo-yo.
I wouldn't mind being that teacher who chooses the fruit,
or that favorite kid who gives the moon its glow.

Stephen Dunn

photo by Matt Valentine

Stephen Dunn is the author of twelve collections of poetry, including *The Insistence of Beauty* (Norton, 2004). His *Different Hours* was awarded the 2001 Pulitzer Prize for poetry.

A Postmortem Guide

For my eulogist, in advance

Do not praise me for my exceptional serenity.
Can't you see I've turned away
from the large excitements,
and have accepted all the troubles?

Go down to the old cemetery; you'll see
there's nothing definitive to be said.
The dead once were all kinds—
boundary breakers and scalawags,
martyrs of the flesh, and so many
dumb bunnies of duty, unbearably nice.

I've been a little of each.

And, please, resist the temptation
of speaking about virtue.
The seldom-tempted are too fond
of that word, the small-
spirited, the unburdened.
Know that I've admired in others
only the fraught straining
to be good.

Adam's my man and Eve's not to blame.
He bit in; it made no sense to stop.

Still, for accuracy's sake you might say
I often stopped,
that I rarely went as far as I dreamed.

And since you know my hardships,
understand they're mere bump and setback
against history's horror.
Remind those seated, perhaps weeping,
how obscene it is
for some of us to complain.

Tell them I had second chances.
I knew joy.
I was burned by books early
and kept sidling up to the flame.

Tell them that at the end I had no need
for God, who'd become just a story
I once loved, one of many
with concealments and late-night rescues,
high sentence and pomp. The truth is

I learned to live without hope
as well as I could, almost happily,
in the despoiled and radiant now.

You who are one of them, say that I loved
my companions most of all.
In all sincerity, say that they provided
a better way to be alone.

The Last Hours

There's some innocence left,
and these are the last hours of an empty afternoon
at the office, and there's the clock
on the wall, and my friend Frank
in the adjacent cubicle selling himself
on the phone.
                I'm twenty-five, on the shaky
ladder up, my father's son, corporate,
clean-shaven, and I know only what I don't want,
which is almost everything I have.
                A meeting ends.
Men in serious suits, intelligent men
who've been thinking hard about marketing snacks,
move back now to their window offices, worried
or proud. The big boss, Horace,
had called them in to approve this, reject that—
the big boss, a first-name, how's-your-family
kind of assassin, who likes me.
                It's 1964.
The sixties haven't begun yet. Cuba is a larger name
than Vietnam. The Soviets are behind
everything that could be wrong. Where I sit
it's exactly nineteen minutes to five. My phone rings.
Horace would like me to stop in
before I leave. *Stop in.* Code words,
leisurely words, that mean *now*.
                Would I be willing
to take on this? Would X's office, who by the way
is no longer with us, be satisfactory?

About money, will this be enough?
I smile, I say yes and yes and yes,
but—I don't know from what calm place
this comes—I'm translating
his beneficence into a lifetime, a life
of selling snacks, talking snack strategy,
thinking snack thoughts.
                         On the elevator down
it's a small knot, I'd like to say, of joy.
That's how I tell it now, here in the future,
the fear long gone.
By the time I reach the subway it's grown,
it's outsized, an attitude finally come round,
and I say it quietly to myself, *I quit*,
and keep saying it, knowing I will say it, sure
of nothing else but.

Empathy

Once in a small rented room, awaiting
a night call from a distant time zone,
I understood one could feel so futureless
he'd want to get a mermaid

tattooed on his biceps. Company
forever. Flex and she'd dance.
The phone never rang, except for those
phantom rings, which I almost answered.

I was in D.C., on leave from the army.
It was a woman, of course, who didn't call.
Or, as we said back then, a girl.
It's anybody's story.

But I think for me it was the beginning
of empathy, not a large empathy
like the deeply selfless might have,
more like a leaning, like being able

to imagine a life for a spider, a maker's
life, or just some aliveness
in its wide abdomen and delicate spinnerets
so you take it outside in two paper cups

instead of stepping on it.
The next day she called, and it was final.
I remember going to the zoo
and staring a long time

at the hippopotamus, its enormous weight
and mass, its strange appearance
of tranquility.
And then the sleek, indignant cats.

Then I went back to Fort Jackson.
I had a calendar taped inside my locker,
and I'd circle days for which I
had no plans, not even hopes—

big circles, so someone might ask.
It was between wars. Only the sergeants
and a few rawboned farm boys
took learning how to kill seriously.

We had to traverse the horizontal ladder,
rung after rung, to pass
into mess hall. Always the weak-handed,
the weak-armed, couldn't make it.

I looked for those who didn't laugh
at those of us who fell.
In the barracks, after drills,
the quiet fellowship of the fallen.

B. H. Fairchild

B. H. Fairchild is the recipient of Guggenheim, Rockefeller, and NEA fellowships. *Early Occult Memory Systems of the Lower Midwest,* from which these poems were taken, received the National Book Critics Circle Award and the Gold Medal of the California Book Awards.

Rave On

> *...wild to be wreckage forever.*
> —James Dickey, "Cherrylog Road"

Rumbling over caliche with a busted muffler,
radio blasting Buddy Holly over Baptist wheat fields,
Travis screaming out *Prepare ye the way of the Lord*
at jackrabbits skittering beneath our headlights,
the Messiah coming to Kansas in a flat-head Ford
with bad plates, the whole high plains holding its breath,
night is fast upon us, lo, in these days of our youth,
and we were hell to pay, or thought we were. Boredom
grows thick as maize in Kansas, heavy as drill pipe
littering the racks of oil rigs where in summer boys
roustabout or work on combine crews north as far

as Canada. The ones left back in town begin
to die, dragging main street shit-faced on 3.2 beer
and banging on the whorehouse door in Garden City
where the ancient madam laughed and turned us down
since we were only boys and she knew our fathers.
We sat out front spitting Red Man and scanned a landscape
flat as Dresden: me, Mike Luckinbill, Billy Heinz,
and Travis Doyle, who sang, *I'm gonna live fast,*
love hard, and die young. We had eaten all the life
there was in Seward County but hungry still, hauled ass
to old Arkalon, the ghost town on the Cimarron
that lay in half-shadow and a scattering of starlight,
and its stillness was a kind of death, the last breath
of whatever in our lives was ending. We had drunk there
and tossed our bottles at the walls and pissed great arcs
into the Kansas earth where the dust groweth hard
and the clods cleave fast together, yea, where night yawns
above the river in its long, dark dream, above
haggard branches of mesquite, chicken hawks scudding
into the tree line, and moon-glitter on caliche
like the silver plates of Coronado's treasure
buried all these years, but the absence of treasure,
absence of whatever would return the world
to the strangeness that as children we embraced
and recognized as *life. Rave on.*
                              Cars are cheap
at Roman's Salvage strewn along the fence out back
where cattle graze and chew rotting fabric from the seats.
Twenty bucks for spare parts and a night in the garage
could make them run as far as death and stupidity
required—on Johnson Road where two miles of low shoulders
and no fence line would take you up to sixty, say,
and when you flipped the wheel clockwise, you were there
rolling in the belly of the whale, belly of hell,
and your soul fainteth within you for we had seen it done
by big Ed Ravenscroft who said you would go in a boy
and come out a man, and so we headed back through town
where the marquee of the Plaza flashed CREATURE FROM
THE BLACK LAGOON in storefront windows and the Snack Shack
where we had spent our lives was shutting down and we

sang *rave on, it's a crazy feeling* out into the night
that loomed now like a darkened church, and sang loud
and louder still for we were sore afraid.
                                        Coming up
out of the long tunnel of cottonwoods that opens onto
Johnson Road, Travis with his foot stuck deep into the *soul*
of that old Ford *come on, Bubba, come on* beating
the dash with his fist, hair flaming back in the wind
and eyes lit up by some fire in his head that I
had never seen, and Mike, iron Mike, sitting tall
in back with Billy, who would pick a fight with anything
that moved but now hunched over mumbling something
like a prayer, as the Ford lurched on spitting
and coughing but then smoothing out suddenly fast
and the fence line quitting so it was open field, then,
then, I think, we were butt-deep in regret and a rush
of remembering whatever we would leave behind—
Samantha Dobbins smelling like fresh laundry,
light from the movie spilling down her long blonde hair,
trout leaping all silver and pink from Black Bear Creek,
the hand of my mother, I confess, passing gentle
across my face at night when I was a child—oh yes,
it was all good now and too late, too late, trees blurring
past and Travis wild, popping the wheel, oh too late
too late
                and the waters pass over us the air thick
as mud slams against our chests though turning now
the car in its slow turning seems almost graceful
the frame in agony like some huge animal groaning
and when the wheels leave the ground the engine cuts loose
with a wail thin and ragged as a bandsaw cutting tin
and we are drowning breathless heads jammed against
our knees and it's a thick swirling purple nightmare
we cannot wake up from for the world is turning too
and I hear Billy screaming and then the whomp
sick crunch of glass and metal whomp *again back window*
popping loose and glass exploding someone crying out
tink tink of iron on iron overhead and then at last
it's over and the quiet comes
                        Oh so quiet. Somewhere

the creak and grind of a pumping unit. Crickets.
The tall grass sifting the wind in a mass of whispers
that I know I'll be hearing when I die. And so
we crawled trembling from doors and windows borne out
of rage and boredom into weed-choked fields barren
as Golgotha. Blood raked the side of Travis's face
grinning rapt, ecstatic, Mike's arm was hanging down
like a broken curtain rod, Billy kneeled, stunned,
listening as we all did to the rustling silence
and the spinning wheels in their sad, manic song
as the Ford's high beams hurled their crossed poles of light
forever out into the deep and future darkness. *Rave on.*

I survived. We all did. And then came the long surrender,
the long, slow drifting down like young hawks riding on
the purest, thinnest air, the very palm of God
holding them aloft so close to something hidden there,
and then the letting go, the fluttering descent, claws
spread wide against the world, and we become, at last.
our fathers. And do not know ourselves and therefore
no longer know each other. Mike Luckinbill ran a Texaco
in town for years. Billy Heinz survived a cruel divorce,
remarried, then took to drink. But finally last week
I found this house in Arizona where the brothers
take new names and keep a vow of silence and make
a quiet place for any weary, or lost, passenger
of earth whose unquiet life has brought him there,
and so, after vespers, I sat across the table
from men who had not surrendered to the world,
and one of them looked at me and looked into me,
and I am telling you there was *a fire in his head*
and his eyes were coming fast down a caliche road,
and I knew this man, and his name was Travis Doyle.

A Photograph of the Titanic

When Travis came home from the monastery,
the ground had vanished beneath him,
and he went everywhere in bare feet

as if he were walking on a plane of light
and he spoke of his sleepless nights
and of a picture in *National Geographic*:

a pair of shoes from the *Titanic* resting
on the ocean floor. They were blue
against a blue ground and a black garden

of iron and brass. The toes pointed outward,
toward two continents, and what had been
inside them had vanished so completely

that he imagined it still there, with the sea's
undersway bellying down each night
as each day after compline he fell into

his bed, the dark invisible bulk of tons
pushing down on the shoes, nudging them
across the blue floor, tossing them aside

like a child's hands in feverish sleep
until the shoestrings scattered and dissolved.
Sometimes he would dream of the shoes

coming to rest where it is darkest,
after the long fall before we are born,
when we gather our bodies around us,

when we curl into ourselves and drift
toward the little sleep we have rehearsed
again and again as if falling we might drown.

Nick Flynn

photo by Joyce Ravid

Nick Flynn is the author of two collections of poetry, *Some Ether* and *Blind Huber* (Graywolf Press, 2000, 2002) as well as a memoir, *Another Bullshit Night in Suck City* (Norton, 2004).

Ago

I don't even know
      how a telephone works, how your voice reached
all the way from Iron River, fed

across wires or satellites, transformed

& returned. I don't understand
      the patience this takes, or anything
about the light-years between stars.

            An hour ago
you cupped your hands in the tub & raised them up,
      an offering of steam. Now

we're driving 66 mph
& one maple is coming up fast, on fire. I begin,
          it's like those fireworks over

the East River, but it's not enough

to say this. By the time I find the words
          it will already be past, rushing away as if falling

into a grave, drained
of electricity, the world between *something is happening*

& *something happened.* Think of an astronaut, big silver hands
& gravity boots, the effort spent

          to keep from flying off into space. Think of

the first time your grandparents listened
to a phonograph, the needle falling to black

vinyl, a song without a body. Think of the names

          you see on a map, think of these towns & rivers
before they were named, when "Liberty" & "New Hope"

were a large rock, a stand of birches. It's what

          I'm afraid of, the speed with which everything
is replaced, these trees, your smile, my mother
                    turning her back to me before work
asking over her shoulder,
how does this look?

You Ask How

      & I say, *suicide,* & you ask
how & I say, *an overdose, and then*
she shot herself,
& your eyes fill with what?
wonder? so I add, *in the chest,*
so you won't think
her face is gone, & it matters somehow
that you know this...

         & near the end I
eat all her percodans, to know
how far they can take me, *because*
they are there. So she
won't. Cut straws
stashed in her glove compartment,
& I split them open
to taste the alkaloid residue. Bitter.
Lingering. A bottle of red wine
moves each night along
as she writes, *I feel too much,*
again & again. Our phone now

      unlisted, our mail
kept in a box at the post office
& my mother tells me to always leave
a light on so it seems
someone's home. She finds a cop
for her next boyfriend, his hair
greasy, pushed back with his fingers.
He lets me play with his service revolver
while they kiss on the couch.
As cars fill the windows, I aim,
making the noise with my mouth,
in case it's them,

& when his back is hunched over her I aim
between his shoulder blades,

in case it's him.

Emptying Town

—after Provincetown

Each fall this town empties, leaving me
drained, standing on the dock, waving *bye-
bye,* the white handkerchief
stuck in my throat. You know the way Jesus

rips open his shirt
to show us his heart, all flaming and thorny,
the way he points to it. I'm afraid

the way I miss you will be this obvious. I have

a friend who everyone warns me
is dangerous, he hides
bloody images of Jesus around my house

for me to find when I come home—Jesus
behind the cupboard door, Jesus tucked

into the mirror. He wants to save me
but we disagree from what. My version of hell
is someone ripping open his
shirt & saying,

look what I did for you.

Frank X. Gaspar

Frank X. Gaspar is the author of four collections of poetry, most recently *A Field Guide to the Heavens* (Brittingham Prize, 1999) and *One Thousand Blossoms* (Alice James Books, 2004). His novel, *Leaving Pico,* was a Barnes and Noble Discovery Award winner and won the California Book Award for First Fiction.

Hurricane Douglas, Hurricane Elida

Here they come again, those Pacific hurricanes,
and here I go in the old white Jeep, sandy and musty
with boards and wetsuits and damp towels, down
the boulevard, down the bougainvillea and the jacaranda,
the red lights and green lights, the Shell station and
the Union 66 station, the 7-11, Anna's Escrows,
Pacific Coast Medical Group, Tiny Naylor's Restaurant,
the Los Altos YMCA, houses and houses behind their
honeysuckled walls, and rows of palm trees curving up
to the muggy sky. A left turn on the highway and watch
the rivers in their concrete bunkers, glassy now because the
wind has not shifted onshore yet. Good. And then turn down
toward the pier and wedge into a parking space and then

down the sand, and there they are again, rolling in like
boxcars, swell after swell, angling off the bar under the
pier, half-again over my head, and then for the first time
ever the thought that I am too old, too weak, too short of
breath. This is fear. How comely, how appealing it is! How
it slows me pulling on the wetsuit and fins, waxing the board,
how it makes my pragmatic heart so ready, knocking against my
ribs in a way that I can hear it all the way up in my head. But
Bang Bang go the breakers, and in *I* go and dig in with my arms,
and get stuck inside a big set, pulling and pulling and getting
nowhere, duck-diving under the whitewater, heaving a breath
into myself when I come up, digging again to take back the distance
I've already lost, digging and breathing like there's no turning
back because, after all, there isn't now, and this is where I prefer
to leave it, this plain, small poem, digging and breathing like
it wants to avoid some classic fate or some failure of will or some
defect of character, bragging into all the noise and commotion, all
the rips and undertows, that there will be a last time, but this is not it.

February

My stepfather coming home
from the wharves to draw his unemployment
and smoke Pall Malls in the sagging
overstuffed wing-chair, cheeks softening
with a beard that grew brindled now,
his life getting on, going nowhere,
sometimes a listless game of checkers
that I never wanted to play with him,
but mostly his drinking coffee from
a chipped bowl and brooding and sending
me once a week down to the boats
with a bucket to ask the luckier men
for flounder or haddock, and always
their wind-darkened faces staring
away from me at the wet decks
as they hoisted the brimming bucket back,

those weeks of fish and eggs and onions
and only cold water running in the taps,
the sun never getting above the line
of the woodshed roof, starlings flapping
down to croak on the crusty backyard snow,
the dank walls muttering to one another
when they thought no one listened, hats
and scarves awake on a nail by the door,
but nothing to dress for and no place to go.

Bodhidharma Preaches the Wake-up Sermon

> *There's no language that isn't the Dharma. Language is*
> *essentially free. It has nothing to do with attachment.*
> *And attachment has nothing to do with language.*
> —Bodhidharma

Somehow or another, something is missing in me. I should
be satisfied with the household gods. I should learn my place
and understand that they are enough for any one man or woman.
Of course we are at their mercy. They suffer us every small thing.
And we thank you, god of the kitchen drainboard and goddess of
the gas-log hearth. We thank you for your benevolence and kindness,
and god of the grocery sacks for your capacious heart, and goddess
of linoleum and green lawns, and winged goddess of the laughter
of neighborhood children, but always we are wandering from
your groves and bowers, your gardens, your abundant pantries.
For instance, what does anyone's life mean, now, in this third
millennium, so-called? I am talking about what you can and can't
live without, which is a way of talking about attachment. Is there
a language that isn't the Dharma? *To seek nothing is bliss,*
said the saint Bodhidharma, but isn't he the one who cut off his eyelids
in the search for a more perfect meditation? No, no, this is not
the way, in the heat of night, in the heat of fevers, the blue gas jets
wavering in the hot breeze on the kitchen range (the goddess of
the four burners, the goddess of the coffee pot, our acknowledgment,

our gratitude), not the way when we open the door to the small empty street and look down its length, first one way and then the other. It's what you can or can't live without. It's all streetlight and crickets on this particular night. It's all language and breath in this particular trial. It's all delicacy and power lines. It's all asphalt and glass. That's why I am up night after night. That's why I walk so softly on the floors and rugs. I am bowing and kneeling in every little corner, at every little helpful shrine, but I couldn't say if I am praying or if I am simply looking for some small button or short piece of string that I've lost. Most nights I really couldn't tell you what on earth I'm doing.

Elton Glaser

photo by Betty Greenway

Elton Glaser, a native of New Orleans, edits the Akron Series in Poetry. He has published six full-length collections of poems, most recently *Pelican Tracks* (Southern Illinois, 2003) and *Here and Hereafter* (Arkansas, 2005). His poems have appeared in the 1995, 1997, and 2000 editions of *The Best American Poetry*. Among his awards are two fellowships from the National Endowment for the Arts, five fellowships from the Ohio Arts Council, the Iowa Poetry Prize, the Crab Orchard Award, and the Ohioana Poetry Award.

Smoking

I like the cool and heft of it, dull metal on the palm,
And the click, the hiss, the spark fuming into flame,
Boldface of fire, the rage and sway of it, raw blue at the base
And a slope of gold, a touch to the packed tobacco, the tip
Turned red as a warning light, blown brighter by the breath,
The pull and the pump of it, and the paper's white
Smoothed now to ash as the smoke draws back, drawn down
To the black crust of lungs, tar and poisons in the pink,
And the blood sorting it out, veins tight and the heart slow,
The push and wheeze of it, a sweep of plumes in the air
Like a shako of horses dragging a hearse through the late centennium,
London, at the end of December, in the dark and fog.

The Worst High School Marching Band in the South

We've seen you all before,
A spectacle of spectacles, thick
As the skull of a cheerleader in midleap—

The horn-rimmed owls, the harlequins
Of brassy hair, the round
Astonished look of wired eyes.

Even at the homecoming game,
You never felt at home, not with
The bell curve of your horn

Turned up in the rain, so deep
No spit valve could shake it off,
Three spindly fingers and two left feet

Making of the muddy football field
Squeals and pleats between the lines,
A hidden message in the halftime mess.

Even then, you never knew the score.
In caps and epaulets, frogged out in braid,
Cuffs at highwater over loose shoes,

You brought up the sweaty rear
Of the Independence Day parade, always
A block behind the other bands, trailing

The waxed convertibles of the livestock queens
And politicians perched on the back seat
Like birds of prey, their cheap suits

Soggy in the noonday sun, their grins
Glinting like the gunsights of assassins,
Always at the tail end, following the firetruck

And the cop car, always missing the beat,
Snares and glockenspiels carried low as
Heavy shovels after the circus elephants.

The flag girls and the majorettes,
Tassels on their boots, batons and bunting
Stalled out like planes in a nose dive,

Shuffle and squint, a rictus fixed
In the face, as if they'd all tied for last
At the Scarlett O'Hara Look-a-Like pageant.

What big drums will wake you
To the life that lies impossibly beyond
The beehive hallways of high school?

What cymbals will go off
Inside your heads, like alarm clocks,
Spun metal ringing in the future's news?

For now, there's nothing you can do
But stagger in broken columns,
Like the ruined temple of forgotten youth,

Defiling the file, losing a step
With every bar, soused on Sousa,
Rapping out the cold cacophonies of pomp.

There's no law against bad music,
No tuba litigation, no policies forbidding
Saxophone harassment in the practice room,

Though we can hope, before you weave around
The wrong goal post in the wrong end zone,
That someone somewhere

Will put his foot down in time,
And two sudden flutes out of ten
Will sweeten the evening air.

Junkyard Blues

My father, who could heave
The hood from an old car
High on his flatbed truck,
Is flat in his bed now, is now
As thin as rain, rain
On a tin roof over the junk
Stored there for more than
Forty years, as if the price
Went up with every ounce of rust—
Starters and wires and wheels
And God knows what, too much
To name or stumble through,
A legacy we'll have hauled off
For scrap, for whatever
The going rate might be today.
Born a Catholic, like all of us,
He'll die one, too, buried from
That little church on the bayou road,
At whose early mass he kneeled
On Sunday morning, before the crowds
And the heat could gather there.
And yet, some papers found
When my last great-uncle
Lay fresh in his grave
Said that we came to this
From the deep dark of Germany,
So many lives ago we can't remember,
A lost tribe of Jews, stuck on another
Exodus from the stupid and
The cruel. And I said:
Well, that explains everything.
That explains it all. And now
My father's nothing more
Than bones and breath, as if
He stared at us from some cold
Camp in Poland where the wind
Reeked of ashes and boiling fat,
A wreck among the wrecks.
O put him in the ground

And get it over with—
What difference does it make
Which God he prayed to,
Or why he's dying here
Before our eyes, each day
Weaker and less himself.
My father's still out there,
Sweating his way through
The cranky maze of an engine
In the summer sun, his hands
Black with grease and red
From honest blood roughed out
In stubborn labor. Where we live,
Everything around us is ruins,
Broken, gutted, and cut apart.
And now there's no one
To put the pieces together again.

Beckian Fritz Goldberg

Beckian Fritz Goldberg is the author of several volumes of poetry, including *Body Betrayer* (Cleveland State University, 1991), *In the Badlands of Desire* (Cleveland State, 1993), and *Never Be the Horse*, winner of the University of Akron Poetry Prize (University of Akron, 1999). Her collection, *Lie Awake Lake,* was awarded the 2004 Field Poetry Prize from Oberlin College Press. She teaches in the Creative Writing Program at Arizona State University.

Far Away Lake

We can't get there
by road, by rope, by
wing

by time—
though time would be the way

by boat
by please please

time would be the way

then the reed-quiver
a cloud of gnats
mumbling its hypnotic suggestion

by sleep, sleep
until you say
lift my elbow   straighten
my legs

And I
straightened you in this life
like flowers

but the little water
there was
went to air
where it came from

And all my love for you
came back—
you couldn't take it where
you were going

you'd get halfway there
and then you'd drift
arms by your side

like a clock
plucked…

Wren

Once I fished a wren
from the pool
held it

little volt
in my hand

This I won't forget:

my mother's shoulders

I'm in the backseat
holding my brother's hand

my sister is driving

I don't have to see
anyone's face

the box of ashes
queerly heavy
like metal

like
the soaked sleeve of your sweater

long ago

the way something would rather drown
than trust

the hand that would lift it

Fourth Month

Finally, my father's soul came
to rest in the closet.
This is where you want
the dead—out of sight

and within scolding distance.
By now, it was June.
The grass shrank
and whitened. The sun,

the sun, was out every day
until we thought
it would never go…

Soon the nights would be still
and pointless,
too hot for bedsheets.
You want to sleep in air,
you want to sleep in water.

But what you feel is the sheen
of grief
like a sweat.

My aunt telling my mother
she should bring his ashes home,
to the lake where he was born,

my mother asking me is it all right
to wait—

but dear god who am I?

Back

The god of the back
must be a lonely god,
god in the shape of man-headed hawk.

Long ago
a man had been sailing the river
and the hawk had been flying beside him
for days. Mornings,

the man would wake and look,
yes, there it was, dark tip-to-tip, the hawk.
His hawk, he began to think of it.
And after a time

he forgot the point of the journey,
he only woke each morning to see
if the hawk was there, to move if the hawk
moved with him, to not rest

if the hawk did not rest. And all of this love
was done in silence, between animal
and animal. There

beside him in the air and there
beside him in the water, the yoke
of the hawk. Once he had a family. Once
he had a city to go to and something

to bring back. More and more
he began to see his life
as a story the hawk was telling

holding the rat of the field in its claw, meaning
There is another world

and I will take you in it.
This

is when he became the god,
god of the back, the beautiful
brow of leaving.

Sarah Gorham

Sarah Gorham is the author of three books of poetry: *The Cure, The Tension Zone,* and *Don't Go Back to Sleep.* New work has been published in *The Gettysburg Review, Poetry, Virginia Quarterly Review, Southern Review,* and *American Poetry Review.* Gorham is president and editor-in-chief of Sarabande Books in Louisville, KY.

Scotoma

Here it comes, like steelwool
or a cluster of pinpricks,
though the visual's being scoured
not her skin and the pain
arrives later. Little by little
what she loves so well
is erased: honeycombed trees,
grass flickering like emeralds, faces
smudged all the way to the forehead,
to their thin crusts of hair.
So it goes for half an hour or so,

till suddenly there's a break,
a bright spot at the center
like the eye on that primordial fish
which was really just a patch
of light-sensitive skin.
But now she's afraid to look,
would rather stay in the dark
with the digested trees and grass.
She knew a girl once
with a strange disfigurement,
her mouth perpetually ajar.
Because of sweet lymphatic fluids there,
bees flew in to sting her tongue.
This open spot
is a window to her brain,
an unwelcome consciousness,
as when the moon drops
and we understand
we are food for the stars.

Rebound Tenderness

With an abrupt jolt
her lover let up his insistence.
No more name-calling,
no more poking and prodding.
He drew back, and was gone.

For years, she'd been opaque,
cool like an ice lens
under his touch. Presto,
she's flooded with color,
anger and blame,
her body's final attempt
to heal up the rent.

It's a classic symptom—pain
when the pressure is released.
Doctors call it "rebound tenderness"
and in tenderness lies the cure
for her unstable condition.

Or so said the 17th century surgeon,
Wilhelm Hilden.
Everyone thought he was a fool,
applying his medicine to the knife
instead of the wound.
To heal, she must relax, lie back,
wish the bastard well.

Stillborn

She was the accident
born at the edge
of the sun,
snapped off, an ice cold
finger of flame.
I know. I stayed behind.
I watched as she
shed her bloody wrap,
the aluminum calipers.
Watched as she plucked
bead after tiny bead
from their viney
double Helix.

To see her now,
I have to squint.
I close my body eye
like a marksman
and everything turns
clear as reason,

sharp. I see the stain
on her loose silk shirt.
I see the ash, and tumble of
Popeye bones she has
fashioned into a hut.
Tiptoeing towards me
she raises one finger.
She raises a white
and wicked doubt.

Eamon Grennan

photo by Diane Zucker

Eamon Grennan is from Dublin and teaches at Vassar College in Poughkeepsie, NY. His poems have been published widely in Ireland and the U.S. His most recent publications are *Relations* (1998) and *Still Life with Waterfall,* which received the Lenore Marshall Poetry Prize for 2003.

Detail

I was watching a robin fly after a finch—the smaller bird
chirping with excitement, the bigger, its breast blazing, silent
in light-winged earnest chase—when, out of nowhere
over the chimneys and the shivering front gardens,
flashes a sparrowhawk headlong, a light brown burn
scorching the air from which it simply plucks
like a ripe fruit the stopped robin, whose two or three
cheeps of terminal surprise twinkle in the silence
closing over the empty street when the birds have gone
about their own business, and I began to understand
how a poem can happen: you have your eye on a small
elusive detail, pursuing its music, when a terrible truth
strikes and your heart cries out, being carried off.

Woman Sleeping in the Train

Her lips remind me of the mouth Bernini gave
Saint Theresa in ecstasy. Eyes not quite closed,
she barely breathes, and her head keeps falling,
it seems, over a wall of sleep, her whole body
suddenly one thing and open. Whenever the train
gives a sudden jerk, her forehead raps the window
and she opens her eyes, trying to bring things
into focus, then slides away again, and sleeps.

Small wonder the sculptor loved such a moment—
the complete surrender of it, a body hovering
between states, its spirit beating wings of light
and near flying—and set in stone the saint
giving herself to God, with God's young
pitiless angel grinning and leveling his spear
at her center, her face naked and moisting over
with love sweat. But the woman I'm watching

is dry as a bone, a trace of pain in the way her mouth
stays slightly open, in which I think I see the remains
of something spent, let go. When she wakes at last
and looks out the window, all is commonplace
again, she an ordinary traveler as I am, nothing
rushing into her body and filling her to the brim
the way her sleep did and what went on in it—its
blind struggles of breath and flesh, its lick of fire—

and it's just the two of us looking through glass
in silence, like survivors, at the vanishing fields
and the light on the Irish Sea near Drogheda,
catching sight of our own reflected, reflecting eyes
as they catch and shy away from the sight of a man
pissing into a blackberry bush—head down, lost
in himself and his action—our tangled glances
having to take it and each other in as we look away.

Vermeer, My Mother, and Me

Roof and sky and chimney stacks,
the blue, the white, the reddish browns
how he might have seen Westfield Road
and the coppergreen spires of Mount Argus
from the window of my childhood bedroom

I can gather from a little corner
of his *Little Street*, and the almost
unremarkable presence in it
of the woman bent over in her own back yard,
who is leaning for a mop in a wooden bucket

and who just might be my mother
at our kitchen door, her eyes cast down
to the shore that's clogged and stinking again
as she takes in a breath—filled
with the smells of grass and apples,

coal dust, Jeyes Fluid, and the sugary
toffee scent from the factory down the road—
that will, when she raises her head,
come out with my name on it, my own
two syllables making their instant way

back through the kitchen, along the narrow hall,
up the dark-carpeted stairs and into
the small, wallpapered, big-windowed bedroom
where I'll hear that name and her known voice
shaping it, making it quick, making me

be there, myself in the very moment
when our daily life—defined
by cloud-broken blue sky and the ginger
bricks of gable-ends, radiance of roof-tiles
and wet chimneys—has to happen, there

where she's calling me to come, quick, help her.

Robert Hass

Robert Hass, former U.S. Poet Laureate and winner of two National Book Critics Circle Awards, is a professor of English at the University of California at Berkeley.

A Story About the Body

The young composer, working that summer at an artist's colony, had watched her for a week. She was Japanese, a painter, almost sixty, and he thought he was in love with her. He loved her work, and her work was like the way she moved her body, used her hands, looked at him directly when she made amused and considered answers to his questions. One night, walking back from a concert, they came to her door and she turned to him and said, "I think you would like to have me. I would like that too, but I must tell you that I have had a double mastectomy," and when he didn't understand, "I've lost both my breasts." The radiance that he had carried around in his belly and chest cavity—like music—withered very quickly, and he made himself look at her when he said, "I'm sorry. I don't think I could." He walked back to his own cabin through the pines, and in the morning he found a small blue bowl on the porch outside his door. It looked to be full of rose petals, but he found when he picked it up that the rose petals were on top; the rest of the bowl—she must have swept them from the corners of her studio—was full of dead bees.

The Apple Trees at Olema

They are walking in the woods along the coast
and in a grassy meadow, wasting, they come upon
two old neglected apple trees. Moss thickened
every bough and the wood of the limbs looked rotten
but the trees were wild with blossom and a green fire
of small new leaves flickered even on the deadest branches.
Blue-eyes, crane's-bills, little Dutchmen
flecked the meadow, and an intricate, leopard-spotted
leaf-green flower whose name they didn't know.
Trout lily, he said; she said, adder's-tongue.
She is shaken by the raw, white, backlit flaring
of the apple blossoms. He is exultant,
as if some thing he felt were verified,
and looks to her to mirror his response.
If it is afternoon, a thin moon of my own dismay
fades like a scar in the sky to the east of them.
He could be knocking wildly at a closed door
in a dream. She thinks, meanwhile, that moss
resembles seaweed drying lightly on a dock.
Torn flesh, it was the repetitive torn flesh
of appetite in the cold white blossoms
that had startled her. Now they seem tender
and where she was repelled she takes the measure
of the trees and lets them in. But he no longer
has the apple trees. This is as sad or happy
as the tide, going out or coming in, at sunset.
The light catching in the spray that spumes up
on the reef is the color of the lesser finch
they notice now flashing dull gold in the light
above the field. They admire the bird together,
it draws them closer, and they start to walk again.
A small boy wanders corridors of a hotel that way.
Behind one door, a maid. Behind another one, a man
in striped pajamas shaving. He holds the number
of his room close to the center of his mind
gravely and delicately, as if it were the key,
and then he wanders among strangers all he wants.

Misery and Splendor

Summoned by conscious recollection, she
would be smiling, they might be in a kitchen talking,
before or after dinner. But they are in this other room,
the window has many small panes, and they are on a couch
embracing. He holds her as tightly
as he can, she buries herself in his body.
Morning, maybe it is evening, light
is flowing through the room. Outside,
the day is slowly succeeded by night,
succeeded by day. The process wobbles wildly
and accelerates: weeks, months, years. The light in the room
does not change, so it is plain what is happening.
They are trying to become one creature,
and something will not have it. They are tender
with each other, afraid
their brief, sharp cries will reconcile them to the moment
when they fall away again. So they rub against each other,
their mouths dry, then wet, then dry.
They feel themselves at the center of a powerful
and baffled will. They feel
they are an almost animal,
washed up on the shore of a world—
or huddled against the gate of a garden—
to which they can't admit they can never be admitted.

Terrance Hayes

Terrance Hayes is author of *Hip Logic* (Penguin, 2002), which was a National Poetry Series winner and a finalist for both the Los Angeles Times Book Award and the James Laughlin Award from the Academy of American Poets. He received a Whiting Writers Award and the Kate Tufts Discovery Award for his first book of poems, *Muscular Music* (Tia Chucha Press, 1999). *Wind in a Box*, his third book of poems, is forthcoming from Penguin in 2005.

segregate

On the first morning of school there is a young tree-
frog waiting patiently at the front gate.
Since this means there will be no classes for the rest
of the day, the children dump their school gear
in their lockers & hustle to the windows to stare.
The girls are eager to transform him with a kiss; the boys eager
to see him on the basketball court. But their principal greets
him with a "Get the Hell out of here!" A security guard fetches the tear-
gas. Some of the older teachers crowd in the doorway like befuddled geese.
"You belong in our swamps not our schools!" they rage.
But clearly the cool-blooded Amphibian-American does not agree.

The Same City

The rain falling on a night
   in mid-December,
I pull to my father's engine
   wondering how long I'll remember
this. His car is dead. He connects
   jumper-cables to his battery,
then to mine without looking in
   at me & the child. Water beads
on the windshields, the road sign,
   his thin blue coat. I'd get out now,
prove I can stand with him
   in the cold, but he told me to stay
with the infant. I wrap her
   in the blanket staring
for what seems like a long time
   into her open, toothless mouth,
and wish she was mine. I feed her
   an orange softened first in my mouth,
chewed gently until the juice runs
   down my fingers as I squeeze it
into hers. What could any of this matter
   to another man passing on his way
to his family, his radio deafening
   the sound of water & breathing
along all the roads bound to his?
   But to rescue a soul is as close
as anyone comes to God.
   Think of Noah lifting a small black bird
from its nest. Think of a carpenter,
   raising a son that wasn't his.

Let me begin again.
   I want to be holy. In rain
I pull to my father's car
   with my girlfriend's infant.
She was pregnant when we met.
   But we'd make love. We'd make
love below stars & shingles
   while the baby kicked between us.
Perhaps a man whose young child
   bears his face, whose wife waits

as he drives home through rain
    & darkness, perhaps that man
would call me a fool. So what.
    There is one thing I will remember
all my life. It is as small
    & holy as the mouth
of an infant. It is speechless.
    When his car would not stir,
my father climbed in beside us,
    took the orange from my hand,
took the baby in his arms.
    In 1974, this man met my mother
for the first time as I cried or slept
    in the same city that holds us
tonight. If you ever tell my story,
    say that's the year I was born.

for James L. Hayes

The Whale

For P.

Just like that your father's dead,
Half of all the footsteps you've made

In your lifetime swept away by the tide
Gnawing the shore, the bits of shells
Like fragments of bone and teeth sinking

Into the sand beneath you as you walk
Toward the people crowding the body

Of a young whale, a boy on the shoulders
Of his father, a woman slipping film into a camera,
The skin peeling on a lifeguard's neck

As he stoops peering into the animal's eye,
Saying nothing, the audience mute, or muted

By the sound of saltwater sweet-talking the shore
As if sweet-talking the earth from her prom dress,
The tide stroking its hands along her inner thigh

And finding the crop of razor bumps
Like the humped tiny backs of shells

And smiling at the thought of the girl preparing
For her prom date, the hair lathered
And shaved away, the air leaving ripples inside

The dress as the knee-high hem is lifted
Above the girl's waist and breasts,

The sound of the silk passing over her body
Like the sound of the tide uncovering
And then covering the hard news of the day,

The news returning each time it's washed away.

Pine

> *I still had two friends, but they were trees.*
> —Larry Levis

In the dark we lugged someone's farfetched bounty
From a truck's black cab and it was a bad idea
And a bedevilment better than the rocks we'd thrown

At the dogs behind each low fence, the branches we'd torn
From saplings barely rooted to the fields, Boomie and I,
Our heads in a swivel of trouble, our two tongues

Swigging distractions, a few hour's worth of wrong turns
Behind us, we were restless and miles from home,
Dark boys roaming in the dark. We found a pickup truck

Unlocked outside a small hotel and in its cab: trash bags
Fat with clothing and housewares, a toaster and vacuum,
Waiting to be used again by someone checked in for the night,

Maybe a runaway wife reversing her dreams, a streak
Of red wine sleeping on her tongue while elsewhere
Her husband was in the dark because he didn't know yet:

She was gone, she was gone. For no good reason
We took the bags from the truck and propped them
Below the pine trees which, like everything in the dark,

Belonged to us. And to anyone approaching, our laughter
Must have sounded like the laughter of crows, those birds
That leave everything beneath them trampled and broken open,

Those birds dark enough to bury themselves in the dark.
But we were not crows, and we were not quiet until it was too late.
I was thrown against a tree as if I weighed less than a shadow,

A hand clutched the back of my neck as if it wasn't a neck.
Cuffed later inside the break-proof glass, I watched
The policemen nuzzling everything we'd touched,

Slithering, their faces calculating absolutes while the trash bags
Shimmered in a fiasco of light. When I looked up,
I saw Boomie nearly twenty feet high in the arms of a pine,

Almost nothing visible, but his white shirt and white shorts.
I could feel him feeling as sorry for me as I felt for him,
And I said nothing. Think of what the tree might have said

If it could speak: *Hold me for a moment then, let me go…*
Something an unhappy housewife might say
To her husband on the last night of their marriage,

Or a boy to policemen when he's locked in a squad car.
I heard a voice between their voices issuing numbers,
Codes or uninterpretable verses, addresses in a bewildered city.

I was to be taken somewhere and given a name
More bona fide and afflicted, I was to be shot
Through the knee and then shot through the jaw,

Boomie must have thought. Even when the scene was clear,
He must have remained. It must have been like clinging
To the massive leg of God—

If the leg of God is covered in bark, if prayer is like waiting
For the darkness beneath you to change into something else,
If it's like waiting in the darkness to be changed.

Samuel Hazo

Sam Hazo's many books of poetry include *Just Once,* published by Autumn House Press. He is the Director of the International Poetry Forum in Pittsburgh, McAnulty Distinguished Professor of English Emeritus at Duquesne University, and the first State Poet of the Commonwealth of Pennsylvania.

But You Were Wrong

Not typically a thought, not
    anything conceived or earned
    but totally gratuitous....
                    It happened
    in your sleep, and, while it stayed,
    it made you memorize each minute.
Later, there was coffee to be drunk,
    your chin and cheeks to shave,
    slacks to be belted, shirts
    to be buttoned, ties to be knotted,
    and a world to awaken and name.
You watched a chief of state
    whose lone credential was audacity.

You listened every hour on the hour
    to the news.
             You read the telegrammic
    headlines and the columned texts
    that answered everything but why.
The more the present tense
    responded to the reveille of your complete
    attention, the more the echo
    of that perfect thought receded.
You said it would return
    with even greater emphasis,
    but you were wrong.
             Days
    intervened, then months, then years...
That thought was like the first girl
    you loved who loved you back.
Distance undid you both, proving
    that separation weakens a weak
    love as surely as it strengthens
    a strong one.
             You felt
    more bitter than bereft.
             The world
    remained the world where no one
    stays twenty and desirable
    for long.
             But still a pressure
    and an ache endured for half
    a century as something undefinable
    but unrepeatable that came
    when you were least expecting it
    and named its memory and left.

Casanova to God

I thought of women basically
     as fruit: delectable when ripe,
     dismissible past prime,
     disposable when old.
                      I'm not
    to blame.
              You made young women
    irresistible, not I.
                My sin—
if it was sin at all—was ultimate
enjoyment of Your handiwork.
That girl from Padua—the supple
     once-ness of her kiss....
                  Her cousin
from Trieste—the way her breasts
announced themselves....
               Surely
You appreciate the patience and the skill
it takes to bring a virgin
to the point where shame means nothing.
I'm not a rapist, after all.
The ones I chose were single,
   willing, totally agreeable.
They wanted to be loved deliciously.
Not roughly like those toughs who pinched
     them on the street, but step
     by gentle step and never in a hurry.
First, some conversation.
            Then,
   a kiss on either cheek.
Then everything that You alone
     could see: a jettison of clothes,
     my palm along her inner thigh,
     our loins in juncture as we hugged,
     the mounting puffs and shudders
     on the sheets, the parting, the repose.
It made me marvel at the way
     You fashioned us for mating
     face to face—essentially

two kinds of kissing happening
in one position all at once.
Because I reached perfection in the act,
some called me a philanderer...
Pronounce me guilty if You like...
I'm reconciled.
                    I did what I
alone could do when I could
do it.
              Who says desire dies?
Today I'm tended by a nurse
who spoons me noodles from a cup.
She tells me to relax.
                    Relax?
When a woman naked underneath
her whites and silks is just a breath
away from Giacomo Girolamo
Casanova of Venice?
                    Impossible.

Arms and the Word

Great sailors though they were,
the Greeks abhorred the sea.
What was it but a gray
monotony of waves, wetness
in depth, an element by nature
voyager-unfriendly and capricious?
Sailing in sight of shore,
they always beached at night
to sleep before the next day's
rowing.
            Taming the sea
by beating it with rods
they named the ultimate insanity—
a metaphor too obvious to paraphrase.

In short, they knew a widow-
        maker when they saw one.
                                        Still,
        for honor, commerce or a kidnapped
        queen, they waged their lives
        against what Homer called wine-dark
        and deep.
                        Some came back never.
Some learned too late that pacing
        a deck was far less hazardous
        than facing what awaited them
        at home....
                        Homer would praise
        their iliads and odysseys in song.
Aeschylus, Euripides and Sophocles
        would watch and wait, then write
        of wars much closer to the heart.
They knew the lives of men—
        no matter how adventurous—
        would end as comedies or tragedies.
They wrote that both were fundamentally
        and finally domestic.
                        Homer
        could sing his fill.
                        The dramatists
        dared otherwise.
                        Compared
        to troubles in a family, they saw
        this business with the sea and swords—
        regardless of the risk—as minor.

Bob Hicok

Bob Hicok's most recent book is *Insomnia Diary* (University of Pittsburgh Press, 2004). *Animal Soul* was a finalist for the National Book Critics Circle Award.

photo by Robert Turney

Bars poetica

This is the story I've tried to tell. Guy
exists. Father mother sister brother.
Oh pretty stars, oh bastard moon
I see you watching me. The trembling
years leading to sex, the trembling sex.
Death as garnish. Death as male lead,
female lead, death as a cast
of thousands. God in, on, as, with,
to, around, because who knows
because. All the while feeling air's
a quilt of tongues, that spaces
between words are more articulate
than words. It's not like you'd hope,
that anyone can make sense.

Look around you, let your ears
breathe deep—almost no one does.
Have another drink. When they throw us out
there's a place down the street
that never closes, and when it does,
we'll climb a fire escape and praise
the genealogy of light. The Big Bang
sounds like what it was, the fucking
that got everything under way.
That love was there from the start
is all I've been trying to say.

1935

for Lester Hicok

He rode in the back with apples and wind.
Rumor was a blast furnace in Battle Creek

needed to be fed. He followed the scent
of work, rode in the back with an ax

and pig. In Battle Creek he'd stand with fifty
or a thousand men. They'd shuffle and smoke,

some would talk while others hid in their hats.
After awhile a man with a clipboard

would ask what he asked and stare as long
as he liked. His nod meant food. He rode

in the back on a coil of chain link fence.
It was warm, shadows popped up from the fields.

In Battle Creek he'd stand. A man would come,
he'd wear a tie and his socks would match.

A furnace needed to be fed, a roof had to rise
over dirt, a pile of steel wanted to move

somewhere else. The rumor was work.
He rode without waving to the men

in other trucks. A rumor was often a lock
on a door. He followed the scent,

rode in the back with apples and wind,
with the tools of his hands and the shadow

of his head running beside the truck.
It got to Battle Creek before he did.

He found other men, their hats,
their cigarettes. He found that their eyes

didn't want him. The furnace was happy
and fat, it didn't need to be fed. Rumor

was a man in Flint had a place and a thing
that needed to be done. He followed the scent,

stuck out his thumb. This is how
my grandfather lived. In the back with a pig.

Cutting edge

I can't be in the avant garde
because I cry when dogs die

in movies. Worse, I sniffle
if they're abandoned or hit

with even the rolled and tepid
discipline of *Newsweek*. My dog

is eight. When I do the math
I get weepy. I see the hole

in the back yard I'll dig,
pet her while imagining

how I'll pet her as the vet
slips the needle in. During

these moments she licks tears
and snot from my face, just

as she took menstrual blood
from my wife's finger

this morning for what it is.
Anyway, sorrow about a dog

looks silly in a beret. It
should be plain spoken,

like everything else
I try hard not to say.

Jane Hirshfield

photo by Jerry Bauer

Jane Hirshfield's fifth collection of poems, *Given Sugar, Given Salt* (Harper Collins, 2001) was a finalist for the National Book Critics Circle Award and winner of the Northern California Book Award. Other honors include fellowships from the Guggenheim and Rockefeller Foundations, the Poetry Center Book Award, and multiple appearances in *Best American Poetry* and the *Pushcart Prize* anthologies.

The Bell Zygmunt

For fertility, a new bride is lifted to touch it with her left hand,
or possibly kiss it.
The sound close in, my friend told me later, is almost silent.

At ten kilometers, even those who have never heard it know what it is.

If you stand near during thunder, she said,
you will hear a reply.

Six weeks and six days from the phone's small ringing,
replying was over.

She who cooked lamb and loved wine and wild mushroom pastas.
She who when I saw her last was silent as the great Zygmunt mostly is,
a ventilator's clapper between her dry lips.

Because I could, I spoke. She laid her palm on my cheek to answer.
And soon again, to say it was time to leave.

I put my lips near the place a tube went into
the back of one hand.
The kiss—as if it knew what I did not yet—both full and formal.

As one would kiss the ring of a cardinal, or the rim
of that cold iron bell, whose speech can mean "Great joy,"
or—equally—"The city is burning. Come."

It Was Like This: You Were Happy

It was like this:
you were happy, then you were sad,
then happy again, then not.

It went on.
You were innocent or you were guilty.
Actions were taken, or not.

At times you spoke, at other times you were silent.
Mostly, it seems you were silent—what could you say?

Now it is almost over.

Like a lover, your life bends down and kisses your life.

It does this not in forgiveness—
between you, there is nothing to forgive—
but with the simple nod of a baker at the moment
he sees the bread is finished with transformation.

Eating, too, is a thing now only for others.

It doesn't matter what they will make of you
or your days: they will be wrong,

they will miss the wrong woman, miss the wrong man,
all the stories they tell will be tales of their own invention.

Your story was this: you were happy, then you were sad,
you slept, you awakened.
Sometimes you ate roasted chestnuts, sometimes persimmons.

The Woodpecker Keeps Returning

The woodpecker keeps returning
to drill the house wall.
Put a pie plate over one place, he chooses another.

There is nothing good to eat there:
he has found in the house
a resonant billboard to post his intentions,
his voluble strength as provider.

But where is the female he drums for? Where?

I ask this, who am myself the ruined siding,
the handsome red-capped bird, the missing mate.

Possibility: An Assay

Again I looked out the window.
All around me, the morning still dark.

The mountain's outline there, but not the mountain.

Then a neighbor's facing plate-glass filled
with the colors, acute and tender, of a Flemish painting.
Corals, blues.

Which seemed to be a preview of the future but were,
I knew,
this moment simply looking elsewhere,
like a woman who has wept for weeks who realizes
that she is also hungry.

The Monk Stood Beside A Wheelbarrow

The monk stood beside a wheelbarrow, weeping.

God or Buddha nowhere to be seen—
these tears were fully human,
bitter, broken,
falling onto the wheelbarrow's rusty side.

They gathered at its bottom,
where the metal drank them in to make more rust.

You cannot know what you do in this life, what you have done.

The monk stood weeping.
I knew I also had a place on this hard earth.

Tony Hoagland

Tony Hoagland has published three books of poems: *Sweet Ruin, Donkey Gospel,* and *What Narcissism Means to Me.* He teaches at the University of Houston and in the Warren Wilson low-residency MFA program and has received grants from the NEA and the Guggenheim Foundation.

The News

The big country beat the little country up
like a schoolyard bully,
so an even bigger country stepped in
and knocked it on its ass to make it nice,
which reminds me of my Uncle Bob's
                            philosophy of parenting.

It's August, I'm sitting on the porch swing,
touching the sores inside my mouth
with the tip of my tongue, watching the sun
go down in the west like a sinking ship,
from which a flood of sticky orange bleeds out.

It's the hour of meatloaf perfume emanating from the houses.
It's the season of Little League practice
and atonal high school band rehearsals.
You can't buy a beach umbrella in the stores till next year.
The summer beauty pageants are all over,
and no one I know won the swimsuit competition.

This year illness just flirted with me,
picking me up and putting me down
like a cat with a ball of yarn,
so I walked among the living like a tourist,
and I wore my health
like a borrowed shirt,
knowing I would probably have to give it back.

There are the terrible things that happen to you
and the terrible things that you yourself make happen,
like George, who bought a little red sportscar
for his favorite niece
              to smash her life to pieces in.

And the girl on the radio sings,
You know what I'm talking about. Bawhoop, awhoop.

This year it seems like everyone is getting tattoos—
sharks and Chinese characters,
hummingbirds and musical notes—
but the tattoo I would like to get
is of a fist and a rose.

But I can't tell how they will fit together on my shoulder:
If the rose is inside the fist, it will be crushed or hidden;
if the fist is closed,—as a fist by definition is,—
it cannot reach out and touch the rose.

Yet the only tattoo I want
is of a fist and rose, together.
Fist, that helps you survive.
Rose, without which
                    you have no reason to.

Suicide Song

But now I am afraid I know too much to kill myself
Though I would still like to jump off a high bridge

At midnight, or paddle a kayak out to sea
Until I turn into a speck, or wear a necktie made of knotted rope

But people would squirm, it would hurt them in some way,
And I am too knowledgeable now to hurt people imprecisely.

No longer do I live by the law of me,
No longer having the excuse of youth or craziness,

And dying you know shows a serious ingratitude
For sunsets and beehive hairdos and the precious green corrugated

Pickles they place at the edge of your plate.
Killing yourself is wasteful, like spilling oil

At sea or not recycling all the kisses you've been given,
And anyway, who has clothes nice enough to be caught dead in?

Not me. You stay alive you stupid asshole
Because you haven't been excused.

You haven't finished though it takes a mule
To chew this food.

It is a stone, it is an inconvenience, it is an innocence,
And I turn against it like a record

Turns against the needle
That makes it play.

Phone Call

Maybe I overdid it
when I called my father an enemy of humanity.
That might have been a little strongly put,
a slight overexaggeration,

an immoderate description of the person
who at that moment, two thousand miles away,
holding the telephone receiver six inches from his ear,
must have regretted paying for my therapy.

What I meant was that my father
was an enemy of *my* humanity
and what I meant behind that
was that my father was split
into two people, one of them

living deep inside of me
like a bad king or an incurable disease—
blighting my crops,
striking down my herds,
poisoning my wells— the other
standing in another time zone,
in a kitchen in Wyoming,
with bad knees and white hair sprouting from his ears.

I don't want to scream forever,
I don't want to live without proportion
like some kind of infection from the past,

so I have to remember the second father,
the one whose tv dinner is getting cold
while he holds the phone in his left hand
and stares blankly out the window

where just now the sun is going down
and the last fingertips of sunlight
are withdrawing from the hills
they once touched like a child.

Two Trains

Then there was that song called "Two Trains Running,"
a Mississippi blues they play on late-night radio,
that program after midnight called *FM in the AM*,
—well, I always thought it was about *trains*.

Then somebody told me it was about what a man and woman do
under the covers of their bed, moving back and forth
like slow pistons in a shiny black locomotive,
the rods and valves trying to stay coordinated

long enough that they will "get to the station"
at the same time. And one of the trains
goes out of sight into the mountain tunnel,
but when they break back into the light

the other train has somehow pulled ahead,
the two trains running like that, side by side,
first one and then the other, with the fierce white
bursts of smoke puffing from their stacks,
into a sky so sharp and blue you want to die.

So then for a long time I thought the song was about sex.

But then Mack told me that all train songs
are really about Jesus, about how the second train
is shadowing the first, so He walks in your footsteps
and He watches you from behind, He is running with you,

He is your brakeman and your engineer,
your coolant and your coal,
and He will catch you when you fall,
and when you stall He will push you through
the darkest mountain valley, up the steepest hill,

and the rough *chuff chuff* of His fingers on the washboard
and the harmonica *woo woo* is the long soul cry by which He
pulls you through the bloody tunnel of the world.
So then I thought the two trains song was a gospel song.

Then I quit my job in Santa Fe and Sharon drove
her spike heel through my heart
and I got twelve years older and Dean moved away,
and now I think the song might be about good-byes—

because we are not even in the same time zone,
or moving at the same speed, or perhaps even
headed towards the same destination—
forgodsakes, we are not even trains!

What grief it is to love some people like your own
blood , and then to see them simply disappear;
to feel time bearing us away
                    one boxcar at a time.

And sometimes, sitting in my chair
I can feel the absence stretching out in all directions—
like the deaf, defoliated silence
just after a train has thundered past the platform,

just before the mindless birds begin to chirp again
—and the wildflowers that grow beside the tracks
wobble wildly on their little stems,
                    then gradually grow still and stand

motherless and vertical in the middle of everything.

Marie Howe

photo by Marion Roth

Marie Howe lives in New York
City and is the author of
The Good Thief and *What the
Living Do.*

What the Living Do

Johnny, the kitchen sink has been clogged for days, some utensil probably
    fell down there.
And the Drano won't work but smells dangerous, and the crusty dishes
    have piled up

waiting for the plumber I still haven't called. This is the everyday we
    spoke of.
It's winter again: the sky's a deep headstrong blue, and the sunlight
    pours through

the open living room windows because the heat's on too high in here, and
    I can't turn it off.
For weeks now, driving, or dropping a bag of groceries in the street,
    the bag breaking,

I've been thinking: This is what the living do. And yesterday, hurrying
along those
wobbly bricks in the Cambridge sidewalk, spilling my coffee down my
wrist and sleeve,

I thought it again, and again later, when buying a hairbrush: This is it.
Parking. Slamming the car door shut in the cold. What you called
that yearning.

What you finally gave up. We want the spring to come and the winter to
pass. We want
whoever to call or not call, a letter, a kiss—we want more and more and
then more of it.

But there are moments, walking, when I catch a glimpse of myself in the
window glass,
say, the window of the corner video store, and I'm gripped by a cherishing
so deep

for my own blowing hair, chapped face, and unbuttoned coat that I'm
speechless:
I am living, I remember you.

Practicing

I want to write a love poem for the girls I kissed in seventh grade,
a song for what we did on the floor in the basement

of somebody's parents' house, a hymn for what we didn't say but thought:
That feels good or *I like that,* when we learned how to open each other's
mouths

how to move our tongues to make somebody moan. We called it
practicing, and
one was the boy, and we paired off—maybe six or eight girls—and
turned out

the lights and kissed and kissed until we were stoned on kisses, and
      lifted our
nightgowns or let the straps drop, and, Now you be the boy:

concrete floor, sleeping bag or couch, playroom, game room, train
      room, laundry.
Linda's basement was like a boat with booths and portholes

instead of windows. Gloria's father had a bar downstairs with stools
      that spun,
plush carpeting. We kissed each other's throats.

We sucked each other's breasts, and we left marks, and never spoke of it
      upstairs
outdoors, in daylight, not once. We did it, and it was

practicing, and slept, sprawled so our legs still locked or crossed, a hand
      still lost
in someone's hair. . . and we grew up and hardly mentioned who

the first kiss really was—a girl like us, still sticky with the moisturizer we'd
shared in the bathroom. I want to write a song

for that thick silence in the dark, and the first pure thrill of unreluctant
      desire,
just before we made ourselves stop.

The Copper Beech

Immense, entirely itself,
it wore that yard like a dress,

with limbs low enough for me to enter it
and climb the crooked ladder to where

I could lean against the trunk and practice being alone.

One day, I heard the sound before I saw it, rain fell
darkening the sidewalk.

Sitting close to the center, not very high in the branches,
I heard it hitting the high leaves, and I was happy,

watching it happen without it happening to me.

David Huddle

photo by Chip Riegel

David Huddle's recent books of poems are *Summer Lake: New & Selected Poems* (1999) and *Grayscale* (2004). He teaches at the University of Vermont and the Bread Loaf School of English.

Water

1.

Valley farmland
beside a mountain:

A spring up there sent down
the coldest, sweetest water—

fifty years since my last sip,
my tongue still remembers

that black-dirt-dogwood
taste of the Blue Ridge.

2.

Between Bristol
and East Middlebury

spring water spouts
from a pipe beside the road—

I see people stopped there
filling plastic jugs.

I want what they want,
but I don't stop.

3.

A house, a car, antique furniture,
computers, phones, shelves of books,

stereos on every floor, a thousand CDs,
two TVs: I'm so rich if they were alive

my parents wouldn't know whether
to be proud of or embarrassed

by this life that feels to me
like nearly unbearable loss.

4.

At Costco now I buy cases of plastic
pints tightly sheathed in plastic, I

who once with my brothers, faces dusty
and guts scrambled by a washboard road,

tumbled from the back of our Grandad's
red Dodge pick-up and raced to the cow's

trough where the spigot stayed wide open,
and we thought the flow would never stop.

Desire

Hiroshige's "Yellow Path"
came of such yearning

quite evidently he met her
in late April—she must have

cast her eyes down to show
him she was too young,

she could not meet his bold
stare, nor could she discuss

when they might meet again,
her parents would be coming

down the path any second now
and if her eyes raised again

it would cause an impossible
confusion in her heart

which was why please he must
turn away from her please no

there couldn't be another
time for her to come here

nor could she tell him where
she lived and no she was so

sorry she couldn't give him
even her name and then since

he wouldn't turn away she
turned, though he thought

she stole one last glance
before hurrying up the path

where he knew better than
to follow her, which left

him nothing else but to paint
where she left him, his only

choice—suicide or these
pink-white weeping trees.

No End

A sonnet began the day I started
flirting with the band's youngest majorette
during marching practice—you'd think it'd
be forgotten by now, how the sweat

shone on her forehead, how the director
shouted and cursed as if preparing us
for battle and we were a bunch of soldiers
instead of backwoods kids—gawky, doofus

hillbillies good for homecoming parades
and halftime shows at football games. It came
to something—that flirtation—escapades
of learning to smoke, getting caught, that game

of whistle-stop in her basement. Dead five
years now. Almost unbearably alive.

Andrew Hudgins

Andrew Hudgins is Humanities Distinguished Professor in English at Ohio State University. He has published five books of poetry with Houghton Mifflin: *Babylon in a Jar* (1998), *The Glass Hammer* (1995), *The Never-Ending* (1991), *After the Lost War* (1988), and *Saints and Strangers* (1985), which was a finalist for the 1985 Pulitzer Prize. A new collection, *Ecstatic in the Poison,* was published by The Overlook Press/ Sewanee Writers' Series in 2003.

In

When we first heard from blocks away
the fog truck's blustery roar,
we dropped our toys, leapt from our meals,
and scrambled out the door

into an evening briefly fuzzy.
We yearned to be transformed—
translated past confining flesh
to disembodied spirit. We swarmed

in thick smoke, taking human form
before we blurred again,
turned vague and then invisible,
in temporary heaven.

Freed of bodies by the fog,
we laughed, we sang, we shouted.
We were our voices, nothing else.
Voice was all we wanted.

The white clouds tumbled down our streets
pursued by spellbound children
who chased the most distorting clouds,
ecstatic in the poison.

Out

My father cinched the rope,
a noose around my waist,
and lowered me into
the darkness. I could taste

my fear. It tasted first
of dark, then earth, then rot.
I swung and struck my head
and at that moment got

another then: then blood,
which spiked my mouth with iron.
Hand over hand, my father
dropped me from then to then:

then water. Then wet fur,
which I hugged to my chest.
I shouted. Daddy hauled
the wet rope. I gagged, and pressed

my neighbor's missing dog
against me. I held its death
and rose up to my father.
Then light. Then hands. Then breath.

Blur

Storms of perfume lift from honeysuckle,
lilac, clover—and drift across the threshold,
outside reclaiming inside as its home.
Warm days whirl in a bright unnumberable blur,
a cup—a grail brimmed with delirium
and humbling boredom both. I was a boy,
I thought I'd always be a boy, pell mell,
mean, and gaily murderous one moment
as I decapitated daisies with a stick,
then overcome with summer's opium,
numb-slumberous. I thought I'd always be a boy,
each day its own millennium, each
one thousand years of daylight ending in
the night watch, summer's pervigilium,
which I could never keep because by sunset
I was an old man. I was Methuselah,
the oldest man in the holy book. I drowsed.
I nodded, slept—and without my watching, the world,
whose permanence I doubted, returned again,
bluebell and blue jay, speedwell and cardinal
still there when the light swept back,
and so was I, which I had also doubted.
I understood with horror then with joy,
dubious and luminous joy: it simply spins.
It doesn't need my feet to make it turn.
It doesn't even need my eyes to watch it,
and I, though a latecomer to its surface, I'd
be leaving early. It was my duty to stay awake
and sing if I could keep my mind on singing,

not extinction, as blurred green summer, lifted
to its apex, succumbed to gravity and fell
to autumn, Ilium, and ashes. In joy
we are our own uncomprehending mourners,
and more than joy I longed for understanding
and more than understanding I longed for joy.

The Long Ship

Death's settled in my suburbs: weak ankles
just a little weaker and the fingers of my right hand just
a little more like unoiled hinges in the cold.
Death's moved into my right shoulder as a flame.
I tease it, taunt it, test it: Can I carry wood?
Can I still throw the ball? How far and for how long?
What's the new price? Higher, but not too high.

Death, darling,
                         you've been gentle up till now.
But after the first kiss I return, we know
how your seductions go: each tender kiss
a little coarser. Each night a little further:
caress to rough insistent stroke. Each qualm
and modest scruple brushed aside till metaphor
gives way to metamorphosis—from one
hard, lived cliché to one nobody lives:
Death's built his long ship, he's raised his black
sail over me, and what ship doesn't love
a steady wind, and what ship doesn't love the white
wake curled behind it like lilies on a black stem?

Richard Jackson

Richard Jackson is the author of eight books of poems, most recently *Half Lives: Petrarchan Poems* (Autumn House, 2004). He has edited two anthologies of Slovene poetry and in 2000 was awarded the Order of Freedom Medal for "literary and humanitarian work" in the Balkans by the President of Slovenia.

The Loss of Breath

I've breathed everything I have into these difficult hills
that overlook the flood plain where she was born,
that woman who held my heart in her hand with delicate skill,
who held that heart budding or bearing fruit, who has gone,
maybe forever, so that now even breathing takes too much will,
so that even seeing is something I fear to do because the stars warn
against what I'm thinking, and the moon itself refuses, still,
to reveal the cliffs and rivers, the towers and windows of scorn.
There's not a shrub or stone in these hills, not a leaf
left on these trees, not a flower left from what I gave her,
not a single blade of grass that does not mean her name,
not a spring, not a cabin, no fire, not even the smoke of belief
to hope she might return, not even the wildest beast, no tiger
in the shadows that would make this wild grief seem more tame.

The Trial

Not the late shift stars sweeping the aisles of darkness,
not the sloops that seem to iron flat the distant harbor,
not the deer threading their delicate scent through the forest,
not all of History marching, raising glorious shouts like banners,
not the news he brought of you, tonight, love's best witness,
news that I expected all along, that no love ever lingers—
the way Diana's troop, spied upon, made such a fuss
they set the dogs on Acteon, tore him apart, blunderer
on their sacred plot— like him, my own heart's ambushed,
like his, buried beside my Love— so, no, nothing here
can save me now, not your eyes, not the memory of your smile,
nothing can save me from this mistake, my life, this disgust
for everything, this desire to be swept away like those dark stars
at dawn, whose life is a constant test, whose every breath is a trial.

The Waking

Now that the earth, sky and wind settle into night's still pool,
now that Sleep tightens its reins on every dream and scans
the stars that whisper as they slip below the fading horizon,
now that the sea freezes its waves and makes the tides stall,
I wake within a thought whose fire chars all dreams, all
hopes, a cold fire, a sweet pain, for Love has won
and lost, battled and sued for peace, posted bond
and released me to sleep only to wake again, a smoldering coal.
From Love's clear fountain I can drink both life and death,
can drink a sweet desire or choke on its acrid poison:
the touch of my Love's single helping hand can stab or heal.
It never ends, a waterfall that lives by falling to its death.
A thousand times a day I rise to die within this prison.
Each day I feel death's life, and die to feel.

Gray Jacobik

Gray Jacobik's book, *The Double Task* (University of Massachusetts Press, 1998), received The Juniper Prize. *The Surface of Last Scattering* (Texas Review Press, 1999) won the X. J. Kennedy Poetry Prize. *Brave Disguises* (University of Pittsburgh Press, 2002) won the AWP Poetry Series Award. She teaches in the Stonecoast MFA Program.

The Tapeworm

It rushes out of you the way Magritte's train engine
rushes out of a fireplace; something
illogical and fast, the long freight of embarrassing
incident coupled to fear. Groceries left at the checkout
because a roommate took your cash, a car wasting
without repairs, the dog saved by a vet
you can't pay, so can't bring home. The ugly humiliating
chewed-up rag of it. Deadweight of trinkets
bought to console that don't console. How you can't get
enough of what you don't really want,
yet in the make-do, grab. Recompense that's supposed
to stave off— what?— the flush of shame
that stipples your neck. Two babies asleep on blankets
on a cold linoleum floor, no furniture,
no food in the fridge, none on shelves— the quick hysteria
of suppose. Suppose you borrow?
Suppose you take. . . ? But worse is the man who
promises work and delivers rape,

though he throws two twenties at you afterwards
that feed you a week. The gut-wrack of
can't-afford, primal yelp that keeps you swallowing hard.
Credit bureaus, bill collectors, taxes, bank.
The old stumble-and-fall-down, temp awhile, whore
awhile, give The Man his due. And here,
at last, you shit it out: the blind-eyed parasite who
bloodies you, the sharp-toothed gnawing
worm of desperation.

Skirts

Women spin and dance in skirts, sleep and wake
in them sometimes, ascend and descend stairs.
Some have walked into the sea in skirts,
which is like tossing a skirt over a man's head,
or pressing his face against the tent of one.
Some woman, maybe wearing a velvet skirt,
has embraced another woman—so that one skirt brushes
against another. Women wash and wring and hang
skirts up to dry, spray them, iron them, hem them,
slip them over slips, over tights. Once, I confess,
I owned six black ones: rayon, wool, gabardine,
linen, cotton, silk. The wind can blow the bulk of a skirt
between a woman's legs, or wrap her in
a twist, or billow underneath so skirls of wind touch
faintly, delightfully. Some women hear skirts
murmuring or sighing, conversing with the flesh
they cover. But most skirts drape in silence, the silence
of slow snow falling, or the hushed liquid glide
of a woman's body through a sunlit pool, the sweet
descent to sleep, or passion, or passion's nemesis,
ennui. A woman's spirit lengthens or widens in a skirt,
magnified by cloth and cut and her stride through
the quickened space. If instead a woman wears
a tight skirt, she feels containment and its

amplification— reduction's power to suggest.
Right now my favorite is a crimpy cinnabar silk
I twist into wrinkles to dry. I wear it walking in
the evenings. I vanish as its folds enfold the sky.

The 750 Hands

Mar de lagrimas (Sea of Tears)
—Osvoldo Yero

Each is cast in porcelain, fired, glazed a shade
of blue or greenish-blue, some left hands,
but mostly right, and each is the hand
of a Cuban artist. Some left during
the great flight of the mid-sixties
and the lesser flights of the seventies
and eighties. And some, forced to work
in mines and canefields, stayed in their
homeland. The hands hang a dozen deep,
a great wave on a long wall, each turned
slightly, thumb up, palm exposed.
From the side we see fingernails,
knuckles, knotted ridges of arteries,
scars of accidents and toil. Inert and cold,
signaling from stony depths, disembodied
yet overarching, as if each lived more
in the sky than in the flesh, more in
the sea than on the shore; the hands
of its people, the sky and sea that hold Cuba.
Each man or woman kept a hand in plaster
long enough to form a mold, each mold
received the poured clay, the glaze, the fire,
filling the void of absence with existence—
I lived through sorrowful times and made art
with this hand. Nothing can stop
a hand from finding what it needs.
Nothing can stop the maker.

Mark Jarman

photo by Eric England

Mark Jarman's latest collection of poetry is *To the Green Man* (Sarabande Books, 2004). His collection, *Questions for Ecclesiastes* (Story Line Press, 1997), won the Lenore Marshall Poetry Prize for 1998. He teaches at Vanderbilt University.

Butterflies Under Persimmon

I heard a woman
   State once that because
He peered so closely

At a stream of ants
   On the damp, naked
Limb of a fruit tree,

She fell for her husband.
   She wanted to be studied
With that attention,

To fascinate as if
    She were another species,
Whose willingness to be

Looked at lovingly
    Was her defense, to be
Like a phenomenon

Among leaves, a body
    That would make him leave
His body in the act of loving,

Beautifully engrossed.
    I can't remember what
She looked like. I never met

The husband. But leaning close
    To the newly dropped
Persimmon in the wet grass,

And the huddle of four
    Or five hungry satyrs,
Drab at first glance, the dull

Brown of age spots, flitting
    Away in too many
Directions, too quickly

To count exactly, small
    As they are, in the shade
At the tree's base; leaning

Out of the sunlight, as if
    I could take part in the feast there,
Where, mid-September,

The persimmons drop,
    So ripe and taut a touch
Can break the skin;

Leaning close enough
   To trouble the eye-spotted
Satyrs, no bigger than

Eyelids, and the fritillaries,
   Their calmer companions,
Like floating shreds of fire,

Whose feet have organs
   Of taste that make their tongues
Uncoil in reflex with

Goodness underfoot,
   I thought of that woman's
Lover, there on my belly

In sun and shadow,
   And wished I could be like that.

In the Tube

They beat the edge
   Of the dawn light,
      The pearly pre-glow

Right at their heels,
   The three boys
      Carrying the fourth

Rolled in a sheet.
   They all had taken
      Something the night

Before in a beach
   House and this one
      Drowned in his sleep.

They acted quickly,
  These instinctive
    Athletes who cross

The faces of tons
  Of crushing water
    Which refrain

From curling over
  And burying them
    Alive because they

Are nimble, quick,
  Tuned to the wit
    Of their survivors'

Bodies. They hurried
  From the running car
    And laid their friend

Like a Sunday paper
  On his parents' doorstep,
    And drove off to

The place where the sharp
  New light would score
    The wave crests and they

Would ride below them,
  Dodging the onrush.

The Wind

Worrying about the children I kept waiting
  To be relieved and walked to the gallery
On a frigid morning in the nation's capital.
  Great clouds of vapor smoking from the street-vents

Unraveled the long stone views of public buildings.
  And small among them, private and insistent,
My fretting was a nightmare nakedness,
  Which must be obvious but no one sees.
I'd come to town on business. It was finished.
  I had a little time and stalked through rooms
Of likenesses and paint that still looked wet
  On the old masters and the younger masters.
I looked around, wanting to be changed,
  And passed the pictures as if they were stalled traffic
And I had chosen to get out and walk.
  Then faced the modest painting by Vallotton,
"The Wind," in the East Wing, and walked on,
  And then returned and stood before it, feeling
A southern breeze begin, hearing a hymn,
  "Breathe on me, breath of God." Eight trees were bending
From right to left across the picture plane.
  So wind-altered I couldn't give them names,
They bowed away yet faced what made them bow.
  The undergrowth beneath them caught the sunlight
And handled it with fronds of yellow shining.
  We were looking up from the floor of Paradise—
I saw that suddenly— and God was calling,
  Warming the cool of the day with his vast breath.
The trees, his angels, pointed where he was looking.
  It wasn't clear if we had fallen yet.
But if we had, this green half-kneeling stir,
  In which things rooted and inevitable were swaying,
Might soothe his wrath and make him think again.
  The sympathetic magic of the paint
Was like a prayer sent both from the past,
  A gift from the dead artist, and from the future,
Vaulting the barrier of all that had been done
  And fixed forever, bathing the judged world
In a wish to soften harshness, everything leaning.
  This wind, painted by Felix Vallotton,
In 1910, somewhere in France, conveyed
  Counsel like a draft of medicine.
And in that counsel, drawn over my anger,

So that it passed through every leaf of it,
(For anger is what I felt, a cloudy ire
    At children who were ceasing to be children)
Came what I had to do. The picture said,
    "Forgive them. And let them live their lives."

Astragaloi

We know there must be consciousness in things,
    In bits of gravel pecked up by a hen
To grind inside her crop, and spider silk
    Just as it hardens stickily in air,
And even those things paralyzed in place,
    The wall brick, the hat peg, the steel beam
Inside the skyscraper, and lost, forgotten,
    And buried in ancient tombs, the toys and games.
Those starry jacks, those knucklebones of glass
    Meant for the dead to play with, toss and catch
Back of the hand and read the patterns of,
    Diversions to beguile the endless time,
Never to be picked up again . . . They're thinking,
    Surely, all of them. They are lost in thought.

Honorée Fanonne Jeffers

Honorée Fanonne Jeffers is the author of two books of poetry, *The Gospel of Barbecue* (Kent State, 2000), which was chosen by Lucille Clifton as the winner of the 1999 Wick Poetry Prize, and *Outlandish Blues* (Wesleyan, 2003). A native Southerner, she now lives in Oklahoma.

Confederate Pride Day at Bama (Tuscaloosa, 1994)

The first time, my liberal white friends try
to prepare me. I might feel ashamed when I hear
rebel yells, see the too familiar flag waving.
You know they're going to sing the song, don't you?

The fraternity boys dressed in gray uniforms,
marching boldly around the yard, then coming home to black
maids, their heads tied up in bright handkerchiefs.

Faces greased to perfection once a year. *Can you believe
they make those women dress up like mammies?*
Southern meals prepared with eye-rolling care.
You should stage a protest. For me or my mama?

Come day, go day, God sends Sunday and I see those
sisters at the grocery store buying food every week.
We smile and sometimes meet each other's gaze.

Nod.
At the very least, write a letter. Some kinds of anger
need screaming. Some kinds just worry the gut
like a meal of unwashed greens, peas picked

too early from the field. Or a dark woman, her brow
wrapped in red, smiling to herself, then hawking
and spitting her seasoning into a Dixie cooking pot.

Don't Know What Love Is

My mother can't recall the exact
infamous year but Mama does know
that she and her friends were teenagers
when they sneaked out to an official joint
in the middle of the woods to listen
to Dinah Washington sing their favorite
love song. They wanted to dance together
so close they'd be standing behind
each other but Mama says, *Dinah showed
up late and acted ugly and on top of
that she didn't want to sing the song.*
This is supposed to be the story of Mama's
blues and how she threw good money
after bad but this is South Georgia
and Dinah's standing in high heels on a Jim
Crow stage two feet off the ground.
She's sniffing the perfume of homemade
cigarettes, chitlin plates, hair grease one
grade above Vaseline and the premature
funk wafting up from the rowdy kids
with no home training. Can't even pee

straight much less recognize a silver lamé
dress. All they know to do is demand
one song because they risked a certain
butt-whipping to be in this joint, in these woods.
Dinah won't sing it, though.
She just won't sing the song.
I'm an evil gal, she hollers out instead.
Don't you bother with me!

Hagar to Sarai

Don't give me nothing in
exchange for a beating
in my belly, sore nipples
way after the sucking is gone.
Don't thank me for my body,
a fine drinking skin
turned inside out for you.
Don't thank me for the back
that don't break from Abram's weight.
I know what you need— a baby's
wail in the morning,
smile on your man's face,
his loins full of much obliged.
I know what you need;
don't give me your grief
to help this thing along.
I know how emptiness feels.
Woman, I know how
to make my own tears.

Joy Katz

Joy Katz was trained in industrial design. She held a Stegner Fellowship at Stanford and the Nadya Aisenberg Fellowship at the MacDowell Colony. She is a senior editor at *Pleiades* and teaches poetry writing at The New School. She lives in Brooklyn, NY.

Some Rain

Freud saw his first patient on a gray morning in Vienna;
cobblestones glistened feebly.
And it was pouring as Pollock dragged red onto *Full Fathom Five*.
Patty Hearst's face was grainy and soft, on closed-circuit,
as if we were watching her through a wet screen door,
but Socrates, as he died, looked sharply into the distance.
Early evening. Water coursed the gutters.
Remember the morning after, when Benjamin Franklin
did nothing in particular?
And how light loved the wipers on the bus to Selma?
Showers ruffled the Potomac as the burglars
were led over the Watergate lawn;
you could hear horses plashing as Galileo upended his telescope
to peer at the enormous, hairy legs of a housefly.
Watson, come here, I need you. Drops clung to the railings,
ran over the roof in thin streams.

In a soaking mist, the *Lusitania* gently sank;
bicycles stood in the rain as the students left Tiananmen Square.
The Lindbergh baby vanished through a wet, streaked window.
A few pale-green leaves were stuck to it.
Jane Eyre came back to find Rochester fumbling in a storm,
the yard full of fallen branches.
The tulip market crashed during a terrible downpour
but oxen grazed patiently at Lascaux, not minding.
If, as Hitler was declared chancellor, the crowd opened their umbrellas,
people stood barefoot in the mud sometimes at Birkenau.
The banality of evil, Hannah Arendt wrote, crushed out her cigarette
and got up to shut the windows.
As Marie Curie set out a small, glowing dish of radium
with her poisoned fingers, a line of storms was moving east;
faintly it thundered while my grandparents listened,
for the first time, to a phonograph.
Lewis Carroll wrote Alice onto the riverbank
while he floated downstream. The first drops were falling;
it was cool and still as the morning Alaric sacked Rome
or the one— it was June— Dickinson looked out at the grass
and said— something. What? Now that was some rain.

The Lettuce Bag

The loveliest lettuce comes in a plastic sleeve that expands, weblike, to
cradle the largest red-leaf or the smallest butterhead. If a rose were the
size of a head of romaine, its petals would be held unbruised. The lettuce
bag would not distort the most bouffant beehive hairdo; indeed, you
could slip it over an actual beehive— a small one— and its grid of plastic
tethers would barely impress the delicate wax. If labias were in season,
their tender interiors, their roundness, would be touched by the grocer's
mist. The lettuce bag has the same selflessness that a good translator has
for a French poem. The little plastic sleeve moves me like a suffragette!
But I am being too grand. Abundantly soft and pliant, its perforations
clean, the bag has a modest beauty. In the modern refrigerator, though,
lettuce goes limp as a peignoir unless stored in an astronaut helmet.

Colophon

Just now the typographer's *a* comes into being.
Her hands have ached to shape its curves:
many strokes of black, then white, then again black, taking
a long time to dry in between: flawless,
the letter has always belonged to the world.

Typeface does not correspond to *a*, or *b*, or *c*, nor the shoulders of *m*,
nor the sweet hooks of lower-case *g*s, but to all the letterforms—
"The beauty that radiates from the work of men," said Eric Gill,
making the slope of the buttocks and shoulders and the small tight backs
of his lovers into the Gill Sans type that letters the London Underground,
"is the beauty of holiness." The typographer's *a*, now finished,

will be reproduced digitally and set into text columns,
sale circulars, billboards. If a word is elegy to what it signifies,
does *woman* disappear? Words say what they will against us
but the serif of *a* hangs still as an earring. My body is here
at the end of *idea*, at the center of *eat, say, dance*.

Café

A downpour has ended and now the peaceful,
steady kind of light that's after,
little spits of rain left in the wind still.
                                    A child,
crying and crying hysterically, until he is shuddering
convulsively, leaves off and when this happens
the same feeling of steadiness. He sits across from his mother,
shivering every now and then.
In a minute he will return to his drawing.

If you are with someone who does not say anything to you,
who does not touch you or ask anything of you
but goes on sitting across from you and after a time
goes back to her book, that's grace.

It returns the world
already in progress: steaming milk, opening newspapers.
And a man walks in carrying a birdcage.

Brigit Pegeen Kelly

Brigit Kelly's third book of poems, *The Orchard*, was published by BOA Editions, Ltd., in April of 2004. She currently teaches in the creative writing program at the University of Illinois.

Black Swan

I told the boy I found him under a bush.
What was the harm? I told him he was sleeping
And that a black swan slept beside him,
The swan's feathers hot, the scent of the hot feathers
And of the bush's hot white flowers
As rank and sweet as the stewed milk of a goat.
The bush was in a strange garden, a place
So old it seemed to exist outside of time.
In one spot, great stone steps leading nowhere.
In another, statues of horsemen posting giant stone horses
Along a high wall. And here, were triangular beds
Of flowers flush with red flowers. And there,
Circular beds flush with white. And in every bush

And bed flew small birds and the cries of small birds.
I told the boy I looked for him a long time
And when I found him I watched him sleeping,
His arm around the swan's moist neck,
The swan's head tucked fast behind the boy's back,
The feathered breast and the bare breast breathing as one,
And then very swiftly and without making a sound,
So that I would not wake the sleeping bird,
I picked the boy up and slipped him into my belly,
The way one might slip something stolen
Into a purse. And brought him here....
And so it was. And so it was. A child with skin
So white it was not like the skin of a boy at all,
But like the skin of a newborn rabbit, or like the skin
Of a lily, pulseless and thin. And a giant bird
With burning feathers. And beyond them both
A pond of incredible blackness, overarched
With ancient trees and patterned with shifting shades,
The small wind in the branches making a sound
Like the knocking of a thousand wooden bells....
Things of such beauty. But still I might
Have forgotten, had not the boy, who stands now
To my waist, his hair a cap of shining feathers,
Come to me today weeping because some older boys
Had taunted him and torn his new coat,
Had he not, when I bent my head to his head,
Said softly, but with great anger, "I wish I had never
Been born. I wish I were back under the bush,"
Which made the old garden rise up again,
Shadowed and more strange. Small birds
Running fast and the grapple of chill coming on.
There was the pond, half-circled with trees. And there
The flowerless bush. But there was no swan.
There was no black swan. And beneath
The sound of the wind, I could hear, dark and low,
The giant stone hooves of the horses,
Striking and striking the hardening ground.

The Dragon

The bees came out of the junipers, two small swarms
The size of melons; and golden, too, like melons,
They hung next to each other, at the height of a deer's breast,
Above the wet black compost. And because
The light was very bright it was hard to see them,
And harder still to see what hung between them.
A snake hung between them. The bees held up a snake,
Lifting each side of his narrow neck, just below
The pointed head, and in this way, very slowly
They carried the snake through the garden,
The snake's long body hanging down, its tail dragging
The ground, as if the creature were a criminal
Being escorted to execution or a child king
To the throne. I kept thinking the snake
Might be a hose, held by two ghostly hands,
But the snake was a snake, his body green as the grass
His tail divided, his skin oiled, the way the male member
Is oiled by the female's juices, the greenness overbright,
The bees gold, the winged serpent moving silently
Through the air. There was something deadly in it,
Or already dead. Something beyond the report
Of beauty. I laid my face against my arm, and there
It stayed for the length of time it takes two swarms
Of bees to carry a snake through a wide garden,
Past a sleeping swan, past the dead roses nailed
To the wall, past the small pond. And when
I looked up the bees and the snake were gone,
But the garden smelled of broken fruit, and across
The grass a shadow lay for which there was no source,
A narrow plinth dividing the garden, and the air
Was like the air after a fire, or the air before a storm,
Ungodly still, but full of dark shapes turning.

Elegy

Wind buffs the waterstained stone cupids and shakes
Old rain from the pines' low branches, small change
Spilling over the graves the years have smashed

With a hammer— *forget this, forget that, leave no*
Stone unturned. The grass grows high, sweet-smelling,
Many-footed, ever-running. No one tends it. No
One comes....*And where am I now?*....Is this a beginning,
A middle, or an end?....Before I knew you I stood
In this place. Now I forsake the past as I knew it
To feed you into it. But that is not right. You *step*
Into it. I *find* you here, in the shifting grass,
In the late light, as if you had always been here.
Behind you two torn black cedars flame white
Against the darkening fields....If you turn to me,
Quiet man? If you turn? If I speak softly?
If I say, *Take off, take off your glasses....Let me see*
Your sightless eyes?....I will be beautiful then....
Look, the heart moves as the moths do, scuttering
Like a child's thoughts above this broken stone
And that. And I lie down. I lie down in the long grass,
Something I am not given to doing, and I feel
The weight of your hand on my belly, and the wind
Parts the grasses, and the distance spills through—
The glassy fields, the black black earth, the pale air
Streaming headlong toward the abbey's far stones
And streaming back again....The drowned scent of lilacs
By the abbey, it is a drug. It drives one senseless.
It drives one blind. You can cup the enormous lilac cones
In your hands— ripened, weightless, and taut—
And it is like holding someone's heart in your hands,
Or holding a cloud of moths. I lift them up, my hands.
Grave man, bend toward me. Lay your face....*here....*
*Rest....*I took the stalks of the dead wisteria
From the glass jar propped against the open grave
And put in the shell-shaped wildflowers
I picked along the road. I cannot name them.
Bread and butter, perhaps. I am not good
With names. But nameless you walked toward me
And I knew you, a swelling in the heart,
A silence in the heart, the wild wind-blown grass
Burning— as the sun falls below the earth—
Brighter than a bed of lilies struck by snow.

Jane Kenyon

Jane Kenyon, who died in 1995, published four collections of poetry, the most recent of which is *Otherwise*. She translated the poetry of Anna Akhmatova and was the recipient of a Guggenheim Fellowship and the PEN Voelcker Award.

Happiness

There's just no accounting for happiness,
or the way it turns up like a prodigal
who comes back to the dust at your feet
having squandered a fortune far away.

And how can you not forgive?
You make a feast in honor of what
was lost, and take from its place the finest
garment, which you saved for an occasion
you could not imagine, and you weep night and day
to know that you were not abandoned,
that happiness saved its most extreme form
for you alone.

No, happiness is the uncle you never
knew about, who flies a single-engine plane
onto the grassy landing strip, hitchhikes
into town, and inquires at every door
until he finds you asleep midafternoon
as you so often are during the unmerciful
hours of your despair.

It comes to the monk in his cell.
It comes to the woman sweeping the street
with a birch broom, to the child
whose mother has passed out from drink.
It comes to the lover, to the dog chewing
a sock, to the pusher, to the basket maker,
and to the clerk stacking cans of carrots
in the night.
                It even comes to the boulder
in the perpetual shade of pine barrens,
to rain falling on the open sea,
to the wineglass, weary of holding wine.

Eating the Cookies

The cousin from Maine, knowing
about her diverticulitis, left out the nuts,
so the cookies weren't entirely to my taste,
but they were good enough; yes, good enough.

Each time I emptied a drawer or shelf
I permitted myself to eat one.
I cleared the closet of silk caftans
that slipped easily from clattering hangars,
and from the bureau I took her nightgowns
and sweaters, financial documents
neatly cinctured in long gray envelopes,
and the hairnets and peppermints she'd tucked among

Lucite frames abounding with great-grandchildren,
solemn in their Christmas finery.

Finally the drawers were empty,
the bags full, and the largest cookie,
which I had saved for last, lay
solitary in the tin with a nimbus
of crumbs around it. There would be no more
parcels from Portland. I took it up
and sniffed it, and before eating it,
pressed it against my forehead, because
it seemed like the next thing to do.

Prognosis

I walked alone in the chill of dawn
while my mind leapt, as the teachers

of detachment say, like a drunken
monkey. Then a gray shape, an owl,

passed overhead. An owl is not
like a crow. A crow makes convivial

chuckings as it flies,
but the owl flew well beyond me

before I heard it coming, and when it
settled, the bough did not sway.

Pharaoh

"The future ain't what it used to be,"
said the sage of the New York Yankees
as he pounded his mitt, releasing
the red dust of the infield
into the harshly illuminated evening air.

Big hands. Men with big hands
make things happen. The surgeon,
when I asked how big your tumor was,
held forth his substantial fist
with its globed class ring.

Home again, we live as charily as strangers.
Things are off: Touch rankles, food
is not good. Even the kindness of friends
turns burdensome; their flowers sadden
us, so many and so fair.

I woke in the night to see your
diminished bulk lying beside me—
you on your back, like a sarcophagus
as your feet held up the covers....
The things you might need in the next
life surrounded you— your comb and glasses,
water, a book and a pen.

Maurice Kilwein Guevara

Maurice Kilwein Guevara was born in 1961 in Belencito, Colombia. He is the author of three collections: *Postmortem*, *Poems of the River Spirit*, and *Autobiography of So-and-so*. He was the first person of Latino descent ever to be elected President of the Association of Writers and Writing Programs (AWP). He is currently Professor of English at the University of Wisconsin, Milwaukee.

Doña Josefina Counsels Doña Concepción Before Entering Sears

Conchita debemos to speak totalmente in English
cuando we go into Sears okay   Por qué
Porque didn't you hear lo que pasó   It say
on the eleven o'clock news anoche que two robbers
was caught in Sears and now this is the part
I'm not completely segura que I got everything
porque channel 2 tiene tú sabes that big fat guy
that's hard to understand porque his nose sit on his lip
like a elefante pues the point es que the robbers the police say
was two young men pretty big y one have a hairy face
and the other is calvo that's right he's baldy and okay
believe me qué barbaridad porque Hairy Face
and Mister Baldy goes right into the underwear department
takes all the money from the caja yeah uh-huh the cash register
and mira Mister Baldy goes to this poor Italian woman that I

guess would be like us sixty o sixty-five who is the section
of the back-support brassieres and he makes her put a big bra
over her head para que she can't see nothing and kneel
like she talking to God to save her poor life
y other things horrible pero the point como dije
es que there was two of them and both was speaking Spanish
y por eso is a good thing Conchita so the people at Sears
don't confuse us with Hairy and Baldy that we speak English only
okay ready
          Oh what a nice day to be aquí en Sears Miss Conception

Fast Forward

     I marry, I divorce, I put three quarters in a parking meter in Milwau-
kee, it's the next year, then the end of spring four years later, and now I'm
married to the woman whose reflection I saw in the dark blue window of
a classroom. We move to the foothills of the Alleghenies, to a farm house
owned by a deaf couple. There are clouds and a blue sky, milking cows.
The old man always has a hammer and a can of nails he rattles; when the
windows are open you can hear him and the old woman screaming at
each other. My new wife complains about the rusty water. She's thirty
and urgent, I want to make a baby too, one night I mount her on the
hard kitchen floor. Three weeks later her period comes heavier than the
months before. By fall, still barren, we both start to see them: The blurred
Amish woman in dark bonnet by the landing, the streak of the infant in
her arms, the x-ray fingers of the baby, the ghost mop luminous in the
corner by the starry window.

How Grammar School is Changing

In the early years all of the teachers were Nouns. They were very strict
Nouns. They wore black robes that reached to the floor and had a fond-
ness for caning the palms of your hands. In the beginning there was very

little light; then a window was placed in the east wall of the school. The first Verb to enter the classroom through our new and only window was a Be. It was yellow and black and buzzed by my ear. One day Be walked vertically up the world map from Santiago to Santa Marta and stopped to smell the salt water. Thinking twice, it flew up to Florida and was eyeing Orange County when my mean third grade Noun squashed Be with her big white reader. She said, "We only need one river in this town," which didn't make any sense. It wasn't long, however, before more stuff started coming in through the windows (there were now four) and through the new fire doors and down the chimney: Adjectives with big, bright, yellow and orange, polka-dot bow ties; Adverbs who yodeled longingly for their homeland; a Pronoun who wore cornrows with green ribbons (I confess I had my first crush on She); a family of Silver Brackets; Question Marks and Periods snowed down the chimney; and, finally, the Invisible Etceteras—pranksters that they are—started moaning sweet nothings in my Noun's ear, which made her grin a little, thank God. By the time I was in the fifth grade, after a vicious fight with the village elders, the principal had hired Dr. Miguel de Sustantivo to make the school bilingual: *y tú sabes lo que pasó después: vinieron las familias Adjetivo y Pronombre y Verbo y más y más....*But yesterday a new little someone came from far, far away who sits sad all alone at lunch. Does anyone know a few words in Vietnamese? I would like to say Good Morning.

Maxine Kumin

Maxine Kumin's newest collections of poetry are *Bringing Together: Uncollected Early Poems 1958-1988* and *The Long Marriage*, in addition to a memoir, *Inside the Halo and Beyond: Anatomy of a Recovery*. In January 2005, W.W. Norton published *Jack and Other New Poems*. Her awards include the Pulitzer and Ruth Lilly Poetry Prizes; Poet Laureate of New Hampshire, 1989-1994; and Consultant in Poetry to the Library of Congress, 1980-81. She and her husband live on a farm in Warner, NH.

Jack

How pleasant the yellow butter
melting on white kernels, the meniscus
of red wine that coats the insides of our goblets

where we sit with sturdy friends as old as we are
after shucking the garden's last Silver Queen
and setting husks and stalks aside for the horses

the last two of our lives, still noble to look upon:
our first foal, now a bossy mare of 28
which calibrates to 84 in people years

and my chestnut gelding, not exactly a youngster
at 22. Every year, the end of summer
lazy and golden, invites grief and regret:

suddenly it's 1980, winter buffets us,
winds strike like cruelty out of Dickens. Somehow
we have seven horses for six stalls. One of them,

a big-nosed roan gelding, calm as a president's portrait
lives in the rectangle that leads to the stalls. We call it
the motel lobby. Wise old campaigner, he dunks his

hay in the water bucket to soften it, then visits the others
who hang their heads over their dutch doors. Sometimes
he sprawls out flat to nap in his commodious quarters.

That spring, in the bustle of grooming
and riding and shoeing, I remember I let him go
to a neighbor I thought was a friend, and the following

fall she sold him down the river. I meant to
but never did go looking for him, to buy him back
and now my old guilt is flooding this twilit table

my guilt is ghosting the candles that pale us to skeletons
the ones we must all become in an as yet unspecified order.
Oh Jack, tethered in what rough stall alone

did you remember that one good winter?

Family Reunion

The week in August you come home,
adult, professional, aloof,
we roast and carve the fatted calf
— in our case home-grown pig, the chine
garlicked and crisped, the applesauce
hand-pressed. Hand-pressed the greengage wine.

Nothing is cost-effective here.
The peas, the beets, the lettuces
hand sown, are raised to stand apart.
The electric fence ticks like the slow heart
of something we fed and bedded for a year,
then killed with kindness's one bullet
and paid Jake Mott to do the butchering.

In winter we lure the birds with suet,
thaw lungs and kidneys for the cat.
Darlings, it's all a circle from the ring
of wire that keeps the raccoons from the corn
to the gouged pine table that we lounge around,
distressed before any of you was born.

Benign and dozy from our gluttonies,
the candles down to stubs, defenses down,
love leaking out unguarded the way
juice dribbles from the fence when grounded
by grass stalks or a forgotten hoe,
how eloquent, how beautiful you seem!

Wearing our gestures, how wise you grow,
ballooning to overfill our space,
the almost-parents of your parents now.
So briefly having you back to measure us
is harder than having let you go.

February

First waking to the gray
of linsey-woolsey cloth
the vivid spotted dogs
the red-fox cattle and
the meeker-colored horses
flattened in snow fog

first waking into gray
flecked with common cock-
crow unfolding the same
chilblain-bruised feet
the old shoulder ache
Mama every day

remembering how you won
the death you wished for

the death you sidled up to
remembering how

like a child in late afternoon
drained from the jubilant sledding
you were content to coast
the run-out to a stop

booted and capped in the barn
joy enters where I haul
a hay bale by its binding string
and with my free hand pull
your easy death along.

On Being Asked to Write a Poem
in Memory of Anne Sexton

The elk discards his antlers every spring.
They rebud, they grow, they are growing

an inch a day to form a rococo rack
with a five-foot spread even as we speak:

cartilage at first, covered with velvet;
bendable, tender gristle, yet

destined to ossify, the velvet sloughed off,
hanging in tatters from alders and scrub growth.

No matter how hardened it seems there was pain.
Blood on the snow from rubbing, rubbing, rubbing.

What a heavy candelabrum to be borne
forth, each year more elaborately turned:

the special issues, the prizes in her name.
Above the mantel the late elk's antlers gleam.

Dorianne Laux

photo by Jeanne C. Finley

Dorianne Laux is the author of three collections of poetry from BOA Editions: *Awake, What We Carry* (a finalist for the National Book Critics Circle Award), and *Smoke.* She is also co-author, with Kim Addonizio, of *The Poet's Companion: A Guide to the Pleasures of Writing Poetry.* Laux is an Associate Professor and works in the University of Oregon's Creative Writing Program.

Pearl

> She was a headlong assault, a hysterical discharge,
> an act of total extermination.
> —Myra Friedman, *Buried Alive:*
> *The Biography of Janis Joplin*

She was nothing much, this plain-faced girl from Texas,
this moonfaced child who opened her mouth
to the gravel pit churning in her belly, acne-faced
daughter of Leadbelly, Bessie, Otis, and the booze-
filled moon, child of the honky-tonk bar-talk crowd
who cackled like a bird of prey, velvet cape blown
open in the Monterey wind, ringed fingers fisted
at her throat, howling the slagheap up and out
into the sawdusted air. Barefaced, mouth warped
and wailing like giving birth, like being eaten alive
from the inside, or crooning like the first child
abandoned by God, trying to woo him back,

down on her knees and pleading for a second chance.
When she sang she danced a stand-in-place dance,
one foot stamping at that fire, that bed of coals;
one leg locked at the knee and quivering, the other
pumping its oil-rig rhythm, her bony hip jigging
so the beaded belt slapped her thigh.
Didn't she give it to us? So loud so hard so furious,
hurling heat-seeking balls of lightning
down the long human aisles, her voice crashing
into us— sonic booms to the heart— this little white girl
who showed us what it was like to die
for love, to jump right up and die for it night after
drumbeaten night, going down shrieking— hair
feathered, frayed, eyes glazed, addicted to the song—
a one-woman let me show you how it's done, how it is,
where it goes when you can't hold it in anymore.
Child of everything gone wrong, gone bad, gone down,
gone. Girl with the girlish breasts and woman hips,
thick-necked, sweat misting her upper lip, hooded eyes
raining a wild blue light, hands reaching out
to the ocean we made, all that anguish and longing
swelling and rising at her feet. Didn't she burn
herself up for us, shaking us alive? That child,
that girl, that rawboned woman, stranded
in a storm on a blackened stage like a house
on fire.

Family Stories

I had a boyfriend who told me stories about his family,
how an argument once ended when his father
seized a lit birthday cake in both hands
and hurled it out a second-story window. That,
I thought, was what a normal family was like: anger
sent out across the sill, landing like a gift
to decorate the sidewalk below. In mine

it was fists and direct hits to the solar plexus,
and nobody ever forgave anyone. But I believed
the people in his stories really loved one another,
even when they yelled and shoved their feet
through cabinet doors or held a chair like a bottle
of cheap champagne, christening the wall,
rungs exploding from their holes.
I said it sounded harmless, the pomp and fury
of the passionate. He said it was a curse
being born Italian and Catholic and when he
looked from that window what he saw was the moment
rudely crushed. But all I could see was a gorgeous
three-layer cake gliding like a battered ship
down the sidewalk, the smoking candles broken, sunk
deep in the icing, a few still burning.

Twilight

My daughter set whatever had begun
to wither or rot on the rail
of the backyard deck. Pear, apple, over-ripe
banana, in October a pumpkin
that by August had gone to dust.
She took photos of the process: pear
with its belly bruised, weekly
growing more squat, the dark spot spreading.
Orange caving in at the navel.
Banana skins tanning like animal hides.
As their outsides grew tough,
their insides grew moist— a crack in the crust
and the dank pudding spewed out.
Pear neck at half-mast, pear bottom black,
pear neck sunk into the drooped shoulders of pear.
She observed and recorded the progress, watched
the realm of the solid transmute and dissolve,
documenting the musk-fragrant, incremental

descent, its delectable inevitability.
She delighted in her entropic world
with complete abandon— never expressing
repulsion or remorse, only taking
her deliberate daily photos: pumpkin
with its knifed hat tipped jauntily
above carved eyes, pumpkin sinking sweetly
into its own orange face, buckling, breaking,
sweating in sunlight, mold webbed and glowing
through a triangle nose, the punched-out smile
a grimace slipping down its furred chin.
When did she become disinterested, distracted
by her life? Where to go? What to do?
Did her socks match? One day she left
her dark harvest behind and walked
to the rink where her skate blades
skimmed the ice, inscribing girlish circles
on the blue skirl of the deserted rink.
Or she lingered at the stalls until twilight,
brushing down her favorite horse, sugar
cubes in her pockets, an apple in her purse.
She actually had a purse. Filled to the clasp
with the evidence of her life: lip gloss,
stubby pencils and colored pens, a little book
she wrote in faithfully, archiving last
names that began with A on the A page,
B's on the B, a billfold with money
and a photo ID, her own face gazing out
through the tiny plastic window.
She stared back at herself like any ordinary girl,
not a girl obsessed with ruin and collapse
who stalked her backyard with a camera.
Something else had caught her eye.
See her lift the tawny jewel
to his whiskered lips, her hand level,
her fingers flat and quivering. Look
at the gratitude in her face
when he takes the first dangerous bite.

Sydney Lea

Sydney Lea is the author of a novel, *A Place in Mind*, two collections of outdoor essays, *Hunting the Whole Way Home* and *A Little Wildness*, and eight volumes of poetry, the most recent of which is *Ghost Pain*. His previous volume, *Pursuit of a Wound*, was a finalist for the 2001 Pulitzer Prize.

Wonder: Red Beans and Ricely

for Christopher Matthews

He blew the famous opening figure of "West End Blues"
and then... A long pause. A long long pin-drop pause.
This sounded like nothing the four of us had been hearing out here
at the Famous Sunnybrook Ballroom in East Jesus, PA,
which was in fact a moth-eaten tent to which in summer
the post-war big bands, then fading into the fifties —
the likes of the Elgars or Les Brown and His Band of Renown —
would arrive to coax the newly middle-aged and their elders
into nostalgia and dance. My cousin, our pretty steadies
and I were younger, cocksure, full of contraband beer,
but the moment I speak of knocked even us in the know-it-all chops.

I suddenly dreamed I could see through the tent's canvas top
clear up to stars that stopped their fool blinking and planets that stood
stock-still over cows and great-eyed deer in the moonlight

and ducks ablaze on their ponds because everything in God's world
understood this was nothing like anything they'd known before.
It's still a fantasy, that sorry tent a lantern,
transparent as glass, through which I beheld the landscape around it
as though it showed in some Low Country more-than-masterpiece
while no one danced. The crassest fat-necked burgher in the crowd
sat rapt, as did his missus, the moment being that strong.
It lingered strong, beginning to end, through the blues that followed.

Then Velma Middleton got up to jive and bellow.
She broke the charm, her scintillant dress like a tent itself,
and people resumed the lindy and foxtrot as she and he
traded the always-good-for-laughs double meanings
of "Big Butter and Egg Man," "That's My Desire,"
and so on. And so we four, or rather we two boys,
resumed our drinking and boasting until the band took its break.
Full enough by now of the Bud and some of the rum
that the cousin had brought— which would take him in too sadly short a time
away to another shore forever— I stood and pledged:
I'll get his autograph. It made no sense at all.

I staggered to and through the canvas's backstage hole,
the mocking jibes of cousin and sweethearts dying behind me,
and beheld a row of semi-trucks: his equipage.
There were two doors as to a house in each, and a little set
of metal steps underneath. Without a hitch, I climbed
one stair of the bunch. It made no sense except it did.
I *knew*.... Something had burned into my reeling brain
when that opening solo started, and the man would have to be
just there where he was when I knocked on one of the several doors
inside the trailer, and the growl was Fate: it didn't surprise me:
Come in, he said. How could he? How could he not? I came.

It was meant to be, and still I stammered with puzzlement, shame.
I'd had a vision, yes, and yet to have the vision
there before me.... Wonder! Great Armstrong at a desk
in an undershirt, suspenders flapping, his face near blinding,
sweatbeads charged by the gimcrack rack of fluorescent lights
so that he seemed to wear an aura— it was all
one supple motion, the way he reached into a drawer,
drew out a jug of Johnny Walker, sucked it down

to the label, squared before him a sheet of paper, ready
for me, it seemed, flourished a fountain pen and wrote:
Red Beans and Ricely Yours at Sunny Brook Ballroom. Pops.

Back at the table they judged it was real enough by the looks.
"I just walked in and got it," I bragged, as if a miracle
hadn't transpired, as great as any I'd ever know.
I bragged as if my part in it all were important somehow,
and God hadn't just looked down and said, *Well okay— him.*
And what remains from then? Not the paper, long since lost,
nor the lovely, silken girls, Sally and Barbara,
nor the cousin, as I've said, who crossed the foulest river,
nor that brash, that truly and stunningly blessèd younger I,
nor the heavenstruck beasts and the trees and the moon and the sky.

Just a handful of opening notes from a horn which are there forever.

Winter Tournament

Our daughters' lay-ups shivered rim or air;
White, their sighs at free throws; passes were
Tropes for awkward prayer.
                                        Georgianna watched
From comfortless cold bleachers set on blocks.
We didn't cry despair or yelp with pain.
Now Coach exhorts the girls to dream of gain
From rout; he clears his throat; the loss, he says,
Should "light a fire" somewhere within the players.
His figure's wrong. Georgianna once was young.
Like them. And he was too. And we. All wrong....

Who'll go on dreaming jump shots, bullet-sure?
Georgianna? No certainty for her,
In dreams or anywhere,
                                        I dare imagine.
(To tell the truth, we haven't spoken.)
Yet here she was, like all of us, to cheer
Or grieve. It's clumsy. Monuments to care,

These mothers, mostly: gone to flesh or bone,
But lovely too. Back-bent, the skinny ones
Have hugged themselves beside their warmer neighbors,
Who've tried to hide sagged parts in upright postures.

Georgianna's simply worn— not thin, not fat.
Someone should prop her up or hold her tight.
Or so she feels tonight,
                    I speculate,
As we collect our children. Those defeats—
Goals rejected, miscues, slips and fouls—
May work their disenchantment on our girls.
Yet I daresay that we imagine beauties
Are at their truest when they're so ungainly.
We cling to daughters, and to that surmise,
As carefully we tiptoe over ice

—Clownish in the dark— to heating cars.
At least in awkwardness they are most ours.

Conspiracy Theory

Through that Taft Hotel window, the local radio station's neonized call letters
over the New Haven Green
now had the alien look of shimmery desert, deep space, one's oddest dream.
First National's carillon was tolling again,
no longer timely, bullets long since cold in the famous cadaver. Those bells

sounded ugly, moreso than ever. Elitists all, we'd come to Yale but inhaled
this murdered Harvardian's meritocratic notions: you could get smart
but have a decent conscience, we thought, could study Locke, Bach, Chaucer
—and later be a Freedom Rider.
Everything, we tried to believe in our hearts, would work itself out in the end.

I didn't recognize it then, but this person had been my only
female friend who *was* pure friend, and nothing besides.
We'd hug and weep and sigh, talk out our own inadequacies, hopes.

And that was that. We were, I suppose, merely lonely.
She must have been no wiser than I, must have known no better what we had.

How but in such ignorance could we two have made our way to bed?
It was an old nexus, sex and death. And faced with this *thing* in Texas,
this sundering of our hopes, however callow,
why shouldn't we be irrational too? But now I wonder why we couldn't value
our never having done what then we did—so pitiable, feckless. Don't ask me.

It was the last place for us, bed. We would never return to where we'd been,
not entirely. We just couldn't do that, before she did herself in.
Not suicide exactly, but not exactly not: she starved herself to death.
By which I don't suggest, or imagine, she did so because of what we'd done,
just before Thanksgiving vacation: crudely, badly done.

A labor it was, of hours, which stopped at last for no reason, except our lust
to stop at last. After which those radio letters, the mumbling walkers below,
the looming Sterling Library towers: each had an off-putting radium glow.
The world felt new, strange, worse, even our conversation
leaping off the point completely,

whatever the point may have been. Our talk turned terse, uncustomary.
For all our so-called education, we didn't have a clue.
Advisors were working in Indochina now, but that wasn't in any course.
A group of Englishmen— across the sea, in some German cellar,
their hair absurd (by the times' standards)—

were ripping off black American rhythms and playing their same three chords
again and again, behind banal words: "I Wanna Hold Your Hand." "Love Me Do."
There lived a sad-sack fellow, James Earl Ray, whom nobody knew.
And I might have noticed, but somehow didn't, the yellow
cast to my woman friend's cheeks or her ribs, which if not yet quite Biafran—

another name we didn't yet speak—were on their way. She ate only aspirin.
Against the smogged night, her profile showed translucent as the drapes.
Her end, I guess, was also on its way: like Watergate, Sirhan, Cambodia, AIDS,
Ali uncrowned by cretins. *Conspiracy* became a watchword, and is so today,
though it means a breathing together, as if women and men

could draw a common air, which was precisely what it seemed back there
no two of them would ever—ever—really do again.

Li-Young Lee

Li-Young Lee was born in Jakarta, Indonesia, in 1957. He is the author of *Book of My Nights, Rose,* and *The City in Which I Love You* (all from BOA Editions, Ltd.). He has also written an autobiography, *The Winged Seed.* He lives in Chicago with his wife and children.

The Hammock

When I lay my head in my mother's lap
I think how day hides the stars,
the way I lay hidden once, waiting
inside my mother's singing to herself. And I remember
how she carried me on her back
between home and the kindergarten,
once each morning and once each afternoon.

I don't know what my mother's thinking.

When my son lays his head in my lap, I wonder:
Do his father's kisses keep his father's worries
from becoming his? I think, *Dear God,* and remember
there are stars we haven't heard from yet:
They have so far to arrive. *Amen,*
I think, and I feel almost comforted.

I've no idea what my child is thinking.

Between two unknowns, I live my life.
Between my mother's hopes, older than I am
by coming before me, and my child's wishes, older than I am

by outliving me. And what's it like?
Is it a door, and good-bye on either side?
A window, and eternity on either side?
Yes, and a little singing between two great rests.

Words for Worry

Another word for *father* is *worry.*

Worry boils the water
for tea in the middle of the night.

Worry trimmed the child's nails before
singing him to sleep.

Another word for *son* is *delight,*
another word, *hidden.*

And another is *One-Who-Goes-Away.*
Yet another, *One-Who-Returns.*

So many words for son:
He-Who-Dreams-for-All-Our-Sakes.
His-Play-Vouchsafes-Our-Winter-Share.
His-Dispersal-Wins-the-Birds.

But only one word for *father.*
And sometimes a man is both.
Which is to say sometimes a man
manifests mysteries beyond
his own understanding.

For instance, being the one and the many,
and the loneliness of either. Or

the living light we see by, we never see. Or

the sole word weighs
heavy as a various name.

And sleepless worry folds the laundry for tomorrow.
Tired worry wakes the child for school.

Orphan worry writes the note he hides
in the child's bag.
It begins, *Dear Firefly....*

Praise Them

The birds don't alter space.
They reveal it. The sky
never fills with any
leftover flying. They leave
nothing to trace. It is our own
astonishment collects
in chill air. Be glad.
They equal their due
moment never begging,
and enter ours
without parting day. See
how three birds in a winter tree
make the tree barer.
Two fly away, and new rooms
open in December.
Give up what you guessed
about a whirring heart, the little
beaks and claws, their constant hunger.
We're the nervous ones.
If even one of our violent number
could be gentle
long enough that one of them
found it safe inside
our finally untroubled and untroubling gaze,
who wouldn't hear
what singing completes us?

Philip Levine

photo by Frances Levine

Phil Levine now divides his time between Fresno and Brooklyn. He published his 17th collection of poems in September of 2004. His collections *Ashes* and *What Work Is* both won the National Book Award. *The Simple Truth* won the Pulitzer Prize. His best book, *One for the Rose,* won nothing.

The Genius

When Jake gave up his job on afternoons
who took up his magical tools so the line
would never stop? Think of the Packard sixteens,
rolling and rolling toward paradise or

Toledo without their upholstery
perfected. Think of it in human terms,
the want of a stitch, the want of a tuck,
Lonnie the foreman howling, "Where's my kike

when I need him?" the heads of the sewers
bowed before the cloth they'll puzzle over
forevermore on earth or in heaven.
Let the whole shop know he won't arrive;

Jacob the cutter missed the streetcar
this very afternoon and no one cried out,
"We're short a passenger, the little kike
whose bad left shoulder tilts to the right."

No one noticed, not even the conductor
busy short-changing & punching transfers,
nor the black assembler nor the typist,
her scalded fingers the color of cinders.

No doubt the god of Detroit looked down
or up, however such a god might look,
and found things as usual, green
the sweet rivers of home, green as raw beer

pissed out, and the air was lavender
and the little kike with a lilt to the right
nowhere in sight. All that afternoon
the men in upholstery did as they might

and nothing got done. The angels of Detroit,
among the silent choirs of engineers,
wept to see their industry unhoused
after so many profitable years.

The answer is: no one took up the tools,
no one took up the craft. The hand-made awls,
the cruel needles, scissors, knives, all he'd sewn,
vanished with him at four in the afternoon.

This has been a short chapter in the tragedy
of my country, one without beginning,
middle, or end, as Aristotle wrote
such tales require— not having lived in Detroit—,

and yet among these details abides a truth
that defines the nature of events on earth,
the perfection of the life or of the work,
and has nothing to do with Uncle Jake.

The Two

When he gets off work at Packard, they meet
outside a diner on Grand Boulevard. He's tired,
a bit depressed, and smelling the exhaustion
on his own breath, he kisses her carefully
on her left cheek. Early April, and the weather
has not decided if this is spring, winter, or what.
The two gaze upwards at the sky which gives
nothing away: the low clouds break here and there
and let in tiny slices of a pure blue heaven.
The day is like us, she thinks; it hasn't decided
what to become. The traffic light at Linwood
goes from red to green and the trucks start up,
so that when he says, "Would you like to eat?"
she hears a jumble of words that means nothing,
though spiced with things she cannot believe,
"wooden Jew" and "lucky meat." He's been up
late, she thinks, he's tired of the job, perhaps tired
of their morning meetings, but then he bows
from the waist and holds the door open
for her to enter the diner, and the thick
odor of bacon frying and new potatoes
greets them both, and taking heart she enters
to peer through the thick cloud of tobacco smoke
to see if "their booth" is available.
F. Scott Fitzgerald wrote that there were no
second acts in America, but he knew neither
this man nor this woman and no one else
like them unless he stayed late at the office
to test his famous one-liner, "We keep you clean
in Muscatine," on the woman emptying
his waste basket. Fitzgerald never wrote
with someone present, except for this woman
in a gray uniform whose comings and goings
went unnoticed even on those December evenings
she worked late while the snow fell silently
on the window sills and the new fluorescent lights
blinked on and off. Get back to the two, you say.
Not who ordered poached eggs, who ordered
only toast and coffee, who shared the bacon

with the other, but what became of the two
when this poem ended, whose arms held whom,
who first said "I love you" and truly meant it,
and who misunderstood the words, so longed
for, and yet still so unexpected, and began
suddenly to scream and curse until the waitress
asked them both to leave. The Packard plant closed
years before I left Detroit, the diner was burned
to the ground in '67, two years before my eldest son
fled to Sweden to escape the American dream.
"And the lovers?" you ask. I wrote nothing about lovers.
Take a look. Clouds, trucks, traffic lights, a diner, work,
a wooden shoe, East Moline, poached eggs, the perfume
of frying bacon, the chaos of language, the spices
of spent breath after eight hours of night work.
Can you hear all I feared and never dared to write?
Why the two are more real than either you or me,
why I never returned to keep them in my life,
how little I now mean to myself or anyone else,
what any of this could mean, where you found
the patience to endure these truths and confusions?

In the White City

After the earthquake the seven hills
remained as before, staring
heavenward without the least
comment. Centuries passed.
My father arrived on the *Tasman,*
out of Alexandria with a load
of fine cotton and one deserter.
February, 1919. He took a room
above a café in the Alfama
where he could unload. Sleep
was impossible, so after dark
he descended on foot to where

the ships groaned and sighed
patiently and he could think
at his ease. The seventh night
low rain clouds blew in from
the sea and broke across the hills
so that when he climbed back
it was against a black river
rushing toward the Tagus. Later,
forty-seven years later, when
I arrived alone at the airport
at dawn, fevered and searching.
I hired a driver, Manuel de Alvaros,
a thief and a smuggler, who drove
only Buicks stolen before the war.
Together we found the room
as it was, my father's suitcase
under the bed, his journal left open
to a blank page on which I wrote
his three names in the one language
we shared. Suddenly I could feel
the land slowly sliding from under me
as though released from Europe
and the past. My father and I,
together once again, heading
somewhere, across the seas or back
to childhood. It was our summer
for one last time, the window
opening on bright flags
of laundry, the cries of vendors,
of kids at play, a trolley gasping
up the staggered hills, all
of Lisbon spread out below
and clarified in exact detail
for those no longer here to see.

Houses in Order

In cardboard boxes under the Williamsburg Bridge
a congregation of mature rats founds a new order
based on the oldest religious principle: they eat
whatever they can get their teeth into. By day
they move slowly about their kingdom, some days
so slowly they seem for hours on end to become
holy relics or the stained brown backgrounds
to events foretold in parables to do with
the savor of salt, the mysteries of mustard seeds,
meat, bones, loaves, and fishes. When you look
back they've gone into water or air, they've joined
the falling rain that makes vision so difficult
even for the visionary. The little houses keep
their secrets the way windowless houses always do
though their walls and roofs proclaim the hour's
holy names—Nike and Converse, Panasonic and Walk-
man—, and though they let light leak in through
their teeth-torn ports and darkness out from under
their lids, they're closed to all but the eyes
of the faithful. These dull pilgrims contemplate
the business of gathering and hunting while the day
hangs on and the traffic drones on the bridge above.
Soon the headlights come on, singly or in pairs,
the rain gleams through the taut cables,
no moon rises above the island where now they are
among us, each one doing a morsel of God's work
until their small jaws ache from so much prayer.

Gospel

The new grass rising in the hills,
the cows loitering in the morning chill,
a dozen or more old browns hidden
in the shadows of the cottonwoods
beside the streambed. I go higher

to where the road gives up and there's
only a faint path strewn with lupine
between the mountain oaks. I don't
ask myself what I'm looking for.
I didn't come for answers
to a place like this, I came to walk
on the earth, still cold, still silent.
Still ungiving, I've said to myself,
although it greets me with last year's
dead thistles and this year's
hard spines, early blooming
wild onions, the curling remains
of spider's cloth. What did I bring
to the dance? In my back pocket
a crushed letter from a woman
I've never met bearing bad news
I can do nothing about. So I wander
these woods half sightless while
a west wind picks up in the trees
clustered above. The pines make
a music like no other, rising and
falling like a distant surf at night
that calms the darkness before
first light. "Soughing" we call it, from
Old English, no less. How weightless
words are when nothing will do.

Larry Levis

Larry Levis, who died in 1996, wrote six books of poetry: *Wrecking Crew* (1972), *The Afterlife* (1976), *The Dollmaker's Ghost* (1981), *Winter Stars* (1985), *The Widening Spell of the Leaves* (1991), and *Elegy* (1997). *The Selected Levis: Selected and with an Afterword by David St. John* was published by the University of Pittsburgh Press in 2000.

The Poet at Seventeen

My youth? I hear it mostly in the long, volleying
Echoes of billiards in the pool halls where
I spent it all, extravagantly, believing
My delicate touch on a cue would last for years.

Outside the vineyards vanished under rain,
And the trees held still or seemed to hold their breath
When the men I worked with, pruning orchards, sang
Their lost songs: *Amapola; La Paloma;*

Jalisco, No Te Rajes—the corny tunes
Their sons would just as soon forget, at recess,
Where they lounged apart in small groups of their own.
Still, even when they laughed, they laughed in Spanish.

I hated high school then, & on weekends drove
A tractor through the widowed fields. It was so boring
I memorized poems above the engine's monotone.
Sometimes whole days slipped past without my noticing,

And birds of all kinds flew in front of me then.
I learned to tell them apart by their empty squabblings,
The slightest change in plumage, or the inflection
Of a call. And why not admit it? I was happy

Then. I believed in no one. I had the kind
Of solitude the world usually allows
Only to kings & criminals who are extinct,
Who disdain this world, & who rot, corrupt & shallow

As fields I disced: I turned up the same gray
Earth for years. Still, the land made a glum raisin
Each autumn, & made that little hell of days—
The vines must have seemed like cages to the Mexicans

Who were paid seven cents a tray for the grapes
They picked. Inside the vines it was hot, & spiders
Strummed their emptiness. Black widows, Daddy Longlegs.
The vine canes whipped our faces. None of us cared.

And the girls I tried to talk to after class
Sailed by, then each night lay enthroned in my bed,
With nothing on but the jewels of their embarrassment.
Eyes, lips, dreams. No one. The sky & the road.

A life like that? It seemed to go on forever—
Reading poems in school, then driving a stuttering tractor
Warm afternoons, then billiards on blue October
Nights. The thick stars. But mostly now I remember

The trees, wearing their mysterious yellow sullenness
Like party dresses. And parties I didn't attend.
And then the first ice hung like spider lattices
Or the embroideries of Great Aunt No One,

And then the first dark entering the trees—
And inside, the adults with their cocktails before dinner,
The way they always seemed afraid of something,
And sat so rigidly, although the land was theirs.

My Story in a Late Style of Fire

Whenever I listen to Billie Holiday, I am reminded
That I, too, was once banished from New York City.
Not because of drugs or because I was interesting enough
For any wan, overworked patrolman to worry about—
His expression usually a great, gauzy spiderweb of bewilderment
Over his face—I was banished from New York City by a woman.
Sometimes, after we had stopped laughing, I would look
At her & see a cold note of sorrow or puzzlement go
Over her face as if someone else were there, behind it,
Not laughing at all. We were, I think, "in love." No, I'm sure.
If my house burned down tomorrow morning, & if I & my wife
And son stood looking on at the flames, & if, then,
Someone stepped out of the crowd of bystanders
And said to me: "Didn't you once know...?" *No.* But if
One of the flames, rising up in the scherzo of fire, turned
All the windows blank with light, & if that flame could speak,
And if it said to me: "You loved her, didn't you?" I'd answer,
Hands in my pockets, "Yes." And then I'd let fire & misfortune
Overwhelm my life. Sometimes, remembering those days,
I watch a warm, dry wind bothering a whole line of elms
And maples along a street in this neighborhood until
They're all moving at once, until I feel just like them,
Trembling & in unison. None of this matters now,
But I never felt alone all that year, & if I had sorrows,
I also had laughter, the affliction of angels & children.
Which can set a whole house on fire if you'd let it. And even then
You might still laugh to see all of your belongings set you free
In one long choiring of flames that sang only to you—
Either because no one else could hear them, or because
No one else wanted to. And, mostly, because they know.
They know such music cannot last, & that it would
Tear them apart if they listened. In those days,
I was, in fact, already married, just as I am now,
Although to another woman. And that day I could have stayed
In New York. I had friends there. I could have strayed
Up Lexington Avenue, or down to Third, & caught a faint
Glistening of the sea between the buildings. But all I wanted
Was to hold her all morning, until her body was, again,
A bright field, or until we both reached some thicket

As if at the end of a lane, or at the end of all desire,
And where we could, therefore, be alone again, & make
Some dignity out of loneliness. As, mostly, people cannot do.
Billie Holiday, whose life was shorter & more humiliating
Than my own, would have understood all this, if only
Because even in her late addiction & her bloodstream's
Hallelujahs, she, too, sang often of some affair, or someone
Gone, & therefore permanent. And sometimes she sang for
Nothing, even then, & it isn't anyone's business, if she did.
That morning, when *she* asked me to leave, wearing only
The apricot tinted, fraying chemise, I wanted to stay.
But I also wanted to go, to lose her suddenly, almost
For no reason, & certainly without any explanation.
I remember looking down at a pair of singular tracks
Made in a light snow the night before, at how they were
Gradually effacing themselves beneath the tires
Of the morning traffic, & thinking that my only other choice
Was fire, ashes, abandonment, solitude. All of which happened
Anyway, & soon after, & by divorce. I know this isn't much.
But I wanted to explain this life to you, even if
I had to become, over the years, someone else to do it.
You have to think of me what you think of me. I had
To live my life, even its late, florid style. Before
You judge this, think of her. Then think of fire,
Its laughter, the music of splintering beams & glass,
The flames reaching through the second story of a house
Almost as if to—mistakenly—rescue someone who
Left you years ago. It is so American, fire. So like us,
Its desolation. And its eventual, brief triumph.

Thomas Lux

photo by Claudia Lux

Thomas Lux is Bourne Professor
of Poetry at The Georgia
Institute of Technology. His
most recent book is *The Cradle
Place* (Houghton Mifflin, 2004).

Refrigerator, 1957

More like a vault—you pull the handle out
and on the shelves: not a lot,
and what there is (a boiled potato
in a bag, a chicken carcass
under foil) looking dispirited,
drained, mugged. This is not
a place to go in hope or hunger.
But, just to the right of the middle
of the middle door shelf, on fire, a lit-from-within red,
heart red, sexual red, wet neon red,
shining red in their liquid, exotic,
aloof, slumming
in such company: a jar
of maraschino cherries. Three-quarters
full, fiery globes, like strippers
at a church social. Maraschino cherries, maraschino,
the only foreign word I knew. Not once
did I see these cherries employed: not
in a drink, nor on top
of a glob of ice cream,
or just pop one in your mouth. Not once.

The same jar there through an entire
childhood of dull dinners—bald meat,
pocked peas and, see above,
boiled potatoes. Maybe
they came over from the old country,
family heirlooms, or were status symbols
bought with a piece of the first paycheck
from a sweatshop,
which beat the pig farm in Bohemia,
handed down from my grandparents
to my parents
to be someday mine,
then my child's?
They were beautiful
and, if I never ate one,
it was because I knew it might be missed
or because I knew it would not be replaced
and because you do not eat
that which rips your heart with joy.

An Horatian Notion

The thing gets made, gets built, and you're the slave
who rolls the log beneath the block, then another,
then pushes the block, then pulls a log
from the rear back to the front
again and then again it goes beneath the block,
and so on. It's how a thing gets made—not
because you're sensitive, or you get genetic-lucky,
or God says: Here's a nice family,
seven children, let's see: this one in charge
of the village dunghill, these two die of buboes, this one
Kierkegaard, this one a drooling

nincompoop, this one clerk, this one cooper.
You need to love the thing you do—birdhouse building,
painting tulips exclusively, whatever—and then
you do it

so consciously driven
by your unconscious
that the thing becomes a wedge
that splits a stone and between the halves
the wedge then grows, i.e., the thing
is solid but with a soul,
a life of its own. Inspiration, the donnée,

the gift, the bolt of fire
down the arm that makes the art?
Grow up! Give me, please, a break!
You make the thing because you love the thing
and you love the thing because someone else loved it
enough to make you love it.
And with that your heart like a tent peg pounded
toward the earth's core.
And with that your heart on a beam burns
through the ionosphere.
And with that you go to work.

Amiel's Leg

We were in a room that was once an attic,
tops of trees filled the windows, a breeze
crossed the table where we sat
and Amiel, about age four, came to visit
with her father, my friend,
and it was spring I think, and I remember
being happy—her mother was there too,
and my wife, and a few other friends.
It was spring, late spring, because the trees
were full but still that slightly lighter
green; the windows were open,
some of them, and I'll say it
out loud: I was happy, sober, at the time childless
myself, and it was one
of those moments: just like that, Amiel
climbed on my lap and put her head back against my chest.

I put one hand on her knees
and my other hand on top of that hand.
That was all, that was it.
Amiel's leg was cool, faintly rubbery.
We were there—I wish I knew the exact
date, time—and that
was all, that was it.

Dystopia

For shoes: rat skins duct-taped around a foot.
Shirts: sacks used to haul corn
to High Feast Day dinners.
The same corn's husks
used to polish the boots of the adjutants
and baked into bread by the adjutants' adjutants.
There are no ribs without elbows in them.
There is no shoulder without the breath of another on it.
Coughing carries across seas and sod.
The Dysentery Ward fights the Typhus Ward
for a melon rind which, in the confusion,
is stolen by a leper
who silences his bell's clapper
with his thumb's stub.
When two love
here, and sometimes two do love here,
they are famished for each other
but too weak to rise from their pallets of straw
to kiss. It is by their serene looks
and one-eighth smiles
the grave crews
honor them—placing one first, the other second,
in a twenty-person trench.
No casseroles for the mourners.
The three or four remaining haves
are quickly eaten by the have-nots.

Gary Margolis

Gary Margolis is Director of Counseling and Associate Professor of English (part-time) at Middlebury College. A former staff member at the Bread Loaf and University of Vermont Writers' Conferences, his most recent book of poems is *Fire in the Orchard* (Autumn House Press). He was awarded the first annual Sam Dietzel Award by St. Michael's College for mental health practice in Vermont.

Self-Portrait in the Garden, 1847

Hippolyte Bayard (1801-1886) rests his arm
On the wooden barrel as if he were leaning
On the body of a grand piano. He's placed
A vase and tilted flower pot beside him
And leaned a ladder against a trellis, as aware
Of the large tin watering can he's put to
His right, as he is of himself, looking out
To something he made that doesn't know
It's a camera. Surely, he believes he'll be
Perceived, if not known, by someone like me,
Who's thinking of who might read this
One day hoeing the garden, mulched in hay
And scraps of paper, drafts of poems
And bits of letters. The curator suggests

He could have surrounded himself with swords
And a fountain or stood in front of a ministry,

Instead of the things of his life he gathered
From a shed next to his neighbor's cottage.
Bayard appears to be a man unafraid of not
Being remembered, arranged this way because
He knew he could see himself and eventually be
Seen looking out through time in the theater
Of his vest and waistcoat, dress shirt and necktie,
Posed and imposing himself in this row
Of things, like a sweet and bitter weed.

Lincoln on the Battlefield of Antietam, October 3, 1862

From a Brady photograph

Oh, my president, tall as a tent-pole,
Standing next to McClellan and Pinkerton,
All top hat and long coat, at attention,
It seems like, trying to be still enough,
To be taken, shot, by Gardner the Scot,
Brady's assistant, trying not to move
More than the wind in the unknown leaves
Or the bodies in front of him, which lay dead
Long enough not to blur.

Shovel and Rake

> *Even in battle, crops and sacred objects must always be spared.*
> —Mohammed

Praise to the prophet I think, looking
    out on my wife's garden, her wavy
rows and beds of mulch.

Praise to this piece of yard she can
    bury her knees and dig her hands into.
Praise to the warrior who walks by her,

weeding, his spear dripping on the dirt
    road, who looks over her way,
in a way I believe he doesn't see her,

snapping peas and pulling up
    the dirty bulbs of the beets.
Who recognizes the way she has

leaned the shovel against the rake
    so they can be seen by anyone
returning with blood on his hands.

Who is looking over the old hay fields
    at the smoke which is having its own trouble
rising and not praising her pepper's fire.

Fall Term

These burrs on the cedar branches are no
    bother. Neither are the curling black
willow leaves the frost tints yellow
    and brown. Before I know it, I can see
my way clear to the gray granite art
    building, where two students are toeing
in to its ragged stone edges, imagining,
    I think, they are on Everest and not a few
yards across from their new dormitory,
    where the spines of their books haven't
been broken yet or anything written
    on a clean sheet of paper. Because no leaf
ever went to college, when there was
    a breeze and the late afternoon sun came
to an open window, like the yellow jackets
    who know enough not to study and the blue
jays who never fail at anything.

Cleopatra Mathis

Cleopatra Mathis is the author of five books of poems. Her sixth collection, *White Sea*, will be published by Sarabande Books in 2005. Widely published in magazines, textbooks, and anthologies, she has been the recipient of many grants and awards, including two National Endowment for the Arts fellowships and the Peter Lavin Award from the Academy of American Poets. She directs the creative writing program at Dartmouth College.

photo by Ted Rosenberg

The Ruin

When I was young, it was enough
to save myself. Childhood's house gave way
to the birds of the night, the rich
Louisiana dark which in its green
carries melody and chorus.
I set my own clock to it, rising
to rain in leaves, a voice
that told me I could leave that place.
Even later, the sun reflecting the image
of water onto a bedroom ceiling
could wake me.

But when my daughter disappeared,
no beauty gave back a reason to live.
I was nothing but mother, I would blow out
the world's candle. No burning,
no fire with its regeneration,
not even ash, that little cold ruin.
It was then I understood
the nothingness of the sea,

the crush of waves driven across miles,
riptides and currents deepening
in a water too vast to freeze.
Thousands of feet, impenetrable:
no diver, no machine, could breathe
in the time it took to reach that bottom;
nothing could live in that black, the descending
zones that cancelled out creatures—
the tiniest slime of protoplasm, eggy scum
on the chalky mud, whatever design
managed to quiver 300 fathoms down
to the zero of the final zone.
And everything above rendered trivial
by the great salt body rocking
through the sea floor canyons and mountains.
All of it a locked tomb, and me
in my iron boat.

Betrayal

Before the dog came, I never knew
about the woods in snow, knee-high; never fell
on the pathless maze that led me in.
Off his leash, he remembered who he'd been—
a raving thing, roaming, and he threw
his whole body in a run, a forward motion
that sank him, rocked him, the long thrust
upward from his hind. He put his snout
down deep in the layered cold
and tunneled, longing after
some hidden thing he knew was there
if only he could dig it out. Some dying smell
guided him to frenzy, and he turned,
pretending not to know me: he was beast, and I
owned the stick, which to him became bone,
the marrow he needed to survive, and so he leapt

in circles around me, pulling closer, madder,
his growls deepening, his eyes going flat
and foreign. I put aside my fear,
put the stick between us and held on
with everything I had. I lowered my head
and fought, laying my flesh on his.
I smelled the hot breath, felt the cold black
tip of his nose; I allowed the two bared fangs
to touch my lower lip: the moment
when he could have had me.
But in that pause, he pulled away
with a long canine sigh, lifted his face
all the way up to the great slow rocking
in the tops of the pines, the sifting ash-like
snow that followed downward like a whisper.
He froze, caught; his open mouth quivered.
Long ago, he raged for meat, knew the damned
before they knew themselves. He stood
with the gods and did their bidding.
Love had nothing to do with it.

Persephone, Answering

The girl in me died.
I watched her go under. In time
I turned back, answering the world
with my dead weight.
I entered the delirious air,
a spring I could make nothing of.

The question is
what is the end of grief?
I knew my mother then
for the first time: the bright self
withers, the soul

whitening like a stem that can't push its way
through rotted leaves, no balmy light
to fatten it into love

—if blooming is what we think is love.
Mother made herself into a bitter root,
living for a few days of flowering.
What art is that, always holding on?

William Matthews

photo by Ted Rosenberg

William Matthews is the author
of a dozen books of poetry,
essays, and translations. He won
the National Book Critics' Circle
Award for *Time & Money*
(Houghton Mifflin, 1995), has
been the recipient of fellow-
ships from the Guggenheim and
Ingram Merrill foundations,
and in April 1997 was awarded
the Ruth Lilly Prize. At the time
of his death in 1997, he was a
professor of English and
director of the writing program
at the College of the City
University of New York.

The Cloister

The last light of a July evening drained
into the streets below. My love and I had hard
things to say and hear, and we sat over
wine, faltering, picking our words carefully.

The afternoon before I had lain across
my bed and my cat leapt up to lie
alongside me, purring and slowly
growing dozy. By this ritual I could

clear some clutter from my baroque brain.
And into that brief vacancy the image
of a horse cantered, coming straight to me,
and I knew it brought hard talk and hurt

and fear. How did we do? A medium job,
which is well above average. But because
she had opened her heart to me as far
as she did, I saw her fierce privacy,

like a gnarled, luxuriant tree all hung
with disappointments, and I knew
that to love her I must love the tree
and the nothing it cares for me.

Housecooling

Those ashes shimmering dully in the fireplace,
like tarnished fish scales? I swept them out.
Those tiny tumbleweeds of dust that stalled
against a penny or a paperclip under the bed?
I lay along the grain of the floorboards
and stared each pill into the vacuum's mouth.
I loved that house and I was moving out.

What do you want to do when you grow up?
they asked, and I never said, *I want to haunt
a house.* But I grew pale. The way cops "lift"
fingerprints, that's how I touched the house.
The way one of my sons would stand in front
of me and say, *I'm outta here,* and he would mean
it, his crisp, heart-creasing husk delivering

a kind of telegram from wherever the rest of him
had gone—that's how I laved and scoured
and patrolled the house, and how I made my small
withdrawals and made my wan way outta there.
And then I was gone. I took what I could.
Each smudge I left, each slur, each whorl, I left
for love, but love of what I cannot say.

Care

The lump of coal my parents teased
I'd find in my Christmas stocking
turned out each year to be an orange,
for I was their sunshine.

Now I have one C. gave me,
a dense node of sleeping fire.
I keep it where I read and write.
"You're on chummy terms with dread,"

it reminds me. "You kiss ambivalence
on both cheeks. But if you close your
heart to me ever, I'll wreathe you in flames
and convert you to energy."

I don't know what C. meant me to mind
by her gift, but the sun returns
unbidden. Books get read and written.
My mother comes to visit. My father's

dead. Love needs to be set alight
again and again, and in thanks
for tending it, will do its very
best not to consume us.

Landscape with Onlooker

One night shy of full, the moon
looks not lonesome shining through the trees, but replete

with the thoughtless sensuality of well-being.
A chill in the air? No, under the air, like water

under a swimmer. The unsteadfast leaves grow crisp
and brittle, the better to fall away. Some nights

fear, like rising water in a well, fills these hours—
the dead of night, as the phrase goes, when you quicken

and the dank metallic sweat beads like a vile dew.
But tonight you stand at your window, framed and calm,

and the air's as sweet as a freshly peeled orange.
There's a moon on the lake, and another in the sky.

Linda McCarriston

photo by Michael LaCombe

Linda McCarriston has published three collections of poems: *Talking Soft Dutch* (an AWP Award Series selection), *Eva-Mary* (Terrence Des Pres Prize winner and National Book Award finalist), and *Little River*. She has also written essays, especially on the intersection of poetry and class consciousness. A professor at the University of Alaska-Anchorage, she has lived in Alaska since 1994.

To Judge Faolain, Dead Long Enough: A Summons

Your Honor, when my mother stood
before you, with her routine
domestic plea, after weeks
of waiting for speech to return
to her body, with her homemade
forties hairdo, her face purple still
under pancake, her jaw off just a little,
her *holy of holies* healing,
her breasts wrung, her heart
the bursting heart of someone
snagged among rocks deep
in a sharkpool—no, not "someone,"

but a woman there, snagged
with her babies, *by* them,
in one of hope's pedestrian
brutal turns—when, in the tones
of parlors overlooking the harbor,
you admonished that, for the sake
of the family, the wife
must take the husband back to her bed,
what you willed not to see before you
was a woman risen clean to the surface,
a woman who, with one arm flailing,
held up with the other her actual

burdens of flesh. When you clamped
to her leg the chain of *justice*,
you ferried us back down to *the law*,
the black ice eye, the maw, the mako
that circles the kitchen table nightly.
What did you make of the words
she told you, not to have heard her,
not to have seen her there? Almost-
forgivable ignorance, you were not
the fist, the boot, or the blade,
but the jaded, corrective ear and eye
at the limits of her world. Now

I will you to see her as she was, to ride
your own words into the light: I call
your spirit home again, divesting you
of robe and bench, the fine white hand
and half-lit Irish eye. Tonight, put on
a body in the trailer down the road
where your father, when he can't
get it up, makes love to your mother
with a rifle. Let your name be
Eva-Mary. Let your hour of birth
be dawn. Let your life be long
and common, and your flesh endure.

A Thousand Genuflections

Winter mornings when I call her,
out of falling snow she trots
into view, her tail and mane
made flame by movement, carrying,
as line and motion, back into air
her shape and substance—like fire
into heat into light, turns
the candle takes, burning.
And her head—her senses,
every one is a scout sent out
ahead of her, behind, beside:
her eye upon me, over the distance,
her ear, its million listeners,
delicate and vast her nose, her mouth,
her voice upon me, closing the distance.
I could just put the buckets down
and go, but I kneel to hold them
as she eats, as she drinks, to be
this close. For something of myself
lives here, stripped of the knowing
that is not knowing, a single thing
from the least webbed tissues
of the heart straight out to the tips
of the guardhairs that shimmer off
beyond my sight into air, the grasses,
grain, the water, light.
I've come like this each day
for years across the hard winters,
seeing a figure for the thing itself,
divine—appetite and breath,
flesh and attention. This morning
her presence asks of me: *And might
you be your body? Might we be
not the figure, but the thing itself?*

Healing the Mare

Just days after the vet came,
after the steroids that took
the fire out of the festering
sores—out of the flesh that in
the heat took the stings too
seriously and swelled into great
welts, wore thin and wept, calling
more loudly out to the green-
headed flies—I bathe you
and see your coat returning,
your deep force surfacing in a
new layer of hide: black wax
alive against weather and flies.

But this morning, misshapen
still, you look like an effigy,
something rudely made, something
made to be buffeted, or like
an old comforter—are they both
one in the end? So both a child

and a mother, with my sponge and
my bucket, I come to anoint, to
anneal the still weeping, to croon
to you *baby poor baby* for the sake
of the song, to polish you up,
for the sake of the touch, to a shine.

As I soothe you I surprise wounds
of my own this long time unmothered.
As you stand, scathed and scabbed,
with your head up, I swab. As you
press, I lean into my own loving
touch, for which no wound
is too ugly.

Jo McDougall

Jo McDougall is the author of
five books of poetry. Her awards
include a Reader's Digest DeWitt
Wallace writing award, an
Academy of American Poets
Award, and fellowships from
the MacDowell Colony and the
Arkansas Arts Council. She has
published in *The Georgia Review,
The Hudson Review, The Kenyon
Review, The Midwest Quarterly,
New Letters,* and others.

The Ferry

Whenever we needed to cross the Arkansas,
we had to take the dirt road to the ferry.
My father would drive.
My mother would fret
about missing the on-ramp,
driving off the other end,
getting caught by the dark.

After we bumped ourselves on
with a few other cars,
after the ferry coughed us away from shore,
the operator would shut the motor off
to drift as long as he dared.
Then we'd hear the motor again,
arguing with the current.

Thus we kept our course—
the river suffering us,
the sun easing down,
darkness closing over us
merciless as water.

A Woman Tires of Hearing Acorns on the Roof

All October they have dinged our roof
like berserk goats.

Today my doctor has phoned.
The tests have come back positive;
he'll see me in his office
tomorrow.

Hungry for snow to lay down
its quiet tarpaulins,
I recall the dirt I was instructed to scatter
as a child, how it rang
on my grandfather's lowered coffin.

Dirt

Its arrogance will break your heart.
Two weeks ago
we had to coax it
into taking her body.
Today,
after a light rain,
I see it hasn't bothered
to conceal its seams.

Taxidermy

Let us mourn the giraffe and zebra,
dead during heavy bombardment
in a Gaza Strip Zoo—
one of terror,
one of tear gas.
There is no money to replace them,
so they will be stuffed
and put back in their cages
for children to see
how it was when these were animals—
although someone who can remember
will have to explain
how the brusque tails sent flies reeling;
how, like barley in an evening wind,
they bent their necks to water;
how the eyes were not glass then,
and darker.

Campbell McGrath

Campbell McGrath is the author of six books, most recently *Pax Atomica* (Ecco/HarperCollins, 2004). His awards include the Kingsley Tufts Prize and a MacArthur Fellowship. He lives in Miami and teaches at Florida International University.

Girl with Blue Plastic Radio

The first song I ever heard was "The Ballad of Bonnie and Clyde."
There was a girl at the playground with a portable radio,
lying in the grass near the swingset, beyond the sun-lustred aluminum slide,

kicking her bare feet in the air, her painted toenails—toes
the color of blueberries, rugburns, yellow pencils, Grecian urns.
This would be when—1966? No, later, '67 or '68. And no,

it was not the very first song I ever heard,
but the first that invaded my consciousness in that elastically joyous
way music does, the first whose lyrics I tried to learn,

my first communication from the gigawatt voice
of the culture— popular culture, mass culture, our culture— kaboom!—
raw voltage embraced for the sheer thrill of getting juiced.

Who wrote that song? When was it recorded, and by whom?
Melody lost in the database of the decades
but still playing somewhere in the mainframe cerebellums

of its dandelion-chained, banana-bike-riding, Kool-Aid-
addled listeners, still echoing within the flesh and blood mausoleums
of us, me, we, them, the self-same blades

of wind-sown crabgrass spoken of and to by Whitman,
and who could believe it would still matter
decades or centuries later, in a new millennium,

matter what we listened to, what we ate and watched, matter
that it was "rock 'n' roll," for so we knew to call it,
matter that there were hit songs, girls, TVs, fallout shelters.

Who was she, her with the embroidered blue jeans and bare feet,
toe-nails gilded with cryptic bursts of color?
She is archetypal, pure form, but no less believable for that.

Her chords still resonate, her artifacts have endured
so little changed as to need no archeological translation.
She was older than me, worldly and self-assured.

She was, already, a figure of erotic fascination.
She knew the words and sang the choruses
and I ran over from the sandbox to listen

to a world she cradled in one hand, transistorized oracle,
blue plastic embodiment of our neo-Space Age ethos.
The hulls of our Apollonian rocket ships were as yet unbarnacled

and we still found box turtles in the tall weeds and mossy grass
by the little creek not yet become what it was all becoming
in the wake of the yellow earth-movers, that is:

suburbia. Alive, vibrant, unselfconsciously evolving,
something new beneath the nuclear sun, something new in the acorn-
    scented dark.
Lived there until I was seven in a cinderblock garden

apartment. My prefab haven, my little duplex ark.
And the name of our subdivision was
Americana Park.

Iowa

First trip alone across the country: a dream of driving
through driving rain in Iowa, sodden Iowa,
miles of drenched earth passed through in the gloaming,

roads of pickup trucks, hogpens, cornbins, silos,
a grocery where I stop for apples and white bread,
streetlights reflected on asphalt and dented iron,

on a bright orange Subaru I acknowledge with a nod
as I acknowledge myself, behind the wheel,
Woody Guthrie and the Ramones, the open road,

all that, the scope of the world, its gravity and zeal
beyond rain-wet windows, its diverse
and circumstantial passage, even the familiar become unreal

in light of that unscrolling: taste of liverwurst
and sweet pickle sandwiches; tears of a woman
on a payphone beside a piebald horse

in some city flashing past, gone,
perhaps Cedar Rapids; atavistic vision of deepest greenness,
the summoning sheen and wavelength of the corn,

as if the kernels radiated an oceanic luminescence
the husks worked to cocoon and sequester
back into the dark. Of course it was

all much stranger than that, richer and sadder
in its unique and particular word-defying actuality
than my familiar penciled grid of sequential semesters.

Different how, in what way? I can't say.
I mean that it is unsayable, a string of precious shells
or trading beads—*cow, brook, hay*—

not the coinage of names but the things themselves,
their totality, their scale and dimension,
the knowledge that there are spheres and levels

one has never conceived: so this is what the rain
feels like in Iowa, in California; this is another way,
another state, another life, another vision.

And then what? What to equal that revelatory awe?
Elizabeth's beauty like an exhibition
of blown-glass roses, her heart's raw glory,

the birth of our children,
that great awakening, leaving the hospital
our first morning together like a vestal procession

passing from the lobby into the lightfall
of a pure blue Chicago spring
as if crossing some threshold of universal

import, powered by mysterious agency, a door opening
silently as the future opens its automatic portal
before us, second by second, invisible and astonishing.

My son is born and I am no longer immortal.
The ring shall be closed, the cycle fulfilled.
I am bound over, as in a fairy tale,

to the will of time, pledged to this world
by an oath of fearful enchantment.
Pledged. Promised. Bound over. Beguiled.

Rock and Roll

Been a long time since I rock & rolled
Led Zeppelin says in its famous song called,
quite rightly, "Rock and Roll,"

as so many are, so far so good,
but then what? *Been a long time since I did the stroll,*
as Robert Plant would have it understood,

or *been a long time since the Dead Sea Scrolls?*
Both, in their way, are intelligible,
both possess sense-making apparatus and obey syntactical protocols,

both signify, both are full
of meaning,
both call to us across the void—*hell-*

o!— but their ways and means
of meaning what they mean and saying what they say are as different
as night from day, the first a formulaic, stripped-clean,

boogie-woogie rant,
the second an implicit commentary on the historicity of the text,
a not uncommon species of lit-crit cant,

coy reference to the complexity
of deciphering what we hear and what we read
in or out of context,

like the time in Verona we could have seen Lou Reed
in the Roman amphitheater that is one of the glories of western civilization
but Elizabeth wouldn't go because she thought I meant Lou Rawls.

Rennie McQuilkin

Rennie McQuilkin's poetry has appeared in *The Atlantic, Poetry, The American Scholar,* and other publications. He is the author of five poetry collections and has received grants from the NEA as well as the Connecticut Commission on the Arts. For many years he directed the Sunken Garden Poetry Festival and recently received a Lifetime Achievement Award from the Connecticut Center for the Book. He lives in Simsbury, CT.

Regatta

All night beneath the stately turn
of the slooped and schoonered sky,
they rode the star-filled swells

expensively, their halyards chiming,
that now are under jib and spinnaker.
From this hill, this humming top,

it might be ivory queens, bishops,
kings, gowns billowing,
who make their cryptic moves

across the mottled bay.
Overhead, a line of swans,
wings working up the air to whistle,

and this for heraldry—
a blue and silver kite, an osprey,
a redtail rounding out

the sky. How hard to believe
in anything
less heavenly. But there it is,

the dive, direct hit of the hawk
and sudden tangent
to the nest,

that innerspring of rabbit rib,
shrew skin, quail down,
fox fur.

As for the yachts, the swift
white yachts—
how many among us

must be taken, bone and gut,
that these may be
so sleek?

Sister Marie Angelica Plays Badminton

with Sister Marie Modeste most afternoons.
Today, because of lengthy vespers, they are late.
A pale moon has already risen, and early bats
are darting like black shuttlecocks.

Except for low wings whispering from time to time
and the Sisters' hushed encouragement,
the only sounds are the plinking of rackets
and a monotone of mourning doves.

On all sides of the court
the sculpted yew in cubes and columns
might pass for black so deeply green it grows.
And now it moves closer,

Marie Angelica would say,
who has been known to have visions.
Though she moves as aptly as the bats,
doesn't miss a shot,

when she goes back for a long one from Marie Modeste,
sways on her toes, arches her back,
raises one arm
and the other to keep her difficult balance,

she is lost, a long-legged girl again
in mare's tail, mullein, milkweed,
leaning on the sudden sky as if it could sustain her
like a hand in the small of her back. It does.

Her nerve ends quick as a shiver of poplar,
arms like branches in a wind,
she feels a cry begin
to rise, to force the self before it

and burst, all colors one. That white.
It vaults straight up, a feathered cry
that hovers in the heart of heaven, hovers,
and plummets to the gut

of the racket she sights it in,
the perfect bird, the shuttlecock
Marie Angelica keeps in play, will not let fall
despite the darkness gathering.

An Old Man's Sense

of time is shot. Now he is five in Indian headdress
facing off with the boy across the street
and now he is being born. The frames

blur by—his small head crowning, coming to light
is an old man's, white on hospital
white. Now the film so quickly reeling and unreeling

jams. It fixes on a single frame.
Before a brilliant circle burns out from its center
he sees

a sleeping compartment
elegant in the velvet and brass-fitted style
of the overnight express from Algeciras to Madrid.

He is raising a tasseled, dark green window shade
on the full Spanish moon. The white of it spills
across the cream and umber landscape of his bride.

Inis Meáin

Considering millennia of tooth and bone and carapace
drifting down in a nameless sea to pave
a barren land for boulders rolled by glaciers to inscribe,

considering the generations that hoisted scribbling
stones to wind-breaking, wind-wailing walls
to story the land, scratched up what little soil welled

in cracks, hauled seaweed and goat dung and pulverized
rock in sally baskets tumped to brows to cover
the old stone text with loam—considering this much

revising, I am more than I am who in my minor plot today
raise rhyming rows
of seed potatoes, withered things, and pray
they will translate well, bloom white as tooth and bone.

Jane Mead

Jane Mead's most recent book is
House of Poured-Out Waters
(University of Illinois Press).
She is the recipient of grants and
awards from the Whiting,
Lannan, and Guggenheim
Foundations.

Concerning That Prayer I Cannot Make

Jesus, I am cruelly lonely
and I do not know what I have done
nor do I suspect that you will answer me.

And, what is more, I have spent
these bare months bargaining
with my soul as if I could make her
promise to love me when now it seems
that what I meant when I said "soul"
was that the river reflects
the railway bridge just as the sky
says it should—it speaks *that* language.

I do not know who you are.

I come here every day
to be beneath this bridge,

to sit beside this river,
so I *must* have seen the way
the clouds just slide
under the rusty arch—
without snagging on the bolts,
how they are borne along on the dark water—
I must have noticed their fluent speed
and also how that tattered blue T-shirt
remains snagged on the crown
of the mostly sunk dead tree
despite the current's constant pulling.
Yes, somewhere in my mind there must
be the image of a sky blue T-shirt, caught,
and the white islands of ice flying by
and the light clouds flying slowly
under the bridge, though today the river's
fully melted. I must have seen.

But I did not see.

I am not equal to my longing.
Somewhere there should be a place
the exact shape of my emptiness—
there should be a place
responsible for taking one back.
The river, of course, has no mercy—
it just lifts the dead fish
toward the sea.

Of course, of course.

What I *meant* when I said "soul"
was that there should be a place.

On the far bank the warehouse lights
blink red, then green, and all the yellow
machines with their rusted scoops and lifts
sit under a thin layer of sunny frost.

And look—
my own palm—

there, slowly rocking.
It is *my* pale palm—
palm where a black pebble
is turning and turning.

    Listen—
    all you bare trees
    burrs
    brambles
    pile of twigs
    red and green lights flashing
    muddy bottle shards
    shoe half buried—listen

    listen, I am holy.

Passing a Truck Full of Chickens
at Night on Highway Eighty

What struck me first was their panic.

Some were pulled by the wind from moving
to the ends of the stacked cages,
some had their heads blown through the bars—

and could not get them in again.
Some hung there like that—dead—
their own feathers blowing, clotting

in their faces. Then
I saw the one that made me slow some—
I lingered there beside her for five miles.

She had pushed her head through the space
between bars—to get a better view.
She had the look of a dog in the back

of a pickup, that eager look of a dog
who knows she's being taken along.
She craned her neck.

She looked around, watched me, then
strained to see over the car—strained
to see what happened beyond.

That is the chicken I want to be.

Judson Mitcham

Judson Mitcham is the author of two collections of poems, *Somewhere in Ecclesiastes* (Missouri, 1991), and *This April Day* (Anhinga, 2003), as well as two novels, both from the University of Georgia Press: *The Sweet Everlasting* (1996) and *Sabbath Creek* (2004). He lives in Macon, GA, with his wife, Jean.

Surrender

We were ordinary men,
unable to embrace each other fully—
to bury a face in the other man's neck,
to rock like drunks in the doorway, saying
goodbye. It was always a handshake
and maybe that sideways hug,
with an arm around the shoulders.
        In the hospital
you couldn't understand, didn't know me,
tried to overturn the rack by the bed, tear
the needles from your arm; searched everywhere,
underneath the sheets and the pillow,
for your clothes, *going home*; grew frightened

when confused by the purpose of a spoon, angry
when you couldn't even urinate—failing
to hit the plastic bottle, till I held you.
If I leaned down close
when the baffled agitation started up,
and I smoothed back your hair, or I kissed you
on the forehead or the cheek, whispered "Daddy,"
you'd throw your arms around me.

There's a way a man turns to a woman,
so his lips just barely graze hers, yet in this,
there is everything that follows, each detail
of forgetting where they are.
And today, I am trembling with desire, wild
for the years, when my lips feel yours, cool
as gold. One kiss for the infinite
particulars of love, to tell you this:

I will be with you there, in the darkness.

The Multitude

The woman in the airplane wanted
to talk about Christ. I did not.
I raised my magazine. She continued, saying Christ
promised heaven to the thief
who believed while nailed to the cross.
The clouds looked solid far beneath. She began
the story of her life, and I stopped her
as politely as I could, saying please, right now,
I'd simply like to read. And for a while,
she did keep quiet, then she asked
if I'd ever really given Christ a chance, so I tried
telling her a joke, chose the one
about the Pope and Richard Nixon in a rowboat.
She discovered nothing funny in the story.
Jesus fed the multitude, she said.

I looked around to find an empty seat.
There wasn't one. She asked me if I knew
about the sower and the seed; about Zaccheus;
Legion and the swine; Mary Magdalene;
Lazarus; the rich young ruler. And I did,
I knew about them all. I told her yes,
sweet Jesus; got the stewardess
to bring another bourbon; tried to buy
the missionary one, but she declined.
And when the plane set down,
I'd escaped up the aisle, made the door,
and started walking fast toward the baggage claim,
when I saw them, all at once, on the concourse:
thousands I would never see again, who'd remain
nothing in my life, who would never have names;
and I realized I'd entertained—strangely,
and for no good reason I could see—
the hope of someone waiting there
who loved me.

History of Rain

What if every prayer for rain brought it down?
What if prayer made drunks quit the bars, numbers hit,
the right girl smile, shirts tumble from the dryer
fully ironed? What if God

required no more than a word? Every spot
of cancer would dissolve like peppermint,
every heart pump blood through arteries as clean
as drinking straws then. All grief would be gone,

all reverence and wonder. But if rain
should fall only once in a thousand years, rare
as a comet, if for fifty generations
there was never that sweet hint of metal in the air

until late one April afternoon
when the dust began to swirl above the ballfield,
and the first big drops fell, popping in the dirt,
and sudden as a thought, great gray-white sheets

steamed on the asphalt, fought with the pines,
would we all not walk out trying to believe
our place in the history of rain? We'd be there
for the shining of the world:

the weeds made gaudy with the quicksilver breeze;
the rainbows floating over black-glass streets;
each cupped thing bright with its blessing; and long
afterwards, a noise like praise, the rain

still falling in the trees.

Writing

But prayer was not enough, after all, for my father.
His last two brothers died five weeks apart.
He couldn't get to sleep, had no appetite, sat
staring. Though he prayed,
he could find no peace until he tried
to write about his brothers, tell a story
for each one: Perry's long travail
with the steamfitters' union, which he worked for;
and Harvey—here the handwriting changes,
he bears down—Harvey loved his children.

I discovered those few sheets of paper
as I looked through my father's old Bible
on the morning of his funeral. The others
in the family had seen them long ago;
they had all known the story,

and they told me I had not, most probably, because
I am a writer,
and my father was embarrassed by his effort. Yet
who has seen him as I can: risen

in the middle of the night, bending over
the paper, working close
to the heart of all greatness, he is so lost.

Jack Myers

Jack Myers, 2003 Poet Laureate of Texas, is the author/editor of sixteen books of and about poetry, most recently *The Portable Poetry Workshop: A Field Guide to Poetic Technique* and *The Glowing River: New & Selected Poems.* He teaches at Southern Methodist University and in the Vermont College MFA Program.

Bread, Meat, Greens, and Soap

> *It feels like déjà vu all over again.*
> — Yogi Berra

I feel like I'm about to be fired,
or my doctor will say I have
the obstruction he suspected,
or my 2nd-story-divorce-efficiency apartment
will be rubbed out by a clear blue sky
when I get back.

For instance, right now I'm walking around
this brand new cost-saver supermarket
conscious of this weird impingement
of loss, the way amputees feel the ache
of a phantom limb only I'm talking about all of me,
when I stop and ask an illegal alien stockboy
what street is this, and he croons to me
"Larmanda, Larmanda," which means Larmanda,
some nameless City Father's long lost wife,
and I realize, Holy Mackerel, right where I'm standing,

between the fresh fish and the meatcase
is my old bedroom where me and Willa,
which means Willa, made love every day
after laps and breaststrokes in the pool
of our lovely torn-down walk-up.
And not fifty feet away, years ago,
behind the pharmacy, I slipped a disc
but kept on crawling forward, thinking
who on earth has stabbed me in the back?

Right here in the hyped-up screaming
of the cereal aisle, the kids used to fly around
the kitchen like cartoon characters.
I wanted to grab the old lady
blocking my bedroom with her cart
and argue about this, let her know
how it was with us, but then I figured
what's the use, what are you going to do
about a past that is now
hundreds of thousands of tons of processed food,
a seven-billion-pound carrot to keep me going?

See how crazy with excitement I can get,
as if my life were living proof
of the Unified Field Theory,
which, in fact, to anyone who's hungry
is business as usual, a big so what?
Like taking pride in a miserable grocery list.
I mean, if you can feel it
about to rain in your bones,
and goddamn monkeys and geese
can sense a disaster
a priori,
if someone with some cash
can raze the past
and plunk a Safeway down on top of it,
then what else needs to happen before
the future will have me convinced?

I consult my list, the instructions I wrote
that amount to a soap opera on how to keep going,

written with such a magnificent sense of ease,
such amputated detachment, that right here in the store
I'm firing myself, divorcing the past from the present,
saying, Get your things,
just get what you came to get
and get out.

Admitting the Dark

> *Everything that has been said...*
> *is hurled through high windows*
> *into a big hole my father calls* heaven *but I call* the sky.
> — John Engman, "Atlantis"

The old Jewish men of my town
with their breath stinking of fish tins
and nasty dispositions, and debts,
and abstinence from everything
ever called lovely had it right.

Even as a child they seemed short to me
in their baggy suits and songs droning
like locust swarming the desert, their dance,
a rock trying to free itself from running away.

I'd slip by their moaning synagogue at dusk
as if it were the lair of larvae, pass quietly
by my fright thinking I had escaped the day
they finally pulled me in and stuck me
in my place and made me kiss the black
Book of the Dead that praised the Glory of God
in such saturating colors it made no sense.

Now all those who sang for the dead
are dead. And the boys who ran away,
emptied the town of marriages and shops
and abandoned it to commuters, have laid pain

to sleep, and sleep in a life that walls out death
and so made death surround them.
What strength it took to feel so weak, to rock
in place and sing of death. Of course it was dark.
That's what they sang about. Even my heart,
surrounded by darkness like way back then,
which is always beating faster in spite of me, knows that.

Taking the Children Away

They will pack the sky blue car
with blankets and pillows
and puzzles and snacks,
enough to end a life,
and the last thing I will see
will be the stuffed animals
pressed against the window,
like a happy ending in a Muppet movie,
tiny hands like wings
waving goodbye, little voices
trailing out the sides like streamers.

I will stand there
in the suicidal, accelerating, horizontal draft
of the car longer than is natural,
feeling liberated,
like a bombed-out town,
as the sad blue car dwindles and darkens
and inhales itself,
and I enter the house,
turn off the lights,
sit in foreclosure,
watching the twinkling half-life
of fallout begin floating down the years,
scattered toys appearing one by one
the way the first evening stars
look left behind.

This must be the missing that begins
inside the waiting for something larger
to take over, the being over to be over
that feels like the cobalt hand of air
I think my soul must be. I am afraid
that it will take a breath and then another
and another, like steps, until I begin to glow
like the small dull bulb inside a doorbell
as the evening sun slowly, simply disappears.

The Rules

My son is playing baseball.
He misses a high pop-up
and feels bad.
Then he strikes out
and we both feel bad.

But since when has paying attention
and doing well always been good for me?
I ask my dog who looks up to me
as we walk through traffic
"How many tragedies have I escaped
by not paying attention?"

My son's errors at play
are moments of pure air and light.
Isn't that what missing is?
That seems just as lovely and interesting
as getting it right.

Marilyn Nelson

Marilyn Nelson's most recent
books include *Fortune's Bones:
The Manumission Requiem* (Front
Street, 2005), *The Cachoeira Tales
and Other Poems* (LSU Press,
2005), *A Wreath for Emmett Till*
(Houghton Mifflin Children's
Division, 2005), and *The Ladder*
(Candlewick, 2005). She is the
Poet Laureate of Connecticut.

photo by Rohan Preston

Egyptian Blue

From red clay spotted on a hillside
Carver came up with a quadruple-
oxidized pigment the blue
of a royal mummy's innermost windings,
an Egyptian blue
no artist or scientist had duplicated
since the days of old King Tut.
It's the bluest blue,
bluer than lapis.
Paint factories and manufacturers
of artists' materials
begged him for the formula,
offering the top floor of Fort Knox.
He sent it
for the cost of the two-cent stamp
it cost him to mail it.

It's an indescribable blue.
You see it every day
on everything from shutters
to a child-sized flowered dress.

We've learned to live with it
without loving it, as if it were
something ordinary,
that blue the world sought
for five thousand years.
Look around with me: There it is
in the folder on my desk,
in my close-up photo of a fairy tern,
in the thumbtacks in my corkboard
holding up photos, poems, quotes, prayers,
a beaded ancestral goddess juju doll
(it's the blue of the scarab in her hand).
It's the blue of that dictionary
of American Regional English,
of the box of eighty standard envelopes,
the blue of that dress waiting to be ironed,
the blue of sky in that Guatemalan cross,
it's the blue of the Black Madonna's veil.

Bedside Reading

for St. Mark's Episcopal, Good Friday 1999

In his careful welter of dried leaves and seeds,
soil samples, quartz pebbles, notes-to-myself, letters,
on Dr. Carver's bedside table
next to his pocket watch,
folded in Aunt Mariah's Bible:
the Bill of Sale.
Seven hundred dollars
for a thirteen-year-old girl named Mary.

He moves it from passage
to favorite passage.
Fifteen cents
for every day she had lived.

Three hundred fifty dollars
for each son.
No charge
for two stillborn daughters
buried out there with the Carvers' child.

This new incandescent light makes
his evening's reading unwaveringly easy,
if he remembers to wipe his spectacles.
He turns to the blossoming story
of Abraham's dumbstruck luck,
of Isaac's pure trust in his father's wisdom.
Seven hundred dollars for all of her future.
He shakes his head.

   When the ram bleats from the thicket,
       Isaac...   like me...   understands
   the only things you can ever
     really...   trust...
  are...
       the natural order...
          ...and the Creator's love...
    spiraling...
  out of chaos...

Dr. Carver smoothes the page
and closes the book
on his only link with his mother.

He folds the wings of his spectacles
and bows his head for a minute.
Placing the Bible on the table
he forgets again at first, and blows at the light.
Then he lies back dreaming as the bulb cools.

Cafeteria Food

*Iowa State College of Agriculture
and Mechanic Arts, 1891*

Even when you've been living on
wild mushrooms, hickory nuts,
occasional banquet leftovers sneaked
out of the hotel kitchen by a colored cook,
and weeds; even when you know it feeds you,
mind and body, keeps you going
through the gauntlet
of whispered assault
as you wait in line;
even when it's free
except for the pride
you have to pay by eating
alone in the basement,
hot meat or chicken and potatoes
and fresh baked bread and buttery
vegetables; even when there's dessert;
even when you can count on it day after day;
even when it's good,
it's bad.

D. Nurkse

D. Nurkse is the author of eight
books of poetry, most recently
Burnt Island (Knopf, 2005), *The
Fall* (Knopf, 2002), *The Rules of
Paradise* (Four Way Books, 2001),
Leaving Xaia (Four Way Books,
2000), and *Voices over Water* (Four
Way Books, 1996). His poems
have appeared in *The New Yorker*
and *The Atlantic Monthly*.

The Last Husband

I met him at one of those receptions
I haunted after my divorce,
in a district of ballbearing factories,
stockyards, binderies and distilleries:

a man remarkably like me,
perhaps even more exhausted,
nibbling intently on a jumbo shrimp
as if watching a great secret
disappear before his eyes.

Was I eager to be exposed?
My tie was creased and threadbare.
I knew nothing of semi-pro hockey
or put-shares in the bauxite industry.

I had to drink almost as much
to talk to him as once to you,
but the chill wine was astonishing

and I found myself dreaming of home,
of the white bed and shivering curtain,
the breeze and the mysteries of sacred love:

as I drained my glass
he emptied his, and side by side
we gobbled the Calamata olives,
sushi, scones, melon cubes impaled
on toothpicks wrapped in green cellophane,
squid, rhubarb, endives, strawberries:

we spoke softly, like children in a trance,
of the starting line-up of the Harrisburg Huskies,
the vast deserted mines in Zambia
and the movements of money via satellite,

until the bay window darkened
and we saw our ghostly bodies
exchanging statistics, blessing each other,
unwilling to part or pronounce your name.

The Latch

A dog barked at me
from behind the dingy white fence.
I glimpsed its flashing teeth,
dull white like surf.
It threw its body against the slats
in play or rage. I rang again.
Lights kindled in a high window.
A man with my face
came out buttoning his shirt

sleepily. He shone his flashlight
straight at the gate,
then to the right and left of me,
then in the trees.
My wife appeared beside him
with our child in her arms.
She too looked up
at the tossing elms, heavy with south wind,
swinging like bells, but with no noise
except twigs splintering.
The dog hurled itself
again and again, like die cast,
the child stared straight at me
crying in silence, lips framing
my name, my father's name, the word
Father. Then the rain came.
They called the dog
and it went to them
tail tucked, the door closed,
the green curtain cinched shut
on nothing, but I stayed
at the gate, my right hand
on the oiled latch.
Sometimes a car passed
and the light enveloped my body
like a caress, knowing me,
gone, and I knelt
to fix an imaginary lace
or grope for a coin
I might have dropped
if I were still waiting.

The River of Separation

A friend went to the famine zone.
When he came back his eyes
would not meet mine.

Once he let me into his silence
and told of standing on a bridge
watching the bodies pass
bloated with hunger, faces
blank from the current.
When he finished I dreamt
of that bridge every night
until I spoke of it
as if I'd been the one
standing there— especially
to a woman, and she believed,
and was marked, and asked
for news; long after
I was gone, she begged for news
from everyone who knew me.

Naomi Shihab Nye

photo by Stephen Davis

Naomi Shihab Nye grew up in St. Louis, Jerusalem, and San Antonio, where she now lives. Her poetry books include *19 Varieties of Gazelle* (a National Book Award finalist), *Fuel*, *Red Suitcase*, and *Words Under the Words*. She also writes children's books, essays, novels for teens, and short stories, and has edited seven poetry anthologies including *This Same Sky* and *What Have You Lost?*

Sure

Today you rain on me from every corner of the sky.
Softly vanishing hair, a tiny tea set from Mexico
perched on a shelf with the life-size cups.

I remember knotting my braid on your bed,
ten months into your silence.
Someone said you were unreachable,
we could chatter and you wouldn't know.
You raised yourself on magnificent dying elbows
to speak one line,
"Don't— be— so— sure."
The room was stunned.
Lying back on your pillow, you smiled at me.
No one else saw it.
Later they even denied they heard.

All your life, never mind.
It hurts, but never mind.
You fed me corn from cans, stirring busily.
I lined up the salt shakers on your table.
We were proud of each other for nothing.
You, because I finished my meal.
Me, because you wore a flowered dress.
Life was a tablet of small reasons.
"That's that," you'd say, pushing back your chair.
"And now let's go see if the bakery has a cake."

Today, as I knelt to spell a word for a boy,
it was your old floor under me,
cool sections of black and white tile,
I'd lie on my belly tracing their sides.
St. Louis, movies sold popcorn,
baby lions born in zoos,
the newspapers would never find us.

One moth lighting on the sink
in a dark apartment years ago.
You point, should I catch it?
Oh, never mind.
A million motions later, I open my hand,
and it is there.

Lunch in Nablus City Park

When you lunch in a town which has recently known war
under a calm slate sky mirroring none of it,
certain words feel impossible in the mouth.
Casualty: too casual, it must be changed.
A short man stacks mounds of pita bread
on each end of the table, muttering
something about more to come.
Plump birds landing on park benches
surely had their eyes closed recently,
must have seen nothing of weapons or blockades.

When the woman across from you whispers
I don't think we can take it anymore
and you say there are people praying for her
in the mountains of Himalaya and she says
Lady, it is not enough, then what?

A plate of cigar-shaped meatballs, dish of tomato,
friends dipping bread—
I will not marry till there is true love, says one,
throwing back her cascade of perfumed hair.
He says the University of Texas seems remote to him
as Mars, and last month he stayed in his house
for 26 days. He will not leave, he refuses to leave.
In the market they are selling
men's shoes with air vents, a beggar displays
the giant scab of leg he must drag from alley to alley,
and students gather to discuss what constitutes
genuine protest.

In summers, this cafe is full.
Today only our table sends laughter into the trees.
What cannot be answered checkers the tablecloth
between the squares of white and red.
Where do the souls of hills hide
when there is shooting in the valleys?
What makes a man with a gun seem bigger
than a man with almonds? How can there be war
and the next day eating, a man stacking plates
on the curl of his arm, a table of people
toasting one another in languages of grace:
for you who came so far;
for you who held out, wearing a black scarf
to signify grief;
for you who believe true love can find you
amidst this atlas of tears linking one town
to its own memory of mortar,
when it was still a dream to be built
and people moved here, believing,
and someone with sky and birds in his heart
said this would be a good place for a park.

Famous

The river is famous to the fish.

The loud voice is famous to silence,
which knew it would inherit the earth
before anybody said so.

The cat sleeping on the fence
is famous to the birds
watching him from the birdhouse.

The tear is famous, briefly, to the cheek.

The idea you carry close to your bosom
is famous to your bosom.

The boot is famous to the earth,
more famous than the dress shoe,
which is famous only to floors.

The bent photograph is famous to the one who carries it
and not at all famous to the one who is pictured.

I want to be famous to shuffling men
who smile while crossing streets,
sticky children in grocery lines,
famous as the one who smiled back.

I want to be famous in the way a pulley is famous,
or a buttonhole, not because it did anything spectacular,
but because it never forgot what it could do.

Ed Ochester

Ed Ochester's most recent books are *The Land of Cockaigne* (Story Line Press, 2001) and *Snow White Horses: New And Selected Poems* (Autumn House Press, 2000). He edits the Pitt Poetry Series, is a core faculty member of the Bennington MFA Program and, with Judith Vollmer, edits the poetry magazine *5 AM.*

The Canaries in Uncle Arthur's Basement

In the white house in Rutherford
the ancient upright piano never worked
and the icy kitchen smelled of Spic 'N Span.
Aunt Lizzie's pumpkin pie turned out green
and no one ate it but me and I did
because it was the green of the back porch.
That was the Thanksgiving it rained and I first thought
of rain as tears, because Aunt Lizzie was in tears
because Arthur came home from the soccer game drunk
and because he missed dinner brought a potted plant
for each female relative, and walked around the table
kissing each one as Lizzie said "Arthur, you
fool, you fool," the tears running down her cheeks as
Arthur's knobby knees wobbled in his referee's
shorts, and his black-striped filthy shirt wet from the rain
looked like a convict's. What did I know?
I thought it meant something. I thought
if I were Uncle Arthur I'd never again
come out from the dark basement where he raised canaries,
the cages wrapped in covers Aunt Lizzie sewed,
and where, once, when I was very small and because Uncle Arthur
loved me or loved his skill or both he slowly removed the cover
from a cage and a brilliant gold bird burst into song.

The Relatives

Holidays, I'd look out the window for them
gathering like a flock of black-coated birds:
at Christmas, Fat Charlie, all red-faced and boozy,
who always told jokes about outhouses and
parted his sparse hair down the middle;
crippled Marie, who didn't want to be a bother,
and Uncle George, the fierce fire chief and
Evelyn Number One with her warbling voice;
Lotte of the high Hungarian cheekbones,
who was beautiful and pious, and Uncle Arthur
who did not always know where he was but is
the only one left of the old ones, 94 this week.

I want to name them all before they go utterly,
young women with gold at their breasts,
the men in their pride and small schemings,
songs after drink and the gossip,
old stories late into the night
as they praised their dead
as best they could, absolving
themselves with their repetitions
for never having had adequate words,
becoming thus, though clumsy,
like the *scop* in the meadhall,
like Nestor in the Pylian camp,
rescuing something from death, for the young,
for me eating cakes with ginger ale,
listening, and it was all new:
the immigrants sailing in steerage to the New World—
"The ocean is big," my grandmother said,
who spent her whole life washing clothes—
the German builder of the bakery in Kingston,
the Wife Who Died From Grief When Her Husband Died,
the Son Who Supported His Mother and Three Brothers.

I never understood their sadness, I felt
a generation too late, at the edge of the world,
and when they left and walked out into the black
and under the street lamps on Woodhaven Blvd.

it was as though they were walking through spotlights
the way Jimmy Durante did on television
at the end of the program slowly walking,

his back bent, from spotlight to spotlight
stopping at each to turn and wave and
walk again into an infinite regression
of lights, turning and waving,
kissing goodbye.

All I have left are a few stories
and an image of a long parade,
George and Sybil, Charles, Ernest
who always smelled of kerosene,
little people joining the famous
in shrinking as they go backward
through the abyss with the others,
older, all traveling: Ruprecht,
Harthacnut, Wang-Wei, and before them,
Arzes, Sextus Marcius, waving and bowing,
Praxithea, Agathocles, an immense crowd
kissing and walking away
until each is tiny as
one neuron
or gone.

Poem for Dr. Spock

I too when I die do not wish
to encumber my friends with the burdens
of sorrow: I want a simple ceremony,
twenty minutes or so, a few poems,
a brief testimonial, a tear or two
against plain black velvet and
as for the corpse burn it, scatter
the ashes around my asparagus plants,

which need large infusions of lime,
or throw them in the eyes of my enemies,
and let the mourners go off to a party,
a staid one where the waiters pour rivers
of Dom Perignon and nobody has to worry
about money for once, and later
a wild one with live music, a reappearance
of the Bonzo Dog Band, if possible, and
recapitulations of every drug popular
for the last fifty years, laughter
and solidarity for days. Let them stay
as long as they wish and then go
satiated, prepared again for the world,
and let the mouse of grief
gnaw at their hearts forever.

Saying Goodbye to the Old Airport

Greater Pittsburgh International Airport
looks like it was built by Mussolini:
giant bronze eagle over the entry,
fat black marble columns squatting
like the entrance to Hell. I'll miss it,
old terminal of the steel petit bourgeois.
I hear it's going to be converted
to food boutiques: boutique bakeries,
boutique souperamas, perhaps boutique meatshops
selling gutted rabbits, like empty pink purses
magically transformed into Lapin Provence
so the provincials will have something
to write reviews about, though I miss
the ugly places with blood on them
that tell us where we came from, what was done
to our grandparents, and our rude uncles who wore
handlebar moustaches and swore at the bosses.

My grandmother scrubbed floors her whole life
and her finest possession was a chip of diamond
on a wire ring. She'd be amazed at this place,
how town after town there's no failure visible,
gleaming miles of steel and glass so that
only if you search for the hidden places,
the towns in valleys we don't visit, the shacks
in the shadows of the rusting mills, like medieval
lackeys around their fallen lord, do you find
the fat mutti sitting in her broken web chair,
the grange halls, windowframes peeling and the glass
loose, where the poor danced.

I used to tell visitors how
the great magnate Frick on his deathbed
said: "Tell Mr. Carnegie I'll see him in hell,"
and surely he has, if there is a hell beyond the Ohio.
Or maybe there isn't, or maybe the sleepwalkers
in the malls are what we know of it, deracinated,
deodorized, in their eternal artificial spring.
The last joke of history on those who don't know it
is that it writes us. In all the great malls
sad, desperate or blank faces, as though
the Pinkertons were coming up river again
with their guns, as though history were repeating
itself, as Groucho said, but this time as farce.

I used to laugh with visitors at this hideous
terminal, its fascist flag bank flapping and flapping
but I always said "Somehow it grows on you" and later
getting out of the car at the place where I work, I'd say
"Before the university paved this space over
for parking there was a cemetery here."
But of course the authorities didn't remove the remains,
just smoothed asphalt over what after all
were nameless immigrant graves. Painted straight
white lines. Put up signs. Stuck meters,
starved wingless angels, all over it.

Sharon Olds

Sharon Olds is the author of seven books of poetry, most recently *The Father; Blood, Tin, Straw;* and *The Unswept Room.* She teaches poetry workshops in the Graduate Creative Writing Program at New York University and was the New York State Poet Laureate from 1998 to 2000. A recipient of the Harriet Monroe Prize, the Lamont Selection of the Academy of American Poets, the San Francisco Poetry Center Award, and the National Book Critics Circle Award, she lives in New York City.

Cambridge Elegy

(for Henry Averell Gerry, 1941-60)

I hardly know how to speak to you now,
you are so young now, closer to my daughter's age
than mine—but I have been there and seen it, and must
tell you, as the seeing and hearing
spell the world into the deaf-mute's hand.
The tiny dormer windows like the ears of a fox, like the
long row of teats on a pig, still
perk up over the Square, though they're digging up the
street now, as if digging a grave,
the shovels shrieking on stone like your car
sliding along on its roof after the crash.
How I wanted everyone to die if you had to die,
how sealed into my own world I was,
deaf and blind. What can I tell you now,
now that I know so much and you are a
freshman still, drinking a quart of orange juice and
playing three sets of tennis to cure a hangover, such an
ardent student of the grown-ups! I can tell you

we were right, our bodies were right, life was
really going to be that good, that
pleasurable in every cell.
Suddenly I remember the exact look of your body, but
better than the bright corners of your eyes, or the
light of your face, the rich Long Island
puppy-fat of your thighs, or the slick
chino of your pants bright in the corners of my eyes, I
remember your extraordinary act of courage in
loving me, something no one but the
blind and halt had done before. You were
fearless, you could drive after a sleepless night
just like a grown-up, and not be afraid, you could
fall asleep at the wheel easily and
never know it, each blond hair of your head—and they were
thickly laid—put out like a filament of light,
twenty years ago. The Charles still
slides by with that ease that made me bitter when I
wanted all things hard as your death was hard;
wanted all things broken and rigid as the
bricks in the sidewalk or your love for me
stopped cell by cell in your young body.
Ave—I went ahead and had the children,
the life of ease and faithfulness, the
palm and the breast, every millimeter of delight in the body,
I took the road we stood on at the start together, I
took it all without you as if
in taking it after all I could most
honor you.

The Promise

With the second drink, at the restaurant,
holding hands on the bare table,
we are at it again, renewing our promise
to kill each other. You are drinking gin,
night-blue juniper berry

dissolving in your body, I am drinking Fumé,
chewing its fragrant dirt and smoke, we are
taking on earth, we are part soil already,
and wherever we are, we are also in our
bed, fitted, naked, closely
along each other, half passed out,
after love, drifting back
and forth across the border of consciousness,
our bodies buoyant, clasped. Your hand
tightens on the table. You're a little afraid
I'll chicken out. What you do not want
is to lie in a hospital bed for a year
after a stroke, without being able
to think or die, you do not want
to be tied to a chair like your prim grandmother,
cursing. The room is dim around us,
ivory globes, pink curtains
bound at the waist— and outside,
a weightless, luminous, lifted-up
summer twilight. I tell you you do not
know me if you think I will not
kill you. Think how we have floated together
eye to eye, nipple to nipple,
sex to sex, the halves of a creature
drifting up to the lip of matter
and over it— you know me from the bright, blood-
flecked delivery room, if a lion
had you in its jaws I would attack it, if the ropes
binding your soul are your own wrists, I will cut them.

The Lumens

He is better, he is dying a little more slowly,
his skin gleams like wet silver,
he tilts his face up to me and it
flushes faintly rose, like a tray
reflecting the flowers it holds. They have drained

the blood out of his body and replaced it
with fresh blood from the people of Redwood City,
they have washed his hair and it lifts in a slow
wave above his brow. They shave him
and he glistens more, his skin is glossy,
he puts on his silver reading glasses and he
glitters, he lifts his eyelids and mild
sluices of shining come out of his eyes.
It is frightening to see how much light
this night man has had in him,
but we are not frightened. Luminous,
he sits up for minutes at a time and jokes,
we laugh, the nurses come in, and each
has a lumen around her folded cap, each
particle of air is capped with brightness
and he does not snuff it— before he dies,
my father dies as an extinguisher,
for minutes at a time he shines before he dies.

My Son the Man

Suddenly his shoulders get a lot wider,
the way Houdini would expand his body
while people were putting him in chains. It seems
no time since I would help him to put on his sleeper,
guide his calves into the gold interior,
zip him up and toss him up and
catch his weight. I cannot imagine him
no longer a child, and I know I must get ready,
get over my fear of men now my son
is going to be one. This was not
what I had in mind when he pressed up through me like a
sealed trunk through the ice of the Hudson,
snapped the padlock, unsnaked the chains,
and appeared in my arms. Now he looks at me
the way Houdini studied a box
to learn the way out, then smiled and let himself be manacled.

Alicia Ostriker

Alicia Ostriker has published ten volumes of poetry, including *The Imaginary Lover, The Crack in Everything, The Volcano Sequence,* and *No Heaven.* She has won the William Carlos Williams Award and other prizes, and has twice been a finalist for the National Book Award. She lives with her husband in Princeton, NJ.

Mother in Airport Parking Lot

This motherhood business fades, is almost over.
I begin to reckon its half-life.
I count its tears, its expended tissues,

And I remember everything, I remember
I swallowed the egg whole, the oval
Smooth and delicately trembling, a firm virgin

Sucked into my oral chamber
Surrendered to my mouth, my mouth to it.
I recall how the interior gold burst forth

Under pressure, secret, secret,
A pleasure softer, crazier than orgasm.
Liquid yolk spurted on my chin,

Keats's grape, and I too a trophy,
I too a being in a trance,
The possession of a goddess.

Multiply the egg by a thousand, a billion.
Make the egg a continuous egg through time,
The specific time between the wailing birth cry

And the child's hand wave
Accompanied by thrown kiss at the airport.
Outside those brackets, outside my eggshell, and running

Through the parking lot in these very balmy
September breezes— what? And who am I?
The world is flat and happy,

I am in love with asphalt
So hot you could fry an egg on it,
I am in love with acres of automobiles,

None of them having any messy feelings.
Here comes a big bird low overhead,
A tremendous steel belly hurtles over me,

Is gone, pure sex, and I love it.
I am one small woman in a great space,
Temporarily free and clear.

I am by myself, climbing into my car.

Move

Whether it's a turtle who drags herself
Slowly to the sandlot where she digs
The sandy nest she was born to dig

And lay leathery eggs in, or whether it's salmon
Rocketing upstream
Toward pools that call: *Bring your eggs here*

And nowhere else in the world, whether it is turtle-green
Ugliness and awkwardness, or the seething
Grace and gild of silky salmon, we

Are envious, our wishes speak out right here
Thirsty for a destiny like theirs,
An absolute right choice

To end all choices. Is it memory,
We ask, is it a smell
They remember

Or just what is it, some kind of blueprint
That makes them move, hot grain by grain,
Cold cascade above icy cascade,

Slipping through
Water's fingers
A hundred miles

Inland from the easy shiny sea—
And we also, in the company
Of our tribe

Or perhaps alone, like the turtle
On her wrinkled feet with the tapping nails,
We also are going to travel, we say let's be

Oblivious to all, save
That we travel, and we say
When we reach the place we'll know

We are in the right spot, somehow, like a breath
Entering a singer's chest, that shapes itself
For the song that is to follow.

Middle-Aged Woman at a Pond

The first of June, grasses already tall
In which I lie with a book. All afternoon a cardinal
Has thrown the darts of his song.

One lozenge of sun remains on the pond,
The high crowns of the beeches have been transformed
By a stinging honey. *Tell me,* I think.

Frogspawn floats in its translucent sacs.
Tadpoles rehearse their crawls.
Here come the blackflies now,

And now the peepers. This is the nectar
In the bottom of the cup,
This blissfulness in which I strip and dive.

Let my questions stand unsolved
Like trees around a pond. Water's cold lick
Is a response. I swim across the ring of it.

Robert Pack

Robert Pack is the author of 18 books of poetry, most recently *Elk in Winter* (University of Chicago Press). He is the Abernethy Professor of Literature and Creative Writing Emeritus at Middlebury College, where he taught for 34 years and directed the Bread Loaf Writers' Conference.

Evasion

I wait here for my other self, my life,
To join me where, let's say, I'm sitting
On a promontory looking out
Across the wild and wind-swept sea,
The wave crests almost regular
Like those ribbed overhanging clouds.
Wild roses, gnarled and blighted by some bug,
Make up the backdrop of my vantage point,
Though I am focused on the sea,
Watching my mind attend upon itself,
Watching my youthful mother nursing
My new sister in smooth summer shade

As now—seven decades on—my sister
Tucks our deaf-blind mother into bed
And feeds her pills to ease her into sleep
That she both dreads and craves.
What can connect my sense of me
From where my life has been
To where I'm sitting now
Among wild roses staring at the waves
As they come cresting in again?
Who was that person digging in moist April earth
To plant a maple or a birch,
Or should I choose the bending figure
Of a snowy January night
As my right representative, lost
In a book about how stars were formed
Or how the laws for organizing words
Got scripted in the neurons and the synapses
Of the evolving human brain?
Yet everywhere I turn I meet a self
That turns away, evades
My grimly scrutinizing gaze,
As if reluctant to be known,
A self that seems to realize itself
Within a scene composed of its own vanishing
With everything and everybody gone,
Each star, each tree, each rose, each book,
Even the spume-spray of the ocean
Underneath its ghostly clouds
As thought thins out just like
The spreading silence of the universe,
Thins out so lightly everywhere
That I can no longer tell myself
From the white calm of the surrounding air.

Eagle

At dusk, I see an eagle's silhouette
Drifting around her distant nest,
And think how close to stark extinction
She has come, the ultimate defeat,
Contingent on some human whim

Or human greed that would usurp her space.
And yet she floats so seemingly serene
As if the tides of air were everything
That needed to be understood,
As if the whole accumulation

Of the past were now,
And now again, and now forevermore
About to be with nothing
Unfulfilled to long for, nothing
To regret. And without envy, only

With a kind of love because
She helps me almost to forget myself,
I watch her tilted wings glide off and lift,
Swooping in some smooth current
I assume she uses and takes pleasure in

Without the need to say how she enjoys
Herself to make joy true.
And so I listen to my thoughts take flight,
I watch a second silhouette
Give further depth and amplitude to space,

Circling as if their hidden nest
Were the sure center of the universe—
A universe with purpose
And unchanging permanence,
Complete by being only what it is.

And so I try to think myself released
From thinking of myself
By fixing on the eagles' dips and swerves
Around their nest, my mind filled with their forms,
The angles of their silhouettes, their curves.

Distance

Deciduous, yes, that's a soothing word;
It feels smooth like a maple leaf
And shares with sharper evergreens,
Whose needles even to the sight are rough,

A sheen that carries through the forest haze
Yet brings you near, as if you spoke the sound,
Deciduous, from a lost past now so remote,
That smooth is no less sorrowful than rough.

Pine evergreen, and hemlock evergreen,
So distant yet so near, still soothe my heart
And smooth the passageway through rough terrain
That keeps my shadow whispering, *deciduous*,

Far from our first embrace where oaks
Are evergreen in memory,
Receding deep into the forest haze
Where still my unsoothed heart makes its abode.

So I'll take all the soothing
Of deciduous renewal I can get,
For there's not shade enough to smooth
The lingering of kisses lost,

The rough road of relinquishing
That leads into the heart's own haze
Where blurring shadows merge,
Making ongoing sorrow smooth

And all loss so breathtaking near
Love cannot tell if loss is smooth or rough,
Deciduous or evergreen,
As far away as when we met, or here.

Linda Pastan

Linda Pastan's eleventh book, *The Last Uncle*, was published by W.W. Norton. She is the 2003 winner of the Ruth Lilly Poetry Prize and is a former Poet Laureate of Maryland.

Snowstorm

Just watching is enough,
as if the eyes were two headlamps,
the body a stalled vehicle
in all this whiteness;
and every space is filled
and filled again with the silence
of pure geometry.
Until, as in a blink, the clouds
part, the fuse

of the sun ignites a passion
of melting, a roar
down the rooftiles,
and here comes the world

as it was, untransformed,
ordinary; and I am still
at the window, full
of a cold knowledge
I hardly understand.

Why Are Your Poems So Dark?

Isn't the moon dark too,
most of the time?

And doesn't the white page
seem unfinished

without the dark stain
of alphabets?

When God demanded light,
he didn't banish darkness.

Instead he invented
ebony and crows

and that small mole
on your left cheekbone.

Or did you mean to ask
"Why are you sad so often?"

Ask the moon.
Ask what it has witnessed.

Geography

I am haunted by the names
of foreign places: Lvov and its bells;
Galway with its shimmer of green;
Grudnow and Minsk
where my grandfather's famished face
belongs on the tarnished coins.

I am haunted by the weight of all those histories:
coronations and christenings; massacres,
famines—people shoveled
under the dark earth, just so much compost,
the lowly potato failing in Ireland,
like daylight itself failing at noon.

Oh, the vastness of maps,
the perfect roundness of globes—
those bellies pregnant with the names
of unimaginable townships and cities. Atlantis
and the Isles of the Blest are not as haunting to me
as Guangzhou or Xi'an or Santorini.

A for Ancona, an operator intones,
N for Napoli, T for Turino,
and at her voice longitudes and latitudes
become entangled like fishnets, waves
of people migrate across borders and oceans
and through the teeming streets of Buenos Aires.

While I remain quietly here in my anonymous woods
where the stream beyond the kitchen window
is so small it is only visible when it creams to ice,
where even in spring, resurgent with rain,
all it can do is empty itself into another stream,
also small, also nameless.

G.E. Patterson

photo by Lee Stanford

G.E. Patterson is a poet, critic, and translator. His writing can be found in several magazines and anthologies, including *Bum Rush the Page, Poetry 180, American Letters and Commentary, Fence, Five Fingers Review, Xcp: Cross Cultural Poetics, nocturnes: (re)view of the arts, Seneca Review, Open City*, and the webzine of St. Mark's Poetry Project, *Poems and Poets*. A collection of his poems, *Tug*, is available from Graywolf Press. After living for several years in the Northeast and on the West Coast, G.E. Patterson now makes his home in Minnesota, where he teaches.

Remembrance

My parents, being race people, taught me
by example: stand tall, speak up & look
straight in a man's eyes; there is real honor
in keeping the back of your head well-combed,
in old shoes you've polished to a hard shine,
in knowing your history and not telling your business.
My parents, being race people, saw that
things Black were put forward—pushing me on
to copy out the lives of Black heroes:
Benjamin Banneker, Ida B. Wells,
James Forton and Charlotte Forton, John Jasper,
Fannie Lou Hamer, Mary Church Terrell;
Marian Anderson, Henry O. Flipper,
Roy Wilkins, W.E.B. DuBois;
Jackie Robinson, John C. Robinson,

Paul Robeson, Mary McLeod Bethune;
Major Taylor, Matthew Henson, Ralph Bunche.

My parents, being race people, knew things,
in this world, would be changed only by work. Hard work,
they told and told me, was the rock of faith.
Hard work, the whipstitch that kept cloth from fraying.

My parents, being race people, believed that
whatever I needed to know I'd learn
best from those who looked like, and looked out for, me.
There was no good reason to go outside
the neighborhood. Our one hope for salvation—
as a race, as a people—was ourselves.
Men and women fighting for more respect
lived up and down the block in well-kept homes
and low-rent apartments near the new Center
for Black Power. They worked long days and nights
at jobs I knew almost nothing about
except their lawfulness. They were Black
in every imaginable way—yellow,
brown, redbone, blue-black (which we called inky),
oatmeal—colors lumped together like light,
a spectrum of miscegenation, broken
and united by love, like a family.

My parents, being race people, told me,
Everything good in them is good and Black,
I would do well if I learned to be like them,
I would do well to call them *Sir* and *Ma'am.*

This Sock Worn Yesterday

Quit with your sad impression of a dog
And bone, digging it up, burying it
Digging it up. You never had a bone

Running your wet black nose against the ground
All night, all day, all night, for no good reason
That squirrel's been gone a long time now   Long gone

Quit your barking too   You're gonna stay fenced
You ain't gonna catch the cat of your dreams

Stop wasting time with that old tennis ball
Ball ain't got no bounce   No one's gonna throw it

Don't matter what you want: piles of pigs' ears
A bitch in heat, a mint-condition hydrant

Might as well pray a sock falls from the sky
With a note, *Last worn by a teenaged boy*

Cinderella

Seems like some people never get the blues
without Billie Holiday turned up loud
quart of Chivas at their feet—maybe Dewars
cigar   cigarette smoke   cat piss   dark rooms
their man two or three years late coming home
their woman packed up   out of town two days
rotten job no job   either way   no money
some people got to go to school to feel
what I feel every morning every night
I wake up wondering what new shit's coming
to make me wish I had yesterday back
I go to bed wondering how long I'll sleep
before something wakes me— siren, bad dream
I hear them   singing to themselves all night
their lives just turning bad   mine been that way

Lament

Hades

I would like to undo it, to take back
The flower, the red seeds, the words I said—
Alter time in an instant— if I could,
If that would put an end to all the talk.

The talk is mostly women laying blame,
Telling the world how badly I behaved,
Telling lies, claiming the woman I loved
Was wronged the moment I whispered her name.

As if mistakes are not always how things end,
As if anyone could stop things going wrong.
As if I made more trouble than love that spring,
Made a new misery and unleashed an old.

I carried her happy into my home
— Such an ordinary start to my shame.

Norah Pollard

Norah Pollard, the daughter of Seabiscuit's jockey, Red Pollard, has been a folk singer, waitress, nanny, teacher, solderer, print shop calligrapher, and sometime secretary. She has received the Academy of American Poets Prize and for several years edited *The Connecticut River Review*. She lives in Stratford, CT.

Narragansett Dark

for my father

They led the horses away.
They tore down the fences.
The wrecking ball brought down
the grandstand, the clubhouse.
They plowed under the track kitchen,

the tack shop, the bettors' windows.
They burned the green barns.

When there was nothing of Narragansett
but a great empty space, the moon
glittered over it like a Vegas sign
and the wind blew dust across
900 acres to the Newport-Armistice roads.
The next day they paved.

Black asphalt covered the scent
of hay and the horse.
They built a drugstore,
a store for linoleum, and they
threw up subdivisions, aqua and mustard
and pink, whose mailboxes rusted
before they were sold.
Then they built a nursing home

where now the old jockey lay in a narrow bed.
He did not know where he was
so the irony was lost to him,
but he knew his wife would come
and wash him and light him a cigarette
and put the swatches of cotton
between his toes and pour him
a small cup of blackberry brandy.
Long nights alone, after the t.v. was
shut off and the brandy gone,
he'd listen for something.
All the long dark nights, listening.

One night a lean March wind
rattled the gate and his heart labored
in his breast and he rose up
for he heard what he heard—
their soft nickering and blowing, the thin
rustle of silks, the creak
of saddle and the tick
of hoof on stone.

And he left the bed and went out
to where they stood in the grasses.
He stood before them and
their breath fell on him like cloud
and he saw their great eyes pool the moon.
And the one waiting for him,
the one with an empty saddle,
was a bay.

He mounted up and they rode under the moon
and the wind flared the mane of his horse
and was hard and clean on his face.
The others galloped on either side, silently,
as if they were running on moss or flowers,
and he went with them where they took him
into the fields of night.

Salt

I don't care about spirit and
where the spirit goes after the body
quits and turns cold and solid
and there's no comfort there anymore.

I don't care about angels and
how they make their way to heaven
and look down on us from two trillion miles.
That's too far. That is never again.
That is gone.

I want my mother back.
I want her pale blue eyes to look at me
appraisingly. I want once more to hear
her say, "Kid, that's quite a rig."

I want to see her in the evening in
her mauve chenille, smoking her Tareytons,

reading her book by the light of the lamp
whose base is a brass chicken foot.

I want to sit with the blue willow teapot between us
and see her giggle into her napkin like a girl
over a silliness of my father's.

I want to see her scorn again,
the curl of her lip, her voice like an adze
when he'd come home late in a certain state.
I want to see her weeping by the window
while my brother, five years old, reels in the yard
drunk as a skunk on cough medicine. I want to hear
that mother's prayer to St. Monica again.

I want to see her faintly uneven top left lip,
her over-large earlobes, her exquisite nose.

I want to see her as we drive to the doctor
that last time, passing by the thrift shop
with the blue polka dot dress in the window.
I want to hear her say,
"Look at that! Silk, it looks like."
And then, with that hedged smile,
　"Well! I guess I'm not dead yet."

Fuck spirits. Fuck death.
I want to buy her that polka dot dress
and I want her here to fill it with
those breasts and their rose-brown
nipples, her fundamental hips, her
elegant shoulders, those long white thighs.

I want the dress to billow with
her light, her heat,
so those dots move like constellations
around her palpable heavenly body
here,
　　　now,
　　　　　in this manifest world.

Kiss

I was the high schooler awkward and shy
coming from church
on an August morning
in the two-toned DeSoto with the
clank in the rear.
He was the gas pump boy
at the Texaco station who said
he needed to hear the clank
in action.

We are the kids who drive
the hot and dusty country roads
of Seekonk,
windows down, wind flicking
my hat's flocked veil, his arm
out the window holding up the roof.

Past corn stands, watermelon stands,
cows, crows, and barnsmell,
past miles of shade trees,
past old tin trailers rusting in the weeds,
to a small dirt clearing in the sun,
where rock ledge and pines surround us
like an amphitheater.
Here
he stops the car and turns
and, barely smiling,
takes off my little rosette hat
with the veil, my white crocheted gloves,
and lays them carefully on the dashboard.
I am not afraid.

His lips, burnt by the sun,
his hands, the nails oil-edged,
touch me everywhere.
The sun blazes. The yellow dress
with the Peter Pan collar falls away.
Wordlessly we cling and kiss,
sweat and touch. His body
smells of sweat and socks and gasoline.

Bits of tobacco from the cigarette
crushed in his shirt pocket
stick to my shoulders,
fleck my small bare breasts.

He shrugs from the shirt
with the Texaco star,
eels from his oily trousers.
His sweating body glistens
like a molted thing, and
there's a port wine stain
like a Maybelline kiss
high on his thigh near his cullions.

Bees. Sun.
The black and pungent pines.
Yellow haze burning off yellow fields.
When he covers me,
his love cry throws crows in the air.
I bloom in his arms like mimosa.

Lawrence Raab

Lawrence Raab is the author of six collections of poems, including *What We Don't Know About Each Other* (1993), winner of the National Poetry Series and a finalist for the National Book Award, *The Probable World* (2000), and most recently *Visible Signs: New And Selected Poems* (2003). He teaches literature and writing at Williams College.

Some of the Things My Mother Said

It'll never be noticed from a trotting horse,
my mother used to say. Which meant:
Forget about it, nobody's going to look
that close. Or else: We're late,
you don't have time to change your shirt.
And even: Try not to worry so much
about everything. But I did,
brooding and slouching around the house,
determined to resist any kind of advice.
Like being a little nicer to people,
my mother would suggest,
since then they'd be nicer to me.
Who could have used another friend or two.
Who needed to get out more, toss a ball around,
spend less time alone. Of course
I didn't listen. And now
I'm thinking of the life I'd have
if I could do it over: the wild cheers
of my friends when I'd make the catch
that wins the game, the way the girls
would smile at me and blush. And then
I'm sitting in my living room,

trophies on the mantel, the wife out shopping,
all the kids gone, remembering that game,
and other games, which look small
and far away, which don't feel
as important as they should. Sometimes
my mother would laugh and say,
You don't have the sense to come in
out of the rain. Which could have meant
exactly that: a friend and I were out there
in the backyard in the rain, just happy
to be tossing a ball around.
But she probably meant: You need to think
more carefully about what you're doing.
God in heaven, I can hear her saying.
Forget about it. Let it go.

Request

For a long time I was sure
it should be "Jumping Jack Flash," then
the adagio from Schubert's C major Quintet,
but right now I want Oscar Peterson's

"You Look Good to Me." That's my request.
Play it at the end of the service,
after my friends have spoken.
I don't believe I'll be listening in,

although sitting here I'm imagining
you could be feeling what I'd like to feel—
defiance from the Stones, grief
and resignation with Schubert, but now

Peterson and Ray Brown are making
the moment sound like some kind
of release. Sad enough
at first, but doesn't it slide into

tapping your feet, then clapping
your hands, maybe standing up
in that shadowy hall in Paris
in the late sixties when this was recorded,

getting up and dancing
as I would not have done,
and being dead, cannot, but might
wish for you, who would then

understand what a poem— or perhaps only
the making of a poem, just that moment
when it starts, when so much
is still possible—

has allowed me to feel.
Happy to be there. Carried away.

Vanishing Point

You're walking down a road
which someone has drawn to illustrate
the idea of perspective, and you are there
to provide a sense of scale.
See how the road narrows in the distance,
becoming a point at which
everything connects, or flies apart.
That's where you're headed.
The rest of the world is a blank page
of open space. Did you really think
you were just out for an aimless stroll?
And those mountains on the horizon:
the longer you look, the more forbidding
they become, bleak and self-important,
like symbols. But of what?

The future, perhaps. Destiny. Or the opposite.
The perpetual present, the foolishness of purpose.
At evening they recede into the sky
as if they had always been the sky.
Is it a relief to know you'll never reach them?
Is there any comfort in believing
you're needed where you are?

Alberto Ríos

Alberto Ríos, born in Nogales, AZ, is the author of eight books of poetry, three collections of short stories, and a memoir about growing up on the border called *Capirotada*. National Book Award finalist and recipient of the Western Literature Association Distinguished Achievement Award, Ríos teaches at Arizona State University.

Refugio's Hair

In the old days of our family
My grandmother was a young woman
Whose hair was as long as the river.
She lived with her sisters on the ranch
La Calera— the Land of the Lime—
And her days were happy.

But her uncle Carlos lived there too,
Carlos whose soul had the edge of a knife.
One day, to teach her to ride a horse,
He made her climb on the fastest one,
Bare-back, and sit there
As he held its long face in his arms.

And then he did the unspeakable deed
For which he would always be remembered:
He called for the handsome baby Pirrín
And he placed the child in her arms.
With that picture of a Madonna on horseback
He slapped the shank of the horse's rear leg.

The horse did what a horse must,
Racing full toward the bright horizon.
But first he ran under the *álamo* trees
To rid his back of this unfair weight:
This woman full of tears
And this baby full of love.

When they reached the trees and went under,
Her hair, which had trailed her,
Equal in its magnificence to the tail of the horse,
That hair rose up and flew into the branches
As if it were a thousand arms,
All of them trying to save her.

The horse ran off and left her,
The baby still in her arms,
The two of them hanging from her hair.
The baby looked only at her
And did not cry, so steady was her cradle.
Her sisters came running to save them.

But the hair would not let go.
From its fear it held on and had to be cut,
All of it, from her head.
From that day on, my grandmother
Wore her hair short, like a scream,
But it was long like a river in her sleep.

In My Hurry

The curious lavender attentions to itself of the jacaranda
Stopped me, as through the leaves and small avenues

In late summer I made my way in love toward you.
The tree's flowering was an intimacy I had not earned,

A color of undergarment or something from the better
Pages in the book already underlined by classmates.

It was lavender or lilac, something from the hundred blues,
This color without rank and without help, standing there,

Giving me the gift over and again but high up, outside
My reach, which made my desire to touch it all the more.

The color and the tree, the moment and the lateness of season,
They joined in a gang of what I could see was a tangle of sinew,

So much muscle in search of the cover-skin of an arm,
The tree itself seeming all at once an arm unleashed,

Strength itself gone wild in its parts to the sky.
This was an arm that had stopped me—

How could I not have seen it? This tree was an arm
And more than arm, its muscle strung in everything

So that the tree—everything about it—the tree
Made itself of arm and leg, leg and neck, at angles,

At stops and starts and in bends, everything broken,
Everything but the lavender, which was flower,

So much lavender coming from what was left, what must be
A mouth, a thousand mouths, at once speaking

The lavender or the lilac, the blue, understood language.
These were match-tipped words asking the impossible of me,

Whatever I imagined the impossible to be: a bowl of cherries
In winter, or that I might come again by this place and stop.

Absent of reason, I could agree to anything addressing a tree.
The cherries were not much, I know, but what they meant,

Born of this exotic, all lavender and muscle, held me.
It was an equal and other necessity, calling to me in my hurry.

It was a tree in wild color calling to a tree in wild color,
And the lavender, I think you know what the lavender is.

The Gathering Evening

Shadows are the patient apprentices of everything.
They follow what might be followed,

Sit with what will not move.
They take notes all day long—

We don't pay attention, we don't see
The dark writing of the pencil, the black notebook.

Sometimes, if you are watching carefully,
A shadow will move. You will turn to see

What has made it move, but nothing.
The shadows transcribe all night.

Transcription is their sleep.
We mistake night as a setting of the sun:

Night is all of them comparing notes,
So many gathering that their crowd

Makes the darkness everything.
Patient, patient, quiet and still.

One day they will have learned it all.
One day they will step out, in front,

And we will follow them, be their shadows,
And work for our turn—

The centuries it takes
To learn what waiting has to teach.

Mary Ruefle

Mary Ruefle is the author of seven books of poetry, most recently *Among the Musk Ox People* (Carnegie Mellon, 2002) and *Apparition Hill* (Cavankerry Press, 2002). She is the recipient of a National Endowment for the Arts Creative Writing Fellowship, a Whiting Writers' Award, and an Award in Literature from the American Academy of Arts and Letters. She teaches in the MFA in Writing Program at Vermont College.

Funny Story

I don't remember where I was going.
I always worry about driving in the snow.
To the airport I think.
What if my car won't start, cold as it is?
But at five a.m. on the morning of January fifth
I was up and out.
Quite frankly, I can still see it:
the sky a glaze of celadon
with a pink moon set in the corner.
It took my breath away
in small white puffs.
When I get to thinking, I think maybe it was my mood.
But my mood was low-down and mean.
I mean before I saw it.
Afterwards—no, not afterwards:
in the same moment
I realized I have a prerequisite for joy.
It surprised me.
I was surprised to consider everything must be made of glass.
Not only the icy poverty of life on earth

but high, immovable things.
I was afraid to move.
I was afraid I would be late.
I was afraid my car wouldn't start.
What if the moon, awash as it was
in decanted light, was dangerously close
to disappearing altogether
and for good this time?
So I just stood there.
I let it take my breath away.
That's OK I said
take my breath away.
And it was gone.

Naked Ladies

Rousseau wanted: a cottage on the Swiss shore,
a cow and a rowboat.

Stevens wanted a crate from Ceylon full of jam
and statuettes.

My neighbors are not ashamed of their poverty
but would love to be able to buy a white horse,
a stallion that would transfigure the lot.

Darwin was dying by inches from not having anyone to talk to
about worms, and the vireo outside my window wants nothing less
than a bit of cigarette-wool for her nest.

The unattainable is apparently rising on the tips of forks
the world over…

So-and-so is wearing shoes for the first time

and Emin Pasha, in the deepest acreage of the Congo,
wanted so badly to catch a red mouse! Catch one he did

shortly before he died, cut in the throat by slavers who
wanted to kill him. *At last!* runs the diary

and it is just this *at last* we powder up and call progress.

So the boys chipped in and bought Bohr a gram of radium
for his 50th birthday.

Pissarro wanted white frames for his paintings
as early as 1882, and three francs for postage, second place.

Who wants to hear once more the sound of their mother throwing
Brussels sprouts into the tin bowl?

Was it *ping* or was it *ting*?

What would you give to smell again the black sweetpeas
choking the chain-link fence?

Because somebody wants your money.

The medallions of monkfish in champagne sauce…

The long kiss conjured up by your body in a cast…

The paradisiacal vehicle of the sweet-trolley rolling in
as cumulous meringue is piled on your tongue
and your eye eats the amber glaze of a crème brûlée…

The forgiveness of sins, a new wife, another passport,
the swimming pool, the rice bowl

full of rice, the teenage mutant ninja turtles escaping
as you turn the page…

Oh brazen sex at the barbecue party!

Desire is a principle of selection. Who wanted *feet* in the first place?

Who wanted to stand up? Who felt like walking?

Diary of Action and Repose

In some small sub-station of the universe
the bullfrogs begin to puff out their mouths.
The night-blooming jasmine is fertilized
in the dark. I can smell it.
And then someone unseen and a little ways off
picks up his flute and asserts his identity
in a very sweet way.
I'll throw in the fact it's April in China—
ah exotica, soft night—
while the bullfrog, the jasmine and the flute
form a diary of action that explains my repose:
spring, ripening to her ideal weight, has fallen
from the bough and into my lap.
For twenty minutes the world is perfect
while two or three thinks fumble for their glasses
in my cranium—
ah the impulse to hurt and destroy has arrived
and *oh* into pretty and endless strips it pares the place
round and round—

Timberland

Paul's Fish Fry in Bennington, Vermont, is no longer
Closed For The Season Reason Freezin. The umbrellas
have opened over the picnic tables and the bees are
beginning to annoy the french fries, the thick shakes
and real malts of my past:

I am thirteen thousand miles removed, on the delta
of the Pearl River, eating a litchi. Its translucent flesh just
burst in my mouth; shreds of it glitter between my teeth.
I smile but the fruit seller is sour. In fact, he is so sour
the only man on earth he resembles is Paul. But the litchi...

Actually none of this has happened yet. I am nineteen
years old. I am riding in the boxcar of a freight train

hurtling towards Pocatello, Idaho. In a very dangerous move
I maneuver my way back to the car behind me, an open gondola
carrying two tons of timberland eastward out of Oregon:

it is here I will lie all night, my head against the logs,
watching the stars. No one knows where I am. My mother thinks
I am asleep in my bed. My friends, having heard of a derailment
at ninety miles an hour on the eastbound freight, think I am
dead. But I'm here, hurtling across the continent with un-

believable speed. We are red hot and we go, the steel track
with its imperceptible bounce allows us to go, our circuitous
silhouette against the great Blue Mountains and my head in a
thrill watching the stars: I am not yet at a point in my life
where I am able to name them, but there are so many and they are

so white! I'm hurtling toward work at Paul's, toward the litchi-
bite in Guangzhou, toward the day of my death alright, but all
I can say is I am *happyhappyhappy* to be here with the stars and
the logs, with my head thrown back and then pitched forward
in tears. And the litchi! it's like swallowing a pearl.

Natasha Sajé

Natasha Sajé is the author of two books of poems, *Red Under the Skin* (University of Pittsburgh Press, 1994) and *Bend* (Tupelo Press, 2004), and many essays. Her work has been honored with the Towson State Prize in Literature, the Robert Winner Award, and the Campbell Corner Poetry Prize. Sajé teaches at Westminster College in Salt Lake City and in the Vermont College M.F.A. in Writing program.

Wave

A few memories float—
two orange cats entwined on the green armchair,
birthday lunch with my mother in the department store tearoom
when women still wore hats and white gloves—
but most are lost. An only child,
center of her parents' world, whose childhood
seems to have disappeared, except when wind
churns up a shell: the spring I had measles
and lay outside wrapped in blankets,
reading novels. My parents' stories, always the same ones:
I never asked for anything, I wouldn't
eat what they prepared. Someone said childhood
would be a source. But how to access?
That person must have had siblings:
telling a story makes it true, and having no one
care about it makes it disappear.
When my mother and my aunt argue
about what happened, or one of them entirely
forgets a wound, I see I have only
the little I've made myself, and I don't trust it.
Explore the depths and love the difficult, Rilke said.
But when I tell myself to remember
whatever sadness and pain were there, I can't,

the beach glass past tumbled smooth
and opaque from scratches, my childhood
swallowed the way the ocean absorbs
debris, even the occasional ship.

Avatar

She thought of her libido as a bird
in the house, blue-feathered,
with a spun sugar beak. What it lived on
was a mystery, although the house
smelled of bitter almonds, and when it rained
the walls were sticky with syrup.
In the attic it beat its wings against
the glass of the one tiny window.

No one could see it
unless they happened to be staring
in, with binoculars. As far as she could tell,

no one ever did, although some people
are like cats when it comes to birds. She herself
grew whiskers from thinking about it.

I Want But Can't Remember

the name of that wax inside a sperm whale
that's used to fix perfume; it sounds like *amber,*
amber, amber, which delivers through turbid fog
the Baltic Sea, fossils with zeros,
the ring my mother wears,
colored like a cat's iris flecked with black,
along with the summer she bought it
in Austria the year I turned seven

when my hair was still dark and thick.
I was photographed next to the car,
the Alps in the background.
At that mountain pass gift shop,
the first time I remember
coveting something—an amber necklace—
that I didn't ask for or even admire out loud
as if I understood it can be fine
to want something and not get it,
that wanting is a secret hymn, a way
to pass the hour shielded from the glaring sun
and tortuous mountain roads,
that one becomes part of the wanting
like a wasp caught in resin,
buried in sand and waiting to be found.

White

> *Seeing is forgetting the name of the thing one sees.*
> —Paul Valéry

In the air a pen moves
over a milk-white field lined faint green,
and a pair of eyes reads
the long "y's," straight "I's,"
"a's" with mouths open like birds
hungry for worms. Bent within the lines,
each curved letter is marked into place,
a gravestone falling into its row.
The dark road below the snow,
the heart's pulse hammering
at wrists and neck.

One has to remain very still to see.
    One has to remain still.

The hand unfurls laundry on a line,
waits for sun to dry and bleach it,
for someone to take it
down, for anyone to wear it.
Wind blows the cloth off the line
or rain soaks and freezes the cloth,
dragging and breaking the cord,
coming to rest in a field.

In a field. Coming to rest.

        Where does one stand to see
the sheets and small briefs fluttering
or frozen, in a landscape
transformed by weather, themselves
transformed
        by weather?

Sherod Santos

Sherod Santos is the author of five books of poetry, most recently *The Perishing* (W.W. Norton, 2003) and a book of literary essays, *A Poetry of Two Minds* (University of Georgia Press, 2000).

12. [from "Elegy for My Sister"]

Several days after the funeral, while watching
a home movie of my niece's wedding, I feel suddenly
and hopelessly incriminated—like the criminal
in some detective story who discovers his victim's
ghost in the crowd—when the camera pans past
my sister seated in one of the folding chairs.
But what guilt, or sadness, was I hiding from?
The knowledge that nothing I'd done had helped?
The fear that I'd done nothing at all? That brief
but nonetheless clear sensation, when the phone call came,
that it was finally over with, finished, and done?
This evening, while I was downstairs working
at the kitchen table, I could hear my wife scolding our son
for marking with crayons on the bedroom wall.
"Aren't you ashamed of yourself?" she asked him.
And I couldn't help thinking, "Yes, I am."

14. [from "Elegy for My Sister"]

The last time I saw my sister was two days after Christmas.
As my taxi to the airport pulled away from the curb,
she stood at the front door of her apartment house
and watched me go. In memory (which is to say,
in the theater of regret and hopefulness) there is a lightness
about her that is hard to explain by description
or imagination, as if, already, some part of her being
had relinquished its watery hold on her—
as if, like a woman standing under a falling star,
she'd momentarily assumed the stance of someone
whose fate is now certain. Nevertheless, I think:
this is an image that has survived her, a likeness freed
from the raveling constraints of what no longer is. I think:
this is an image she wouldn't have struggled against.

Smoke Tree

Seeking out sun from beneath

A spreading sycamore, it fountains over
    Our front door in a long-limbed,
        Liquid, sideways arc, a kind of airily

Maintained *yogin*'s bend it gains

By virtue of a mystic struggle for the world
    Of light; and having moved there—
        By both heaven and earth, it fulfills in us

The idea of a life

Inclined to assume the burnished illogic
    Of what it believes (and how
        Else could we rise up into an element

So remote from us?) and the spirit in which
      That belief is held. Still, love,
           Lest we should take too seriously the soul's

      Priority in such things,

It makes a game of us each spring when, leaving
      Home in the mornings, we're forced
           To stoop to hurry beneath its dipping limbs,

      The same spare limbs which, pruned back

In October, somehow overnight have grown
      Dense with pale, exfoliate
           Blooms, their million rose-gray filaments tipped, each

      With a pinprick drop of dew:

Little planetaria turned inside out
      Or, touched by sun, a crystal
           Starburst fireworks show which even the most lack-

      Luster breeze, or squirrel's leap

From limb to limb, will shake down on us a sil-
      Very shower of light and rain,
           A chill exhilaration we quicken to

      With a goose-bumped, breathless, earth-

Bound thrill the flesh transfiguring figures through
      A language that imagines
           Our storied bodies come crisply into leaf.

After Catullus

A penknife engraved first your name, then his,
Then a heart around them with a wedded plus,

Then an X across it all, the drawn out chronicle
Of your last uncontested crush still knuckling over,

Twenty years later, in the side yard of your parents'
House. For as I learned this evening, it was your

Crossed heart that broke, not his, and so turned
Romance into something fleshed, impregnable

And almost shameless once those first taboos
Took a backseat to the round chord your plucked

Body struck: that overjoy you've rung so many times
By now you've grown unsure of what it was

You wanted then, before the dream had wearied
Of itself and sex stood through you like an ampersand.

And so, tonight, as you rise from your canopied
Childhood bed, I watch you watch those leafy

Shadows worry across the windowsill, and I feel
For a moment the presence of that lost thing

Out there in the lull of a late rain dying out,
In the moon transfusing through the windowpane,

And as if I'd tasted them myself, I feel for you
Those thousand kisses left upon the lips of other men.

Ruth L. Schwartz

Ruth L. Schwartz's five books include *Dear Good Naked Morning* (selected by Alicia Ostriker for the 2004 Autumn House Prize), and *Edgewater* (HarperCollins 2002), which was Jane Hirshfield's choice for the National Poetry Series. She is a certified Depth Hypnosis practitioner and shamanic counselor in Oakland, CA.

Highway Five Love Poem

for Anna

This is a love poem for all the tomatoes
spread out in the fields along Highway Five,
their gleaming green and ruddy faces like a thousand
moons prostrate in praise of sun.
And for every curd of cloud,
clotted cream of cloud spooned briskly
by an unseen hand into the great blue bowl,
then out again, into a greedy mouth.
Cotton baled up beside the road,
altars to the patron saint of dryer lint.
Moist fudge of freshly-planted dirt.
Shaggy neglected savage grasses
bent into the wind's designs.
Sheep scattered over the landscape like fuzzy confetti,
or herded into stubbled funnels, moving like rough water
toward its secret source.
Egrets praying in the fields like
white-cloaked priests.

A dozen wise and ponderous cows
suddenly spurred to run, to gallop, even,
down a flank of hill.
Horses for sale, goats for sale, nopales for sale, orange groves for sale,
topless trailers carrying horses,
manes as loose and lovely as tomorrow in our mouths,
and now a giant pig, jostling majestic in the open
bed of a red pickup,
and now a fawn-colored coyote
framed between the startled fruit trees
who looks directly at me before loping back
into the world he owns.
Even the bits of trash are alive,
and chase each other in the wind, and show their underwear.
Even the sparrows hop like the spirit,
sustain themselves on invisible specks,
flutter and plummet, rise straight up like God.

Sex

It's the church of pleasure and sorrow.
All its intricate windows have been smashed.
It holds the places where the stars
opened inside us, blood on shattered glass.
It holds the light between us,
brighter than anything—
except for the equal measure of darkness,
sealed inside our bodies,

which eclipses it.
O stubborn animal, celestial, transforming.
O spasm which loves nothing but itself,
aware of nothing but itself, grateful to nothing.
O firefly which asks, What do you most want?
as it sputters out.

Tangerine

It was a flower once, it was one of a billion flowers
whose perfume broke through closed car windows,
forced a blessing on their drivers;
then what stayed behind grew swollen, as we do;
grew juice instead of tears, and small hard sour seeds,
each one bitter, as we are, and filled with possibility.
Now a hole opens up in its skin, where it was torn from the
branch; ripeness can't stop itself, breathes out;
we can't stop it either. We breathe in.

Photograph of the Child

for my sister

Your mouth is open as a world
The skin on your arms is soft as the flowering world
You're jumping barefoot in the grass, no one is
stopping you; no one and nothing has destroyed you yet
Your skinny little belly, its navel an off-center planet
Your shorts bunched-up, your little knees uneven with the jump
Only your toes are touching, your heels have already leapt
I will frame you like this forever before and after
I abandon you
And who's alive who doesn't remember
floating, at least once, above the ordinary street?
And who's never made a promise they couldn't keep?

Tim Seibles

Tim Seibles is the author of *Hammerlock, Body Moves,* and *Hurdy-Gurdy.* His newest collection of poems, *Buffalo Head Solos,* was published by the Cleveland State University Poetry Center in 2004. A former NEA fellow and winner of an Open Voice Award from the 63rd Street Y in New York City, he teaches courses for Old Dominion University's English Department and MFA in Writing Program.

Four Takes of a Similar Situation
or *The World Mus Be Retarded*

Fine as that Mexican mommy was?
Had me thinkin *jalapeño, hot tamale, arroz
con pollo* an' every other Spanish food
I ever heard about. Hell, I gotta
little bit of a accent just looking at'er, homebrew.
Yes, indeedy, sweetie, that girl's stuff
was **sho-nuff** meaty. Talkin 'bout
leave that girl alone—is ya crazy?
Even them gay cats be leanin when she bust in!
Had that cinnamon-colored skin
all squeezed into that tight yellow jump-suit
and that smooth-ass salsa-fied strut:
make a brotha wanna do them no-hand push-ups, yo—
make you wanna put ya shoes on backward
And run over yourself, make you

mus gotta getta new car, a new pair a'pants
or at leas' a new attitude.

Fine as that sista was?
Wit them tight-ass jeans ripped up jus right—
you know the kind: look like somebody
let Tony the Tiger customize them bad boys
till it was just a cryin shame
how them big choclit thighs come screamin
outta there. Shee-it! I was so bent over looking
I coulda tied my shoes wit my teeth—and
she saw that I was seein and she gave me one a'them
uh-huh, yeah looks, like she knew
that I **betta** know she got all the groceries
in one bag. Home-slice, if that honey
had got a holt'a me   it'd been
Humpty-Dumpty all over again—
all the king's horses and all the king's men
woulda jus shook their heads and said, *Yeah, mothafucka,*
you shoulda **known** *you wasn't man enough.*

Fine as that lady was?
Big as China is, they couldn't fit
no more fine behind the Great Wall
than Ms. Asia had in her lef earlobe. I won't even
tell you about that thin little light-blue top
she was wearin—**no** bra   **no**where
no how, home-page!
Nipples hard as trigonometry too—
makin that serious jailbreak. Yo,
I gotta cramp in my gums jus from tonguin
the maybe's, baby! And we most certainly do **not**
wanna discuss that black satin sheet a'hair
she had sheenin till a brotha mus gotta
wear shades. And had the nerve to have them rich,
full-bodied Maxwell House lips—damn near
like a sista. Yeah, you can do the *The Monkey*
and the *Philly Dog* too, but you can't tell me
that that Chinese Chile wasn't sho-nuff bad.
Talkin' bout who I should and shouldn' be checkin out:
The whole world mus be retarded.

Fine as Ms. white girl was?
Fuck all y'all crazy mothafuckas!
I don know if she was prejudice or not,
but the honey had them big, strong-ass
white girl calves—and one a'them slit skirts
that talk to ya when she walk—
and backed it up witta little bit a'bootie:
I'm telling you dead-up, yo—I was ready
to forgive the sins of her fathers right then and **there**!
Had that kinda curly, halfway frizzy red-brown hair.
She coulda been Jewish, Scottish,Octoroon, Italian—
only her hairdresser knows, hometown, but
if the honey had said, *looka'here, mista,*
I think I wanna waltz—brotha, you betta know
I had my dancin shoes wit me.

The Caps On Backward

It was already late inside me.

City air. City light.
Houses in a row.

14-year-olds. Nine of us.
Boys.

Eight voices changed. Already rumbling
Under the governance of sperm.

But *his* voice, bright as a kitten's
tickled our ears like a piccolo.

So, we'd trill ours up—*What's wrong, man?*
Cat got your balls? Then watch him shrink
Like a dick in a cool shower.

Every day. Bit by bit. Smaller.

I think about it now—how bad he wanted to be
with us   how, alone with the radio

he must have worked his throat
to deepen the sound.

The blunt edge of boys   teething on each other.
The serrated edge of things in general.

Maybe he spilled grape soda on my white sneaks.
Can't remember.

But I knocked him down, gashed him with my fists.

It was summer. A schoolyard afternoon.
Older boys by the fountain.

Yeah, kick his pussy ass.

Nobody said it, but it was time.
We knew it   the way trees know shade
doesn't belong to them.

The low voices knew.
And the caps on backward.

It must go something like this:

First, one cell flares in the brain. Then
the two cells next to that. Then more and more.

Until something far off begins to flicker.
Manhood, the last fire lit before the blackening woods.

The weak one separated from the pack.

The painted bird. The bird, painted.

Latin

Words slip into a language the way
white-green vines slide between slats in a fence.

A couple opens the door to a restaurant,
sees the orange and black colors everywhere

and the waitress grins, "Yeah,
a little Halloween overkill, huh."

Overkill, a noun for all of us
fidgeting under the nuclear umbrella—

but for that instant, it just meant too many
paper skeletons, too many hobgobbled balloons.

———————

I know a woman who is tall with dark hair
who makes me think of honeysuckle

whenever she opens her legs. Not just the flower
but dew-soaked music itself *honeysuckle* like a flavor.

And I remember the first time years back
when LaTina told me what it was we had

between our eight-year-old front teeth
that April afternoon, our hands wet

with rain from the vines. "Honey sickle," she said,
while the white flower bloomed from the side of her mouth,

and I had a new sweetness on my tongue and a word
I'd never heard before. How was it decided in the beginning?

This word   for *this* particular thing,
a sound attached to a shape or a feeling forever.

———————

All summer long the cicadas don't know
what we call them.

They sneak from the ground every year after dark,
break out of their shells right into the language,

and it holds them like a net made of nothing
but the need to make strange things familiar.

All summer long they rattle trees like maracas
until they become part of our weather—

quiet in rain, crazy in hard sun,
so we say *those cicadas sure make enough noise, huh.*

And the noise of that sentence   heard ten-thousand times
becomes a name for *us* the cicadas keep trying to say.

―――――――――

I think about dying sometimes,
not the sudden death in the movies—

the red hole in the shirt, the eyes
open like magazines left on a waiting room table—

not that, but withering slowly like a language,
barely holding on until everything

I ever did or said   is just gone, absorbed
into something I would never have imagined—

like Latin. Not lost completely, but moved away
from that bright, small place

between seeing   and naming,
between the slow roll of ocean

and the quick intake of air
that would fill the word *wave.*

Jeffrey Skinner

Jeffrey Skinner has published
five volumes of poetry, the
second of which was a winner
in the National Poetry Series.
Salt Water Amnesia, appearing
in 2005, is his most recent
collection. His poetry has
gathered grants from the
National Endowment for the
Arts, the Ingram-Merrill, and
the Howard Foundations.
He is co-founder and editorial
consultant for Sarabande
Books.

The New Music Concert: A Drinking Dream

The composer began to speak about the aspens
which had inspired his upcoming piece,
but stopped suddenly in the middle of a word
and confessed that he did not know
an aspen from an oak, had never laid eyes,
could not pick one out of a mugbook of trees
if his life depended, etcetera—he really
gave an eloquent apologia, before breaking
completely into sobs, his tux shirt
bending in little waves. The audience
was stunned—excruciating discomfort!—
and did not know where to turn. A man
with shaved head whipped out a cell phone
and whispered calm instructions to an underling.

The opposing hands of newlyweds
drifted toward each others' inner thighs.
The woman who had commissioned
the new music sat grandly motionless,
a Victorian mansion, gutted by fire. Stagehands
did what they could, moving the spotlight
around the floor, but the composer
would wander back into the light, weeping
and looking down at his hands in disgust,
as if he had dipped them in egg batter. Finally
a member of the brass section, a beauty
who had once been the composer's lover,
leapt up and dragged the composer
into the wings. The curtain of burgundy velvet
descended like a soft guillotine, cutting
off the whole sad affair. Then some
pale guy tiptoed out and announced
that after a short intermission the program
would resume. But I'd had enough. I walked
across the avenue to a bar, the dark kind
with knife scars on the mahogany railing,
and ordered a double. "Double what?" asked
the bartender. "Double Aspen," I said, not knowing
what I was saying. But it turns out there is
such a drink, which, the bartender whispered,
if it doesn't kill you will make you famous.

Stay

A clearance sale banner has broken free and risen
momentarily into clouds: *Everything Goes*. Cool air,
Canadian import, silvers the look of grass
and branch, each leaf a tuning fork set humming,
each shadow exact, razor-cut. Across the street
Frank rakes his hosta bed; the scritch
of tines jerks up my dog's head briefly. But it's
a known sound, and she sinks back

into the furred rumple of dream. My daughters
have entered their teens intact, whole shells, rarely
found, waiting to be lifted and filled with a new
element, air breathers now. Everyone alive
is arrayed. I don't say joyous, I say singular
constellation. And I want everything
to stay as it is: stay, cloud pinned
over the slaughterhouse on Market Street,
stay voices of men laying concrete on Mossrose.
Stay Sarah, whose body has sifted mine fifteen years.
Stay sober mind, stay necessary delusions.
Stay shadows, air, rake, dog. Good stay. Good.

Praying Outdoors

Not because it's *natural,* that exhausted word.
No: because he walked to town for coffee and a paper
and forgot his keys.

After the paper bled
its secondhand misery on his hands
there was nothing left to read but the sun
and the green scribble of grass
(which he had read before
as a young man grinning through the forest).

He lit a cigarette and considered the tininess of his problem.

He had no change to make a call.
His personal suffering belonged to past and future,
those twin holographs.
If he so desired
he could retrieve the spackling knife
from the shed and pry open the dining room screen....

Consider his ancestors
who labored centuries to escape
the peasantry: The king was dying, the land barren,
etcetera. Still. Did they have this in mind, this mild text of lawn,
twentieth century, almost over?

He knelt before a chair
cheaply made, and said Thanks

for passing the needle through my heart, Lord,
for holding the thread between thumb
and forefinger....

For a moment he disappeared.

A starling lit on his shoulder. Pecked.

The Winter Generations

When you think back it is all white,
snow falling on previous snow, the fatherly angles
of cornice and split-rail generalized
by accumulation, as if the quiet you suspected
was always there had grown
outward, and a pin dropped anywhere
would sink into its own impression
and snow quickly cover
that flaw with a thin white scar,
so the question of sound never arose.

When you think back your lips freeze
with icy snot and your hands
burn under mittens, which is nothing
compared to the pain when they come off
and blood screams at room
temperature, and the crust of weather melts

from cuffs and Father's Navy cap
left steaming on the radiator,
and you swallow first agony of waiting
as the Hop-A-Long mug of cocoa cools.

When you think back, that man
throwing snow to either side of the walk,
that woman watching, shaping
the mammal plush of your hair with her
curved hand—they could be
your children now, they are so young,
the future has not mentioned
their names, and later when they embrace
in the kitchen you will squirm
between, one of the happy unknowns.

When you think back too long
the present says *feed me, I'm starving*
and your own children tumble
from the bus and hardscrabble through the door,
the notebook leaps from your hand
and falls into that distant winter
where consciousness, lit like a pilot light,
first knew it burned alone,
and your daughters must be driven, *hurry,*
to their soccer practice in the snow.

Deborah Slicer

Deborah Slicer won the 2004 Autumn House Poetry Prize for a first book of poetry. She lives near Missoula, Montana.

photo by Steve Cummings

Skiing Slough Creek, Yellowstone, February 9

Done a dumb thing,
trying to cross the drifted mile meadow down the middle,
break trail through a bowlful of sugar, butt-deep.

Now forward takes the exertion of a glacier,
turning back, a wish
blowing out candles at thirty-six.

And the white-out moving up the valley like the underwing of some
   deranged angel.

Do I take it standing?
Kneel?

A few yards south five cow bison
hunker under blue spruce in an acre basin.
Stretch my arms wide-out, whisper—*Sisters,
save me.*

Then God flips on all the celestial lights.

Meteor showers of wet kisses pelt my bowed head,
while huddled, hugger-mugger, wind wags all of me
like a scolding finger.
Until I love

every cat's paw cruelty, abandonment's ash
mask, my alum
kiss, my
unrequited lust, the begging
baby bird beak of enraged
loneliness,
the slap!—
the copperhead who bit
my bare
heel once. Love
the beating,
love it for its own sake,
then it stops.

Hip-deep,
          six bison
                    breaking trail
behind me.

After Metaphysics, or When the Fly Leaves the Flybottle

Just when I'm ready to call in the day and put it to bed without supper
you send the mockingbird who plays with his musical zipper,
exposing the World's underlife.
You send perfume from the autumn olive
whose septillion flowering ears are full of bees
singing songs for the revolution.
Out back Jake's Creek is speaking in tongues—
Missed you-missed you-missed you.

You wear me down, obsessively
rubbing your hands along my better judgment,
kissing the upturned noses of all my higher principles, until
my clothes are big as a mast sail,
until my longing leavens one-thousand wedding cakes,
my longing is an undertow, and all the tourist beaches are posted: *Danger*.

Come for me—I'll break off my arms and will them to a body
of water, hang my legs up in overalls at night
so they won't come after us, feed
English to the birds in sweet pats of butter.

Then our loving gets raucous—
white moths yapping their wings—you wag, you
    wag in the little fingerbowl of me.

Your verbstem assumes declensions of mythic proportions.
My vowel sounds open on the south-most *hallelujah* side of the mountain.
Then metaphysically speaking we've stopped speaking
metaphorically—Silence

nuanced as a landscape in snow.

Mousey and Me

If you think like a Holstein
who's stood cramped in a grey stall

all six months of winter, waiting
for the first buttercups to push up snow in the pasture

like clabber rising through milk,
then you know the penalty

for swatting the bony man in thick glasses
with a piss-soaked tail

that stings like fire thrown in his face:
You get a beating with

whatever's handy—the bucket, a filthy rope,
his fists—on your rump

and maybe all over the head.
Sometimes, when the pain is unbearable

his brothers will have to stop him, throw him into a snowbank,
with his pride.

(Why do you do it, anyway?
                              Who knows...
  He's such an easy target.)

When he leans his strawberry blonde head against you
as he's milking,

mumbling all his heartache
into your belly, usually

the extra weight there's all right.
But when it gets meaner,

when he threatens to move into Floweree and
get rid a all a ya!

then it's not so easy to stand there, take it, or
the strap.

His freckled hands are a fact of life,
and at least they're efficient. Now and then

there's sugar in those fists
that he makes you work a little for—

haul a wagon of muck from the barn
after he's grappled an hour just to teach you the harness,

maybe lower your head down
like you're grateful, demure—

act interested in the neighbor's prize bull, even though he's certifiably
stupid.

That man?
Mousey and me knew him about the same.

Shiners

I climb toward the headwaters of Mill Creek
and where the Appalachian Trail crosses the creekbed
squat down in the path of the mid-morning sun,
so they can see me in my shadow,
so I can see them.

Because two-legs are supposed to keep walking in the direction of afternoon,
because something that's different is something gone wrong,
it takes a long time,
an almost graveside stillness
before they will come out from under the rocks.

Jesus bugs are oblivious.
Two one-armed crayfish sling silt at woozy moss.
I sit with my mind tucked under my wing like a sleepy heron

until the first shiner melts out of a silvery rock,

then more shiners
in a shallows so clear they seem to levitate just above the gold pea gravel,
shy as new silk.

When I sink my limp fist to the muddy bottom
shiners scatter-burst,
a darting scream, filmy chaos
in which I lose myself, again.

But after some time a shiner enters the hand-house I've built,
and the current in there contracts and expands and it feels as though I
                                                           have hold

of the first pulse of Adam.

Then my own heart beats once less lonely,
ashes in my mouth taste less bitter,
and I remember how even his God had to rebuild covenants with life
                                                         like this.

Tracy K. Smith

Tracy K. Smith's book, *The Body's Question*, won the 2002 Cave Canem Poetry Prize. She has also received awards from the Rona Jaffe and Ludwig Vogelstein Foundations and a Fellowship from the Bread Loaf Writers' Conference. She lives in Brooklyn, NY.

Mangoes

The woman in a blouse
The color of daylight
Motions to her daughter not to slouch.
They wait without luggage.
They have been waiting
Since before the station smelled
Of cigarettes. Shadows
Fill the doorway and fade
One by one
Into bloated faces.
She'd like to swat at them
Like the lazy flies
That swarm her kitchen.

She considers her hands, at rest
Like pale fruits in her lap. Should she

Gather them in her skirt and hurry
Down the tree in reverse, greedy
For a vivid mouthful of something
Sweet? The sun gets brighter
As it drops low. Soon the room
Will glow gold with late afternoon.
Still no husband, face creased from sleep,
His one bag across his chest. Soon
The windows will grow black. Still
No one with his hand always returning
To the hollow below her back.

Desire is a city of yellow houses
As it surrenders its drunks to the night.
It is the drunks on ancient bicycles
Warbling into motionless air,
And the pigeons, asleep in branches,
That will repeat the same songs tomorrow
Believing them new. Desire is the woman
Awake now over a bowl of ashes
That flutter and drop like abandoned feathers.
It's the word *widow* spelled slowly in air
With a cigarette that burns
On its own going.

from "Joy"

It will rain tomorrow, as it rained in the days after you died.
And I will struggle with what to wear, and take a place on the bus
Among those I will only ever know by the shape their shoulders make
Above the backs of the seats before mine. It is November,

And storm clouds ascend above the roofs outside my window.
I don't know anymore where you've gone to. Whether your soul
Waits here—in my room, in the kitchen with the newly blown bulb—
Or whether it rose instantly to the kingdom of hosannas. Some nights,

Walking up my steps in the dark, digging for the mail and my keys,
I know you are far, infinitely far from us. That you watch
In the way one of us might pause a moment to watch a frenzy of ants,
Wanting to help, to pick up the crumb and put it down
Close to their hill, seeing their purpose that clearly.

Thirst

The old man they called Bagre
Who welcomed us with food
And rice-paper cigarettes
At the table outside his cabin
Was the one who told the soldiers
To sit down. They were drunk.
They'd seen the plates on our car
From the road and came to where
You and I and Bagre and his son
Sat laughing. I must have been
Drunk myself to laugh so hard
At what I didn't understand.

It was night by then. We smoked
To keep off the mosquitoes.
There was fish to eat—nothing but fish
Bagre and the other men caught.
The two little girls I'd played with
Were asleep in their hammocks.
Even Genny and Manuel,
Who rode with us and waited
While we hurried out of our clothes
And into those waves the color
Of atmosphere.

Before the soldiers sat down,
They stood there, chests ballooned.
When we showed them our papers,

They wanted something else.
One of them touched the back of my leg.
With your eyes, you told me
To come beside you. There were guns
Slung over their shoulders
Like tall sticks. They stroked them
Absently with their fingers.

Their leader was called Jorge.
I addressed him in the familiar.
I gave him a half-empty bottle
Of what we were drinking.
When it was empty, I offered to fill it
With water from the cooler.
He took a sip, spat it out
And called you by your name.
I didn't want to see you
Climb onto that jeep of theirs—so tall
And broad it seemed they'd ridden in
On elephants yoked shoulder to shoulder,
Flank to flank.

Maybe this is a story
About the old man they called Bagre.
The one with the crooked legs
That refused to run.
Maybe this is a story about being too old
To be afraid, and too young not to fear
Authority, and abuse it, and call it
By its name, and call it a liar.
Or maybe it's a story about the fish.
The ones hanging on branches
To dry, and the ones swimming
With eyes that would not shut
In water that entered them
And became them
And kept them from thirst.

Gerald Stern

photo by Martin Desht

Gerald Stern is the author of
fourteen books of poetry,
including *This Time: New and
Selected Poems*, a National Book
Award winner (1998), and more
recently, *American Sonnets*.
His essays, *What I Can't Bear
Losing: Notes From a Life* was
released in 2003. He was the
first Poet Laureate of New Jersey.

My Sister's Funeral

Since there was no mother for the peach tree we did it
all alone, which made the two of us closer
though closeness brought its loneliness, and it would
have been better I think sometimes to be sterile
from the start just to avoid the pain
which in my life this far has lasted seventy
years for I am in love with a skeleton
on whose small bones a dress hung for a while,
on whose small skull a bit of curly hair
was strung, and what is dust I still don't know
since there was no mother to turn to then and ask
what else was she wearing, did she have on shoes,
and were the two trees from Georgia, and was it
true somebody said the other peach
should have died instead of her; and I could
imagine the nose going first though forty years later
the trees were still there and not as big as you'd think;
and it was my cousin Red with the flabby lips
who said it, he had red eyes, a red monstrosity,
a flabby body, half the house was filled with

male cousins, they were born in rooms a
short distance from the rats, I can't remember
which ones had the accents nor what his
Hebrew name was, nor his English.

Good Boy

An awful thing to do to a dog, tie a
blue lead around his face, say sit,
click your cricket, say good boy and give
him a treat; an awful thing to do to a man,
close the factory when he turns sixty-five
and let him row across the river on social
security alone; I sat on the porch
moaning for nothing or walked down my mud path
through the hordes of geese, their crap *partout*
and no one with a small white plastic baggie
to save the day, and I was followed and hissed at
since geese know and are aggressive sometimes
beyond the issue of bread. You know the guard,
he who lowered his head and opened his mouth
to show his red throat? He saved my life.

Corsets

I was caught in a time warp there in my landlady's
basement apartment struggling with her niece's corset
the which at a dinner party I was instructed by
the woman sitting next to me that *girdles* were the style
in the early fifties, not corsets, but it was a time warp
and even though she was young she came from Corfu
and even though it was 1950 they still wore
corsets there as they did in America in
1930 or even in 1920

among the healthy and flapperless, and I
unhooked her since there were more ways of surrendering
then for she was studying Greek at Hunter College
and I was writing poems of pure endearment
tinged with touches of Utopia that came
from all the places you'd expect, and since I
associated Utopias already with corsets,
having written perfectly at my mother's vanity
amid the perfumes and powders, half sitting on a
wobbly bench on top of *her* corset I confounded
one kind of love with another the way you always
did—and do—land of milk, land of honey.

Loyal Carp

I myself a bottom feeder I knew what
a chanson à la carp was I a lover
of carp music for I heard carp singing
behind the glass on the Delaware River,
keeping the shad themselves company
and always it was a basso, in that range there
was space for a song compleat, it was profundo
enough and just to stop and drink in that
melody and just to hum behind those
whiskers, that was muck enough for my life.

Battle of the Bulge

The way a fly who dies in sugar water,
he couldn't find a way to lift his wings
out of there, they were so heavy, the way
a plant doesn't need that rich a dirt, the way

it chokes from too much love, the way
I lay on the ground, I dug a hip hole, I slept
with grass, and dirt, the way Ammon Hennacy
wore a red flannel shirt, and a tie, he was
Dorothy Day's friend—you knew the saint?—it was
my own costume for years, he was in prison
with Berkman—in Atlanta—Berkman was there
for shooting and stabbing Frick, Hennacy for
conscience; I met Hennacy on Spruce Street
in 1958, the same year I met
Jack Lindeman who lost his hearing in Belgium,
the winter of 1944, he lives in
Fleetwood, P.A. and we communicate by
fax—I never heard him ask for pity
nor did we ever talk about that winter, he
introduced me to Dorothy Day and published
his poems in the *Catholic Worker*—and Marvin Hadburg,
he whom *I* pity, he was drafted when the
government was desperate and sent to
southern Georgia for four weeks training
and then to Bastogne three days before Christmas
where he spent a week in a barn and came home
with both feet frozen a day or two short of two months
some of the flesh cut off, as I remember,
a gold discharge button in his lapel,
selling underwear again in his father's store,
his head very small, his shoulders hunched, his mouth
always open—I would say he was a
collector of feathers for the Achaen archer
Teucer of the incurved bow, whose shoulder
Hector smashed with a rock, just where the clavicle
leads over to the neck and breast, thus deadening
his wrist and fingers, I would say that Ajax
knocked him down when passing by and Zeus,
deflector of arrows and breaker of spears, the father
of slaughter without end, he pissed on him.

Virgil Suárez

photo by Jason Flom

Virgil Suárez was born in
Havana, Cuba in 1962 and has
lived in the United States since
1974. He is the author of over
twenty books of prose and
poetry, most recently *Infinite
Refuge, Palm Crows, Banyan,*
and *Guide to the Blue Tongue.*
The University of Pittsburgh
Press will publish *90 Miles:
Selected and New Poems* in winter
2005. He is currently writing a
new novel and restoring a '55
Chevrolet.

What We Choose of Exile

> *We choose exile as a vantage point;*
> *from exile we look back on the rejected,*
> *rejecting place—to make our poems*
> *out of it and against it.*
> —Donald Hall in his preface to
> *Above the River: The Complete Poems of James Wright*

This rock my father brought over from Las Villas,
    the place of his birth and which he kept in his shoe-
cleaning box kit, a copy of his first full paycheck
    in the United States, $110 in 1974, a month's salary

he brought to my mother as an offering of his love
    to us, no? His blue tongue as he lay dying, entubed
throat, heart, his glands knowing so finally the clasp
    and hold of God's hands upon his body. We choose

nothing, and all. This is the way it is for those lost
   into the eternal haze of dust, cobwebs, broken piano
strings, crow-cawing, a shrieking in the ear. A rusted
   car, a 1965 Dodge Dart. A black comb with a couple

of broken teeth with which to comb the hair, scratch
   that mosquito bite behind his arm. The way our elbows
dry out and become scaly. My mother's arthritic hands,
   fingers gone numb from years of sewing zippers at piece-

meal wages. Cufflinks, their dull glint inside her jewelry
   box, a gift one Valentine's Day, bought from the Avon lady.
What chooses us, that's what my father wanted to know.
   The moment, fate, life? Cold air in Manhattan, a river

in Kentucky. The mesas of New Mexico, where I'd love
   to die one night only to have owls, crows, wolves, foxes
tear me apart, appease their hunger of place with my stolen
   flesh, this exile's heavy, musky meat—our bodies' history

of place, those places left behind and those about to be
   traversed. We can carry our lanterns to light the way,
or we can walk on with our eyes closed, our tongues tied,
   our arms behind our backs, ready to sacrifice or surrender.

Cucuyo Ghazal Razzmatazz

Those Cuban nights of long ago, smoke
   punctuating my father's talk and from tall grass

the cucuyos, fireflies, flashed their beck-and-call
   to me, as I looked, amazed, at the dark grass.

My father, the dissident, persecuted and sad,
   knowing he'd leave his country. No more grass

or these insects of the night that illuminated
    my life with silvery flashes atop the swaying grass.

After forty-three years of exile, my father's dead,
    my mother shrinking in widowhood, the grass

is no longer as green, dark or filled with fireflies,
    though once in a while I see a ghost-flash in grass

growing wild around the lip of my man-made pond.

Apparition

There under the Japanese bridge
    my wife gave me as a gift
one birthday, I saw a green

hand, covered in duckweed.
    I stopped the car and ran
toward the edge of the pond.

It turned out not to be a hand,
    but a dead bird, bloated,
its wet feathers like fingers

clawing at the water reeds.
    I thought if I pulled it out,
I'd drag the body of a man

I watched drown in Cuba
    once. Some said he didn't
drown at all but chose to jump

into a canal after a raging
    storm, to allow the currents
to sweep him under where

water, silt, detritus, all things
    taken down river speak
of what surging water takes

from us, or, years later, shows
    us as a way to remind us
that it takes or gives,

either way we return to it
    and sometimes all we can do
is raise our hand in question.

Julie Suk

Julie Suk is co-editor of *Bear Crossings: An Anthology of North American Poets* and the author of four books of poetry, including *The Dark Takes Aim,* published by Autumn House Press.

Stalking

I could barely see,
but shot at what moved,
followed blood on the leaves
to the place the buck fell,
the body still warm,
eyes not yet glazed.

Kneeling down
I slit the throat
and pushed away
in case he kicked—
the way the dying do,
protesting to the last
regardless of pain.

Baby, my father used to say,
squeeze the trigger gentle-like.

Blood on the kitchen floor,
the smell of neat's-foot oil,
a clean stock.

I relish the flesh
of roasted venison,
its pungent taste
bursting on the tongue.

There isn't a bone
I wouldn't gnaw
to marrow, and suck.

Hungry, hungry—
remember that when I ease
up to you.

Rounds

When I held my first son,
how perfect he seemed.
Driving home late,
we would sing rounds
O how lovely is the evening
his head nodding to my lap.

Blessings on that third
of our lives spent in sleep,
the plots of the day
left dangling.

Once I drove by a woman
clinging to a viaduct's ledge,
police, priest, and the curious

crowded below, the road
curving past into a benign
vista of cows and trees.

Blessings on those moments of reprieve
grabbed before dropping into nightmare.

How could my son fracture,
unaware of the split?
Ominous, the day I waited
on his porch, cake in hand
as if food could assuage
a mind reeling off.

Get out! Get out! The door slammed.
What I dread is a stand-off,
barricades, guns, police
with no choice but to shoot.

Blessings on the daughter
who ripens with a life
that turns us around again,
this time, we hope,
the helix of notes
descending in tune.

For a while we let pass
what Aeschylus said,
how at night
the pain that can't forget
falls drop by drop
upon the heart.

The moon floats off,
the dog whimpers under the steps.
How lovely the evening
with a child on my lap,
a circle of us singing
heedless of the dark taking aim.

A Troubled Sky

I wake to an owl screech,
black feathers scattered,
crows caterwauling around the oak,
one squawking for its lost mate.

My call came at three,
a nightmare crashing through,
your body already cool,
the tick of a fan the only hint
air once stirred with your breath.

Day took over, blazing as it did
on the wheatfield where Van Gogh
shot himself, dying later
cradled in his brother's arms.

The way I held you
in a landscape I can't scumble over,

like the canvas
lashed with cobalt, ocher, black,
the one road dropped by the horizon,
the sky ominous, embittered by crows.

The Dead

The dead sift through us
without flesh, bone, hair,
or whatever else the stars concoct
for us to touch.

Reaching for the velvet muzzle
of a horse, their hands pass on through
never feeling the warm breath in their palms.

Try catching wind as it runs over wheat
leaving it in shocked repose.

Cruel—to see the one you love
and realize neither tongue nor limb.
Desire, an unattached shadow.

Dashing without thought against the day,
we complain at the slightest wound.
The dead drift by longing for a bruise.

Philip Terman

Philip Terman is a Professor of English at Clarion University, where he teaches creative writing and modern poetry. His books include *What Survives* (Sow's Ear Press, 1993), *The House of Sages* (Mammoth Books, 1998), and *Book of the Unbroken Days* (Mammoth Books, 2004). He is currently working on editing a collection of essays on the poet James Wright and directs the Chautauqua Writers' Festival.

My Old and New Testaments

Boisterous with our shrieks and shouts,
my cousin Michael and I, seven years old,
hollered our heads off, chasing and strutting

and squealing under the ping-pong table
and over the bar counter and in and out
of the corner closet where my father stored

his war uniforms. Upstairs, my parents
were sleeping the sleep of adulthood,
far enough away to forget about completely

until we looked up at the mountain
my father was, six foot four, brushing
the ceiling with his thin curly black hairs: *keep*

it low, he ordered, calmly, palm pushing the air
down. He believed in the value of hard work,
he would break the minor laws of his fathers

before he would give up one day of the six
the god of labor had assigned to him—
even the day he was shot in the intestine.

From his bed at St. Luke's Hospital he leaned
over and whispered customers' names and prices
of used cars into the ears of his incompetent sons.

He started back upstairs into that realm
unfamiliar to us as the upper world, that other life
of exhaustion and rustled hair and wanting a peace

on the only morning he could sleep through.
So we went back to our own concerns—
we squeaked and screamed until, suddenly,

from the top of the stairway, the pausing
and the slowly-turning-around
and the descending: two hundred and fifty pounds,

eyebrows furrowed, black eyes fixed the way
I'd seen him stare down a customer who wanted
only to test drive a car for the joy ride.

He reached out his right sergeant's hand and—
not brutal, but quick and definite, a snap and a sting—
he slapped me on the left cheek and returned

back to regain whatever rest he could salvage.
It didn't hurt much. But I screamed and wailed,
I thrashed and dived so deeply into myself

I didn't notice his return, slow and silent,
leaning down to the height of my shivering body,
his skin the odor of cigar smoke, nest of gray hairs

strewn beneath his unbuttoned blue cotton pajamas,
his shadowed face. He stroked the seal on my skin
that was burning with the hand that rebuked me.

He kissed the flame out with his wet lips.

The Oldest Brother Lesson in the World

In the room without heat the desk's cherry wood
warmed his body all night until the pale skin of dawn

found his face pressed beside the book opened
to drawings of the skeleton he studied through

the noises of that house, the screams of our father
calling him down to dinner. Ten years younger,

upset with one crisis or another, I carved our name
in the surface but he said furniture is alive

like us if we allow it to breathe and pass it on
the way it was made. Near an open window he wore

the scratches away with steel wool, his fingers precise as if
treating bruises on skin, brushed on the stain

with delicate surgeon's eyes, the wet streaks shimmering
like roses in the sun. It was what he left me,

smudged with the invisible smoothing of his palms,
the imprint of his ghost-ear listening to the tree in the wood,

what I listen for now, sanding my own splinters
and chipped edges, the flaws he taught me to re-touch.

Some say as brothers get older they get more distant,
meaning we grow out of our childhoods,

when we sat naked in the same waters
and he rubbed my tender flesh with soap.

This will last for as long as memory lasts,
and now that it is here written down, longer,

and any one who cares can imagine an older
brother cleaning the younger as has been done

according to custom throughout the centuries.
It will last as long as the oldest brother lesson in the world will last,

the story our mother taught us about the two sons
who wound up wandering apart in two separate worlds.

Her own two brothers stopped speaking over something
or other and the years hammered the nails of their refusal

harder into their wounds until one died and became
bones that spoke less than the silence of the flesh.

Does his body cry to his brother from the ground?
Is cursing a brother the same as cursing yourself?

Is looking into a brother's face like looking into water
and seeing your own death? Are brothers two wings

of a great bird? Does each carry inside of him the other
half of the secret of how to live a righteous life on earth?

Pinochle

Tonight after an all-day rain the world
seems far off and even my dead father
has retired back to the pinochle game
he plays with his older brother Nate

and that policeman Zuresky and Aunt
Florence's Uncle Joe, who even alive
was always unemployed but wore
the same brown suit and porkpie hat
and always had a stack of *Playboys*
stashed on the floor of the back seat
of his Plymouth. When I glanced at one
he warned that it was a bad habit:
It gets you excited, he said, *and that
costs money.* He'd always visit,
widowed or divorced I never knew,
talking about the track. I was too young
to inquire any further, his body thin
as a shadow, face pale, soft-spoken
and serious, smoking and playing cards
with Uncle Nate and that policeman Zuresky
and my father, who turns back now
from all my inquires and tells Uncle Joe
to stop shuffling and deal.

Sue Ellen Thompson

Sue Ellen Thompson is the author of *This Body of Silk* (Northeastern University Press, 1986), *The Wedding Boat* (Owl Creek Press, 1995), and *The Leaving: New & Selected Poems* (Autumn House Press, 2001). A former resident poet at The Frost Place in Franconia, NH and Visiting Writer at Central Connecticut State University, she is a freelance writer and editor in Mystic, CT.

What Happened After

The day it happened they found me
submerged in a quilt on the sofa watching
t.v. *Why is she all covered up*
on such a warm day? they must
have wanted to ask. Instead,
they sat in the room and watched with me, together
my husband and daughter and I watched men
playing golf, their shirts dots of citrus
when seen from above, in a tree so green
and vast it seemed they could never fall.

Why doesn't she eat? they must have said
to each other as dusk fell and they scraped
the glazed food from my plate. It is
so long ago now I cannot recall
how many hours I lay there, my eyes
perpendicular to their concern, saying
nothing, wondering when I would feel the strength
return to my bones, when I would rise
from my bed and walk, feel the grass pushing up
from the earth and the green coming back to where

it had always lived in me. For how many days
did I cling to my husband like a woman pulled
from the wreck? When he stopped to buy gas
I would brace my body against his back while he
pumped, I'd feel the fuel moving through me
and think, *You're going to live.* Everywhere
he went I went with him, the stripe of his sleeve
pinched hard in my fingers, my steps the shadow of his
and he never asked why. You won't read about me

in the papers. I'm the child who was lost
and found his way back before his parents
missed him, whose ferocious embrace
confounds them, who breaks every night
under the knowledge of where he has been.

At Sixteen

Like a diver who knows it will take a long time
to reach the bottom, she is weighting
herself for the journey, puts on the leather belt
hung with rings the size of giant wedding bands,
the heavy silver umbilicus that sways between waist
and wallet. Around her neck a daisy chain
of safety pins and pop-tops, a penny pendant
with the background to Lincoln's head cut away.
Her ear-rims are pierced at half-inch intervals
with delicate silver hoops, as if she will need
even their sleight freight to get where she is going.

Each tooth has its own little hem-weight,
their fluted edges are laced together with wire
and while she sleeps, their sharp white points
grow yellow and broad for mangling.
But she pushes the rib with its parcel of pink
off to the plate's flowered margin, ignores
the felled stalks of broccoli all lined up and lying down

like the trees on Mount St. Helens. She doesn't need food
or any of the things it has been my life's work

to provide. At Sunday dinner she writhes
in her chair, tilting it backward, exposing
her throat to the chandelier. On her wrists,
the heavy links of my hopes for her;
a cat collar studded with rhinestones, bright
as the least of my fears. She doesn't know
that she's taking me with her. Like the two
black shirts she wears: One stays inside
the other even as they are laundered.

The Visit

I gave her some change, everything
I could dredge from the bottom of my purse,
to buy a cold drink at the college snack bar
the day of the open house for prospective
students. She took the coins without
touching my palm and disappeared
down the long corridor, her loose pants
scooping the dust from the floor,
her sneakers scuffed almost bald
of their suede, and I thought *This is how
she will leave me a year from now—*
my money loose in her fist, my breasts
on her father's body, my tears locked
in her father's eyes. When she returned,
she slammed the money down on the table
before me and said, *What the hell can I get
for sixty-five cents?*

              She walked off
in the direction of the car, turning
her baseball cap backwards, the way
she did as a child bent over a coloring book,
not wanting so much as a shadow to fall

between her and her intent. I should have done
what my mother did, I should have rubbed soap
into the carpet of her tongue, but I didn't.
In silence I drove her all the way down
the New York Thruway, the Mass Pike,
91 South—her head flung back
on its hinges, her mouth ajar, sleeping
the way an infant sleeps when the evening's
last feeding is over—so furious
and blessed was I to have her in my sight.

The Empty Room

Unable to sleep, my husband gropes
for his reading glasses and book.
He tiptoes into our daughter's room—
the bed freshly made in the wake
of her leaving for college, the windows
stripped of their curtains for washing—
and draws back the dinosaur sheets,
slipping into the crescent shape
of her absence.

               I think of him there:
middle-aged, the gray with its fingers
laced deep in his beard, little half-glasses
crouched low on the ridge of his nose.
Just before dawn, I go to him,
lowering my body into his
backwards, pressing my shoulder blades
into his chest, my hips
into the hollow of his, the curve
of my calves against his hard shins,
lashing my body to his as I did
in the tumult of our twenties, when all
we longed for was an end to the storm,
when all we knew of loss was to turn
in the night and find the other one gone.

Natasha Trethewey

Natasha Trethewey, Associate Professor of English and Creative Writing at Emory University, is author of *Bellocq's Ophelia* (Graywolf, 2002) and *Domestic Work* (Graywolf, 2000). She is the recipient of fellowships from the Guggenheim Foundation, the Rockefeller Foundation, and the National Endowment for the Arts.

Photograph of a Bawd Drinking Raleigh Rye

—E.J. Bellocq, circa 1912

The glass in her hand is the only thing moving—
too fast for the camera—caught in the blur of motion.

She raises it toasting, perhaps, the viewer you become
taking her in—your eyes starting low, at her feet,

and following those striped stockings like roads,
traveling the length of her calves and thighs. Up then,

to the fringed scarf draping her breasts, the heart
locket, her bare shoulder and the patch of dark hair

beneath her arm, the round innocence of her cheeks
and Gibson-girl hair. Then over to the trinkets on the table

beside her: a clock; tiny feather-backed rocking chairs
poised to move with the slightest wind or breath;

the ebony statuette of a woman, her arms stretched above
her head. Even the bottle of rye is a woman's slender torso

and round hips. On the wall behind her, the image again—
women in paintings, in photographs, and carved in relief

on an oval plane. And there, on the surface of it all, a thumb-
print—perhaps yours? It's easy to see this is all about desire,

how it recurs—each time you look, it's the same moment,
the hands of the clock still locked at high noon.

(from "Storyville Diary")

2. Father

February 1911

There is but little I recall of him—how
I feared his visits, though he would bring gifts:
apples, candy, a toothbrush and powder.
In exchange I must present fingernails
and ears, open my mouth to show the teeth.
Then I'd recite my lessons, my voice low.
I would stumble over a simple word, say
lay for *lie*, and he would stop me there. How
I wanted him to like me, think me smart,
a delicate colored girl—not the wild
pickaninny roaming the fields, barefoot.
I search now for his face among the men
I pass in the streets, fear the day a man
enters my room both customer and father.

Incident

We tell the story every year—
how we peered from the windows, shades drawn—
though nothing really happened,
the charred grass now green again.

We peered from the windows, shades drawn,
at the cross trussed like a Christmas tree,
the charred grass still green. Then
we darkened our rooms, lit the hurricane lamps.

At the cross trussed like a Christmas tree,
a few men gathered, white as angels in their gowns.
We darkened our rooms and lit hurricane lamps,
the wicks trembling in their fonts of oil.

It seemed the angels had gathered, white men in their gowns.
When they were done, they left quietly. No one came.
The wicks trembled all night in their fonts of oil;
by morning the flames had all dimmed.

When they were done, the men left quietly. No one came.
Nothing really happened.
By morning all the flames had dimmed.
We tell the story every year.

Miscegenation

In 1965 my parents broke two laws of Mississippi;
they went to Ohio to marry, returned to Mississippi.

They crossed the river into Cincinnati, a city whose name
begins with a sound like *sin*, the sound of wrong—*mis* in Mississippi.

A year later they moved to Canada, followed a route the same
as slaves, the train slicing the white glaze of winter, leaving Mississippi.

Faulkner's Joe Christmas was born in winter, like Jesus, given his name
for the day he was left at the orphanage, his race unknown in Mississippi.

My father was reading *War and Peace* when he gave me my name.
I was born near Easter, 1966, in Mississippi.

When I turned 33 my father said, *It's your Jesus year—you're the same
age he was when he died.* It was spring, the hills green in Mississippi.

I know more than Joe Christmas did. Natasha is a Russian name—
though I'm not; it means *Christmas child*, even in Mississippi.

Mark Turpin

Mark Turpin is the author of *Hammer* (Sarabande Books), for which he received *Ploughshares* at Emerson College's Zacharis First Book Award. A 1999 graduate of Boston University's MA in Creative Writing program, he has spent 25 years working construction and building houses as a crew foreman and master carpenter. He lives and works in the San Francisco Bay Area.

Waiting for Lumber

Somehow none of us knew exactly
what time it was supposed to come.
So there we were, all of us, five men
at how much an hour given to picking
at blades of grass, tossing pebbles
at the curb, with nothing in the space
between the two red cones, and no distant
downshift of a roaring truck grinding
steadily toward us uphill. Someone thought
maybe one of us should go back to town
to call, but no one did, and no one gave
the order to. It was as if each to himself
had called a kind of strike, brought a halt,
locked out any impulse back to work.
What was work in our lives anyway?

No one recalled a moment of saying yes
to hammer and saw, or anything else.
Each looked to the others for some defining
move—the way at lunch without a word
all would start to rise when the foreman
closed the lid of his lunchbox—but
none came. The senior of us leaned
against a peach tree marked for demolition,
seemed almost careful not to give a sign.
And I, as I am likely to do—and who
knows, but maybe we all were—beginning
to notice the others there, and ourselves
among them, as if we could be strangers suddenly,
like those few evenings we had chosen to meet
at some bar and appeared to each other
in our street clothes—that was the sense—
of a glass over a fellow creature's fate.
A hundred feet above our stillness
on the ground we could hear a breeze
that seemed to blow the moment past,
trifling with the leaves; we watched
a ranging hawk float past. It was the time
of morning when housewives return
alone from morning errands. Something
we had all witnessed a hundred times before,
but this time with new interest. And all of us
felt the slight loosening of the way things were,
as if working or not working were a matter
of choice, and who we were didn't
matter, if not always, at least for that hour.

Sledgehammer's Song

The way you hold the haft,
The way it climbs a curve,
   A manswung curve,
The way it undoes what was done.

The way a stake sinks,
  Cement splits or a stud
  Spins off its nails.

The way shoulders shrug.
The way the breezes waft
  And wake and tease a cheek,
The way it undoes what was done.
The way a cabinet cracks
  And rakes and bares
  The nail-scarred wall beneath.

The way a stance is spread,
The way the steel head pings
  And thrums and thuds,
The way it undoes what was done.
The way a bathtub breaks:
  Pieces barrowed, porcelain
  Left in a bin.

The way sight is stark.
The way the weight wills the arms,
  The back and heart,
The way it undoes what was done.
The way the weight is weighed,
  Stalling the swing,
  The sorrow mid-arc.

The Furrow

Your father must have held you up beneath the arms
to see your grandfather's body. What you saw
you don't remember, just a memory of yourself
seeing and the feeling of hanging in his hands.
Maybe he believed the only answer was to see,
and raised you up as if to say: Look—nothing

is there. Sadness then was only a lesson to recite
in the heart, wanting earnestly to please, attentive
to the soberness that buttoned a white dress shirt,
snugged a dark tie against your Adam's apple.

Rushing homeward in the dim back seat—anywhere
you might have stopped on the road that night:
those familiar furrows of dust when you got out
to pee in the gloom of the Central Valley, your
figure hidden in the shade of vines while the stars
above the highway churned. Half of everyone you
would ever love waiting back in the car as the engine
cooled, their voices eased beneath the whirr of crickets.
Forty years past. What lessons learned? Few, or none—
mainly the force of life behind now, raising you up.

Jean Valentine

Jean Valentine is the author of nine books of poetry, most recently *Door in the Mountain: New and Collected Poems, 1965-2003* (Wesleyan University Press, 2004). She lives and works in New York City.

High School Boyfriend

You were willing to like me, and I did something,
and blew it,
and your liking me would have saved me,
and my liking you would have saved you,

that was the circle I was walking around,
pushing a bar that moved a wheel
down in the dark, holding my breath,
naked in a long hard army coat of you,
hating my feet, hating my path...

Today my tongue is a fish's tongue,
kissing my friend's light breastbone, his chestnut down;

full of tears, full of light, half both,
nowhere near my old home: no one anywhere
is so wrong.

Barrie's Dream, the Wild Geese

"I dreamed about Elizabeth Bishop
and Robert Lowell—an old Penguin book
of Bishop's poetry—a thick china cup
and a thick china sugar bowl, square,
cream-colored, school stuff.
                                        And Lowell was there,
he was talking and talking to us,
he was saying, 'She is the best—'
Then the geese flew over,
and he stopped talking. Everyone stopped talking,
because of the geese."
                                        The sound of their wings!
Oars rowing, laborious, wood against wood: it was
a continuing thought, no, it was a labor,
how to accept your lover's love. Who could do it alone?
Under our radiant sleep they were bearing us all night long.

Snow Landscape, in a Glass Globe

in memory of Elizabeth Bishop

A thumb's-length landscape: Snow, on a hill
in China. I turn the glass ball over in my hand,
and watch the snow
blow around the Chinese woman,
calm at her work,
carrying her heavy yoke

uphill, towards the distant house.
Looking out through the thick glass ball
she would see the lines of my hand,
unearthly winter trees, unmoving, behind the snow . . .

No more elders.
The Boston snow grays and softens
the streets where you were...
Trees older than you, alive.

The snow is over and the sky is light.
Pale, pale blue distance...
Is there an east? A west? A river?
There, can we live right?

I look back in through the glass. You,
in China, I can talk to you.
The snow has settled; but it's cold
there, where you are.

What are you carrying?
For the sake of what? through such hard wind
and light.
            —And you look out to me,
and you say, "Only the same as everyone; your breath,
your words, move with mine,
under and over this glass; we who were born
and lived on the living earth."

The River at Wolf

Coming east we left the animals
pelican beaver osprey muskrat and snake
their hair and skin and feathers
their eyes in the dark: red and green.
Your finger drawing my mouth.

Blessed are they who remember
that what they now have they once longed for.

A day a year ago last summer
God filled me with himself, like gold, inside,
deeper inside than marrow.

This close to God this close to you:
walking into the river at Wolf with
the animals. The snake's
green skin, lit from inside. Our second life.

Ellen Bryant Voigt

Ellen Bryant Voigt has published six books of poetry—*Claiming Kin, The Forces of Plenty, The Lotus Flowers, Two Trees, Kyrie* (a National Book Critics' Circle Award finalist), and *Shadow of Heaven* (a National Book Award Finalist)—as well as *The Flexible Lyric,* a collection of essays. A Chancellor of the Academy of American Poets, she teaches in the Warren Wilson College low-residency MFA program.

The Waterfall

Meeting after twenty years apart,
I ask my friend to give me back myself
at nineteen, but he can't, or won't:
Sunny, he says, and quick to speak your mind.
Then he asks if he has aged,
if he looks the same—who had always seemed
so satisfied, past need, past harm.
At every stop we stare at each other,
returning to the other's face as though
it were a wind-rucked pond we hope will clear.
And slowly, as we spiral up the mountain,
looking for landmarks, the road

a narrow shelf on the wooded slopes, I realize
he's terrified of me; and since he cannot yet
know who I am, begin to see myself as I was then:
implacable:
                    but that's not the word he flung at me
beside the shaded pool, the blanket smoothed,
the picnic barely opened.
That was years ago;
now we have the usual pleasantries,
trade photographs, his family and mine,
their fixed improbable faces.
                                        Eventually,
we find the general store, the left-turn fork
the hidden waterfall still
battering the rocks,
and the ease of recognition makes me old.
Standing close enough to feel the spray,
looking up at the falls, its powerful
inexhaustible rush of water,
I think that art has ruined my life,
fraught as it is with what's exceptional.

But that's not true; at the start, at nineteen,
I wanted it all,
every exhilaration, every grief—

acquisitive was what he said.
How could I have hurt him?
Such a new candle, just lit, burning, burning.

The Lotus Flowers

The surface of the pond was mostly green—
bright green algae reaching out from the banks,
then the mass of waterlilies, their broad round leaves
rim to rim, each white flower spreading
from the center of a green saucer.

We teased and argued, choosing the largest,
the sweetest bloom, but when the rowboat
lumbered through and rearranged them,
we found the plants were anchored, the separate
muscular stems descending in the dense water—
only the most determined put her hand
into that frog-slimed pond
to wrestle with a flower. Back and forth
we pumped across the water, in twos and threes,
full of brave adventure. On the marshy shore,
the others hollered for their turns,
or at the hem of where we pitched the tents
gathered firewood—
                              this was wilderness,
although the pond was less than half an acre
and we could still see the grand magnolias
in the village cemetery, their waxy
white conical blossoms gleaming in the foliage.
A dozen girls, the oldest only twelve, two sisters
with their long braids, my shy neighbor,
someone squealing without interruption:
all we didn't know about the world buoyed us,
as the frightful water sustained and moved the flowers
tethered at a depth we couldn't see.

In the late afternoon, before they'd folded
into candles on the dark water,
I went to fill the bucket at the spring.
Deep in the pines, exposed tree roots
formed a natural arch, a cave of black loam.
I raked off the skin of leaves and needles,
leaving a pool so clear and shallow
I could count the pebbles
on the studded floor. The sudden cold
splashing up from the bucket to my hands
made me want to plunge my hand in—
and I held it under, feeling the shock that wakes
and deadens, watching first my fingers,
then the ledge beyond me,
the snake submerged and motionless,

the head propped on its coils the way a girl
crosses her arms before her on the sill
and rests her chin there.
                            Lugging the bucket
back to the noisy clearing, I found nothing changed,
the boat still rocked across the pond,
the fire straggled and cracked as we fed it
branches and debris into the night,
leaning back on our pallets—
spokes in a wheel—learning the names of the many
constellations, learning how each fixed
cluster took its name:
not from the strongest light, but from the pattern
made by stars of lesser magnitude,
so like the smaller stars we rowed among.

Plaza del Sol

This is a veterans' ward, here by the pool
in Florida, where every chaise is taken, every frame
stretched out to full extension, the bodies just removed
from cold storage, exposing to light and air
the wound, the scar, the birthmark's crushed grape,
contiguous chins undisguised by pearls,
pitted shoulders plumped or scapular, flesh
pleated under an upper arm, a vast loaf rising
out of the bathing bra, or chest collapsed
and belly preeminent, spine a trough
or a knotted vine climbing the broad cliff-wall.
Down from this pelvic arch five children came;
that suspicious mole, his mother kissed;
but who will finger such calves, their rosaries?
Here's a brace of ankles like water-balloons;
here's a set of toes shingled with horn.
Here is the man, prone, whose back is a pelt,
and the supine woman whose limbs are tinkertoys,
and the man whose tattooed eagle looks crucified,

and his brother with breasts, and his wife with none—
a woman tanned already, dried fruit arranged on a towel—
and her pale sister, seated, bosom piled in her lap,
oiling the lunar landscape of her thighs.
The hot eye over them all does not turn away
from bodies marooned inside loose colorful rags
or bursting their bandages there at the lip of the cave—
from ropy arms, or the heavy sack at the groin,
or the stone of the head—bodies mapped
and marbled, rutted, harrowed, warmed at last,
while everyone else has gone off into the sea.

Winter Field

The winter field is not
the field of summer lost in snow: it is
another thing, a different thing.

"We shouted, we shook you," you tell me,
but there was no sound, no face, no fear, only
oblivion—why shouldn't it be so?

After they'd pierced a vein and fished me up,
after they'd reeled me back they packed me under
blanket on top of blanket, I trembled so.

The summer field, sun-fed, mutable,
has its many tasks; the winter field
becomes its adjective.
                         For those hours
I was some other thing and my body,
which you have long loved well,
did not love you.

Judith Vollmer

Judith Vollmer is the author of three full-length collections of poetry—*Reactor* and *Level Green* (University of Wisconsin Press), and *The Door Open To The Fire* (Cleveland State University Press)—and the limited edition collection *Black Butterfly*, awarded the Center for Book Arts Prize. She is the recipient of grants from the National Endowment for the Arts and the Pennsylvania Council on the Arts, and residency fellowships from Yaddo and the American Academy in Rome. Vollmer directs the creative writing program at the University of Pittsburgh at Greensburg and co-edits the poetry journal *5 AM*.

Early Snow

It was coming down hard so the teacher motioned the flute
then the piano quiet and the children sang

a cappella, teacher's voice was gone, they screaked and worked
their lungs & shoulders like gulls, they swooped and cranked

it up, it was wonderful being all alone,
they could hear pauses, one by two by one, then she

ran to the edge of the world, opened it and thrust the dark
sleeve of her dress out & down into the whirlpools

and when a flake landed crisp & complete on the black
wool she ran to every desk then back for more until

she showed every voice a new jewel, an alien, autotelic
shape. What would you like to be, or who, or would you

go with the wind sweeping the parking lot & small bank of trees.

Spill

Before, I spoke of clear things,
shadows on white tile, men in paper suits
mopping the radiated water with Kotex pads
trucked in through the security dock, 1960. Now
I see blurry grasses swaying in dusk, the starless
sky & vaporous shapes of a Pennsylvania
town behind wire fences, there in the misty
place beyond the woods. I hear a truck
sputtering with cheap gas, & boot soles
slapping cement. *Is that my Uncle Ray*
running toward the truck, away? No, he's inside
with his men cleaning the burning place
protecting the core. Dawn is a swollen eye
they work toward. Those must be cattails
waving over the marshland, those must be geese
making that slapping leather sound of flight.

She Kept Me

wrapped & close & fragrant
in her incense of strange lemon soap.
She carried me down, all the way down
into her solitude, lace & bones was all
she was under the t-shirt

faded to watered black silk, thin
as her night veils, dreams

of wet earth, spring, Amsterdam
where she hung with the houseboat boys,
loading bricks of blond hash safely on;
she nursed their sore throats with concentrations
of aspirin & oranges. Spent her money on
artcards & books with blue wrappers.
Whores in windows moved
their lips like bright candies
and petals drifted down

onto my dark woven shoulders
& the three weeks we had,
hotels, of course, also her parents'
canalside perch where I held her
while she read her Stendhal, her Colette,
the stitches of my devotion
weight she counted on
for *quiet, let's find the exact point of focus, now that's desire,
isn't it?* O it is sex, mother
of all creative energies, books, & companion views.

I liked her
in the cool air of her balcony nights.
I was left on a train and once in a musty café.
I was handed down, yes, but never
taken up so fondly.

Sidney Wade

photo by Marion Ettlinger

Sidney Wade has published four collections of poems, the most recent of which is *Celestial Bodies* (LSU Press, 2002). Her poems appear regularly in a wide variety of journals, including *Poetry, The New Yorker, Grand Street, Paris Review, The New Republic, The Gettysburg Review,* and *Harper's.* She has taught at the University of Florida in the Creative Writing Program since 1993.

Insurance

I'm recklessly flying
my wind-sheared bicycle
no sun-screen no cell phone

I'm loose on the sun-drowned
prairie and chirping *Look
Ma no goddamned helmet*

and Ma at this moment
is standing her fragile-
boned crooked old frame as

straight as she can on the
ledge of her stair-chair and
pushing the button and

rising like a goddess
from the dark undertow
borne upward on a shell

yet bound of course to fall
and it's clear that we need
a policy for when

imagination fails
when an ocean of fact
and white foaming despair

rushes up the hard legs
and submerges the heart
of the headstrong rider

when the tangy salt smell
disaster brings powders
our transported bodies

and threatens our moving
and most always precise
navigations which are

full of prolific doubt
but dazzlingly feathered
and fabulously real

Ants and a Little, Vicious Pig

In a paradigmatic shift in the history
of bloodshed, sacking and carnage,

they liberate the poor from the ferociously horned toad
then nudge them through harm's gate

and call it a blessing. This immaculate perception
issues from the palaver caravan of a foster human

and follows a great bloating of the vital tongue.
Fat hands are thrust deep into pockets of resistance,

where the vulnerable fling stones,
helpless at the edge of billowing death.

Privilege's minions will keep it swelling,
that rushing and lucrative sorrow river.

Snake

A Rough Green Snake daydreams on the bike trail
in the sun, an elegant ribbon of olive light.
We are alone in the world, a solitude of two,
in a formal dimension of our own making, a rite
not of passage but of recognition.
Understood, again, the manumission
of the heart of light, how the body translates heat
into form and color—a fine green tale.

Leaving Train

I'm stepping off the Hallelujah Line.
We've rattled down the concourse trunk and hollered
on the bed but now the ties have followed
that wayward track into an unbenign
new distance. Nostalgia bees are fine
when buzzing round a spray of rhododendrons,
but here they sting and bring to life a somber,
vast and achy past. Let's never mind.

I wish we'd known the great highways of love.
Altissimo in seventh gear. The high,
pure dance of sustenance. Here, though, we seem
to founder in the trackless grass. Above
my head a single star wields its light
like a scimitar. I'm on the road. I steam.

Charles Harper Webb

Charles Harper Webb's most recent book of poems, *Tulip Farms and Leper Colonies*, was published in 2001 by BOA Editions, Ltd. In 2002, the University of Iowa Press published *Stand Up Poetry: An Expanded Anthology*, edited by Webb. *Hot Popsicles,* his book of prose poems, will be published by the University of Wisconsin Press in 2005. Recipient of grants from the Whiting and Guggenheim foundations, he teaches at California State University, Long Beach.

Cocksucker

I thought it was a myth, tied with *motherfucker*
for the World's Most Disgusting Thing.
Just because some poor kid couldn't throw a ball,
or run, or talk without a lisp, didn't make him
a fairy, fruitcake, queen, queer, pansy, homo,
flaming fag—didn't mean he would do *that*.

My opinion made some say I must be one, and let me
practice the right cross-left hook Dad taught me.
When Sammy Blevins, Taft High's choir teacher,
got the spirit and proclaimed he'd been "an evil
Sodomite till saved by Jesus' love" (Jesus Gonzales,
jokers sneered)—I admitted *cocksuckers* were real.

Still, I had doubts until Del Delancey hired me
to play guitar for the Delmations, and we caught rainbow
trout and wrote neo-doowop and roomed together
on the road, and I had girls stay over, but he never did,
and when the band broke up, he said, "I love you, Chuck,"
and cried, certain I'd hate him. "It's hell," he said—

the hot iron boiling in his gut, the dark well
where, like that unkillable giant in Grimm's Tales, he hid
his heart. Remembering times I'd called some slow
driver or loudmouth drunk a cocksucker, I said,
"It's no big deal, Del." But I edged away.
"They do it up the Hershey Highway like I like it,"

he wrote from Mexico—to punish me?—and he was gone,
folded and packed into the chest where I keep painful things
safe, out of sight. But then today I heard a joke
about a cork soaker, a Coke stocker, and a sock cutter.
When I told my wife, she said, "A good cocksucker's
what I pray to be."

                    Please, God, take care of Del.
Lead him safely through the long valley of AIDS.
Give him health, a hacienda, and a man
who worships him and does everything he likes.
Tell him for me—dream, telepathy, vision, it's up to You—
Del, my friend, you cocksucker, I loved you too.

The Lost One

A girl forgets one pill, and you step through
a crimson door into this world. Crisis
who catches hold and grows, you catalyze

long talks: "soul-searching" that is less about
deciding "What is right?" than "How can I
get out of this?" Like Arctic air, your life

brings storms. One future grandfather slaps
the body in which you've appeared;
the other runs to find a doctor and the cash

to undo what his boy has done. Long-distance
calls proliferate as you drift
in the dark: budding astronaut on your umbilical.

Do you sense the airplane leaping
through the air; the small white room with no
mirror, the other girls pushing their big

bellies like prams? Do you hear the nuns'
low voices mix their broth of envy, compassion,
contempt? Each day your walls compress you

more. You share your host's panic
when they contract and squeeze. Shoved into light,
you gasp corrosive air, and howl. The blurs

around you are faces (though you can't focus
your eyes). Your host is wheeled away without
a kiss goodbye. The couple bending over you

coo *Mommy, Daddy,* as they drive you home—
farther from me. Still, sometimes
I think I feel you, as one twin will sense

the other—as if part of me that seemed lost,
still survives. I feel glad unaccountably,
and I think, "Daughter—is that you?"

Vikings

Overran my boyhood dreams—fierce
Blond beards, slab-chests,
Biceps gripped by bronze bands,
Dragon ships which terrorized my ancestors,
Weak Britons who whined to Christ:

No match for Odin, and the hard hammer
Of Thor. While other kids clutched

Toy guns and grenades, I swung
My plastic war ax: immune to bullets,
Refusing to die. While they dreamed

Of rocketing through sunny skies,
I dreamed of fjords, their crags and storms
Matching my dark moods, my doubts
Of God, my rages and my ecstasies.
I snuck in twice to see *The Norseman,*

Wincing but bearing it as the Saxon king
Chopped off Prince Gunnar's right
Hand. I gloried in the sulking gods
And ravens and great trees, roots
Reaching underground to realms

Of dwarfs and trolls. I gloried in the runes
On shields, the long oar strokes
That sliced through ocean cold as steel.
I gloried in the Valkyries, bearing slain
Heroes to the mead halls of Valhalla

To feast and fight and fondle blonde
Beauties forever, while we sad
Methodists plucked harps and fluttered:
Sissies mommy had to dress
For Sunday school. The day before

Christmas vacation, when Danny Flynn
Called me "a fish-lipped fool,"
I grabbed a trashcan lid and slammed
It like a war shield in his face,
Then leapt over his blood and bawling

And—while teachers shrilled their whistles,
And Mr. Bean, the porky principal,
Scurried for his ax—thrust my sword-
Hand in my shirt and stalked out
Into the cruel winter of third grade.

Baron Wormser

Baron Wormser is the author of six books of poetry and the co-author of two books about teaching poetry. He co-directs the Frost Place Conference on Poetry and Teaching and directs the Frost Place Seminar in addition to teaching in the Stonecoast MFA program. He lives with his wife in Hallowell, Maine.

Rudinsky's, 1953

In the back of my grandfather's delicatessen
The waiters talked about the bad things.
Dropping dishes, that was more than bad,
It was a curse, a shame on the profession.
That's what they called it, a profession.
Nowadays that means sitting through college
But there was a lot to it—you had to be swift
And deft, you had to be strong, you had to be patient,
You had to be calm. Lots of qualities.

Like monkeys, diners did all sorts of things.
They weren't just there to eat. The families
Maybe but the couples had other thoughts.
But the bad things—slipping was a bad thing,

Not adding up a check correctly, setting
The wrong dish down, forgetting to pour the water.
The waiters watched for each other and looked out for each other.
They were mothers and brothers to each other.

Have you ever been on your legs for ten hours straight?
Do it for thirty years and we'll talk about it.

The waiters knew everything there was to know
About the human disgrace (as they called it).
To keep their wits alert they bet on the size
Of a tip before a party sat down. They bet
On how many drinks, which desserts, sugar in
The coffee, how many trips to the can.
Clothes, eyes, manners, speech:
Everything was a fact or a hint—
One day or another everything had happened.
Farters, no-tippers, complainers,
Drunks, check-skippers, glass-breakers.
It was a reputable place but people were
Going to be people no matter where they were.
Women stuffed pickles in their pocketbooks,
Men grabbed handfuls of toothpicks.
The worst thing was a lady making eyes at you.
Only misery could come of that. One night
A fellow threw a plate of blintzes at a waiter,
"Bothering my girl, you lousy Jew."
They shook their heads and made disgusted faces.

You could know everything, that was the funny part,
But it didn't help. As in a dream you saw
It before it was going to happen but still it happened.
Like the Nazis or rain or when you go to get
The last piece of cheesecake and it's not there.

A Quiet Life

What a person desires in life
  is a properly boiled egg.
This isn't as easy as it seems.
There must be gas and a stove,
    the gas requires pipelines, mastodon drills,
    banks that dispense the lozenge of capital.
There must be a pot, the product of mines
    and furnaces and factories,
    of dim early mornings and night-owl shifts,
    of women in kerchiefs and men with
    sweat-soaked hair.
Then water, the stuff of clouds and skies
    and God knows what causes it to happen.
There seems always too much or too little
    of it and more pipelines, meters, pumping
    stations, towers, tanks.
And salt—a miracle of the first order,
    the ace in any argument for God.
    Only God could have imagined from
    nothingness the pang of salt.
Political peace too. It should be quiet
    when one eats an egg. No political hoodlums
    knocking down doors, no lieutenants who are
    ticked off at their scheming girlfriends and
    take it out on you, no dictators
    posing as tribunes.
It should be quiet, so quiet you can hear
    the chicken, a creature usually mocked as a type
    of fool, a cluck chained to the chore of her body.
Listen, she is there, pecking at a bit of grain
    that came from nowhere.

Draft Morning (1969)

I'd been taking low-dosage downers for a couple of years—
Not to the point of being melodramatically
Addicted but not able to look life in the face
Without the helpful hand of pharmacology either.
And I'd been talking to a shrink who kept
An unlit cigar in his mouth and went to Wellfleet
For a month in the summer and who nodded
Occasionally as I babbled and even less
Occasionally asked me a question—"When did
That happen, Baron?" or "Who said that to you?"
That upon later reflection seemed so mundane
As to make my stomach churn with grief.

A mellow hell, my mother dying of cancer in bits
And pieces, lying in a hospital bed, her eyes
Unfocused, her spirit buried beneath painkillers
So that she seemed an ethereal zombie or a super-
Annuated piece of machinery, a relic of a purpose.
And the war that followed you into the grocery store
Checkout aisle so that when I looked up from the jars
Of gefilte fish for my grandmother and the newest
Sugar-dosed cereals for my younger sisters,
There were the newsmagazines with photos of leaders,
Helicopters, and increasingly, snapshots from their
High school yearbooks of guys who'd been blown away.
We knew, of course, what we were doing. That's what
The living have the right to say although I wasn't much
Of a true believer and one day when I picked up my
Dodge Dart at the garage where I'd gotten the brake
Shoes replaced, Joe Flaherty, the family mechanic whom
I'd known since childhood asked me how I was doing
And in response, out of the exasperated blue, I said,
"The war bites it" and he walked around the counter
And put his face directly up to mine and told me
I was a poor excuse for an American,
That brave men were dying in that jungle this minute
While I spouted my two-bit opinions. I thought
There was more sadness in his voice than rage.

So when one cool and celestially clear autumn
Morning I walked into a downtown building that seemed
Like a cross between an old hotel and an armory,
I wasn't afraid or confident but numb and zoned-out.
There was instant camaraderie and instant wariness
And most of all a lot of scoffing because that's really all
A nineteen-year-old can do is scoff at the quiet weight
On his tender shoulders, scoffing at death and the army
And girlfriends and parents and other guys, scoffing
At everything. So when I looked in the eyes of the bored
And harassed army shrink, I knew I was at one
Of those bridges that takes you somewhere you didn't know
About or even want to know about if you were willing
To step out of line and be half-honest with yourself.
I told him I couldn't do it, and he said in a voice
Just like his eyes, "Is that so, son? Is that so?"
And wrote something down on a carbon paper form and
Blurted out "next" as he motioned me away from
His uncluttered desk.
                                  Three blocks away in the pale
Late-afternoon light I threw a vial of pills
Into the gutter—a self-conscious, self-loathing gesture—
And I sat a long time at the steering wheel, not
Turning the key, quivering like some bug
In its inordinate flight.

Anti-Depressant

What a pig happiness is. Plus
I'm a body living with an anti-body.
You probably don't know how that goes.
One of my hang-ups is my trying to tell you:

The pills tell me to let sincerity lapse.
I used to talk a true blue streak but now
I honor mute science as dryly as
The next atheist. I'm chemical

And it hurts. The calibrations come and go;
Research works overtime. I should be pleased
And some days am. It wavers and feints
And my smile is ghastly but I can walk down
A street and see the ratty English sparrows
Foraging in the litter and not start to cry.

Mark Wunderlich

photo by Mary Jane Dean

Mark Wunderlich is the author of *The Anchorage,* which received the 1999 Lambda Literary Award, and *Voluntary Servitude,* published in 2004 by Graywolf Press. He teaches at Bennington College and lives in New York's Hudson River Valley.

Soprano Authority

The mist persisted and the fog persisted.
The magnolia held the globes of flowers in its hands,
and the mass with its unavoidable conclusion

played on the stereo—*O Lamb of God,*
with tender steps I tread—
with its progressions—B flat, A flat minor—Rome

did burn again, did burn again.
The two lay on the floor and the fire burned
behind its grate, while the mist thickened the night,

the streetlights held their yellow globes,
and the two listened to the recorded voice
of one of the men, his voice a boy's pure soprano,

notes he will never reach again.
The two listened to the mass, with its inevitable conclusion—
the wood brace hung with the body of a man,

a sorrow so large it could contain the whole world,
the voice on the stereo a voice without ache,
without tremor, gone now,

except for this recording,
which they rewind and listen to again,
one man hearing with quickening intent,

the other listening to what he has lost—
the bell and burn and soft treading steps—
a boy's voice buried in the throat of a man.

Water Snake

My grandmother fed it bits of ground meat,

taught it to come when she clapped her hands, or whistled.

The creature spent its days lolling about the boat house.

Its presence repelled the rats.

The Mississippi lapped its filthy water against corrugated summers

as I jigged my fishing line over the boat house rail.

The snake looped and glided over the tin roof.

It undulated a thousand tiny muscles to do so.

The sight of it nauseated me—

how it moved like waves of heat rising off a road.

I detest anything that crawls on its belly,

harbors a pallid heart wet with cool blood.

At night, it slid among the bulrushes at the rocky shore

or twisted like a cipher through the black water in search of frogs.

Afternoons, it absorbed the heat of the day

rousing itself only when it heard that familiar whistle

and rose up to receive the gift of flesh

arcing toward it through the air.

Dream of Archaeology

On the desert hardpan, we set our brushes twitching
to uncover the chips scattered across what had once been a temple.

Nine gates opened in the wind, nine gates no longer visible.
Soon, I found the broken tibia, the net of bones

I recognized as human and my own brush dusted away
the crumbled attar of the grave.

Dust rose up. A shape announced itself to me. Inside
the cracked bowl of a pelvis my mind sketched in a face.

A thing was carried there that met the world with its wet and blood-tender
face. The sun sent down its burning sentence, even and ill-willed

as we disturbed the sleeping mother I begged would forgive
this intrusion. Though my question would be answered with decay.

Dean Young

Dean Young has published six
books of poetry, most recently,
Elegy on Toy Piano (University
of Pittsburgh Press, 2005).
He teaches in the Iowa Writers'
Workshop and the Warren
Wilson low-residency MFA
program.

I See a Lily on Thy Brow

It is 1816 and you gash your hand unloading
a crate of geese, but if you keep working
you'll be able to buy a bucket of beer
with your potatoes. You're probably 14 although

no one knows for sure and the whore you sometimes
sleep with could be your younger sister
and when your hand throbs to twice its size
turning the fingernails green, she knots

a poultice of mustard and turkey grease
but the next morning, you wake to a yellow
world and stumble through the London streets
until your head implodes like a suffocated

fire stuffing your nose with rancid smoke.
Somehow you're removed to Guy's Infirmary.
It's Tuesday. The surgeon will demonstrate
on Wednesday and you're the demonstration.

Five guzzles of brandy then they hoist you
into the theater, into the trapped drone
and humid scuffle, the throng of students
a single body staked with a thousand peering

bulbs and the doctor begins to saw. Of course
you'll die in a week, suppurating on a camphor-
soaked sheet but now you scream and scream,
plash in a red river, in sulfuric steam

but above you, the assistant holding you down,
trying to fix you with sad, electric eyes
is John Keats.

Cotton in a Pill Bottle

I love the fog. It's not one hundred degrees.
It's not Mary sobbing on the phone or powder-
white mildew killing the rose. My father
lost inside it keeps pretending he's dead
just so he can get a little peace.
It's not made of fire or afraid of fire
like me, it has nothing to do with smoke.
There's never any ash, anything to sift through.
You just put your hand on the yellow rail
and the steps seem to move themselves.
It doesn't have a job to do.
It's morning all afternoon.
It loves the music but would be
just as happy listening to the game.
Still, I don't know what frightens me.

It doesn't blame anyone.
You'll never see tears on its cheeks.
It'll never put up a fight.
I love how the fog lies down in the air,
how it can get only so far from the sea.

How I Get My Ideas

Sometimes you just have to wait
15 seconds then beat the prevailing nuance
from the air. If that doesn't work,
try to remember how many times
you've wakened in the body of an animal,
two arms, two legs, willowy antennae.
Try thinking what it would be like
to never see your dearest again.
Stroke her gloves, sniff his overcoat.
If that's a no-go, call Joe
who's never home but keeps changing
the melody of his message.
Cactus at night emits its own light,
the river flows under the sea.
Dear face I always recognize but never
know, everything has a purpose
from which it must be freed,
maybe with crowbars, maybe the gentlest breeze.
Always turn in the direction of the skid.
If it's raining, use the rain
to lash the windowpanes or,
in a calmer mode, deepen the new greens
nearly to a violet. I can't live
without violet although it's red
I most often resort to.
Sometimes people become angelic when they cry,
sometimes only ravaged.

Technically, Mary still owes me a letter,
her last was just porcupine quills and tears,
tears that left a whitish residue
on black construction paper.
Sometimes I look at used art books at Moe's
just to see women without their clothes.
How can someone so rich,
who can have fish whenever he wants,
go to baseball games,
still feel such desperation?
I'm afraid I must insist
on desperation. By the fourth week
the embryo has nearly turned itself
inside out. If that doesn't help,
you'll just have to wait which
may involve sleeping which may involve
dreaming and sometimes dreaming works.
Father why have you returned,
dirt on your morning vest?
You cannot control your laughter.
You cannot control your love.
You know not to hit the brakes on ice
but do anyway. You bend the nail
but keep hammering because
hammering makes the world.

Acknowledgments

Doug Anderson: "Itinerary," "Blues," and "Xin Loi" are from *The Moon Reflected Fire*. Copyright © 1994 by Doug Anderson. Reprinted by permission of Alice James Books. "New Woman Blues" is from *Blues for Unemployed Secret Police* by Doug Anderson (Curbstone Press, 2000). Distributed by Consortium Book Sales & Dist.

Catherine Barnett: "Refusal," "Evening in the Garden," and "Family Reunion" are from *Into Perfect Spheres Such Holes Are Pierced*. Copyright © 2004 by Catherine Barnett. Reprinted by permission of Alice James Books.

Jan Beatty: "My Father Teaches Me Desire," "My Father Teaches Me Longing," "My Father Teaches Me Light," and "Modern Love" are from *Boneshaker*, by Jan Beatty, copyright © 2002. Reprinted by permission of the University of Pittsburgh Press.

Wendell Berry: "Creation Myth" and "The Current" are from *Collected Poems: 1957-1982*, copyright © 1985 by Wendell Berry. Reprinted by permission of North Point Press, a division of Farrar, Straus and Giroux, LLC. "The Sky Bright after Summer-Ending Rain," "They Sat Together on the Porch," and "The Old Man Climbs a Tree" are from *A Timbered Choir*, copyright © 1998 by Wendell Berry. Reprinted by permission of the author.

George Bilgere: "Pain," "Magellan," and "The Garage" are from *The Good Kiss*, The University of Akron Press, copyright © 2002 by George Bilgere. Reprinted by permission of the University of Akron Press.

Peter Blair: "Litany for Edwin," "Freight Train," and "Death for Breakfast" are from *The Divine Salt*, copyright © 2003 by Peter Blair. Reprinted by permission of Autumn House Press.

Andrea Hollander Budy: "The Hunters," "History," and "A Tree Like This One" are from *The Other Life*, copyright © 2001 by Andrea Hollander Budy. Reprinted by permission of Story Line Press. "Poem in October" first appeared in *Poetry* and is reprinted by permission of the author. Copyright © 2005 by Andrea Hollander Budy.

John Canaday: "By then I'd had it up to here...," "And then the longhairs did it...," and "And I thought I'd seen destruction..." are excerpts from "Major John Dudley." Copyright © 2005 by John Canaday. Reprinted by permission of the author.

Hayden Carruth: "Pittsburgh," "Testament," and "I, I, I" are from *Scrambled Eggs & Whiskey: Poems 1991-1995*, copyright © 1996 by Hayden Carruth. Reprinted with the permission of Copper Canyon Press, P. O. Box 271, Port Townsend, WA 98368-0271.

Judith Cofer: "Gift of a Knife" first appeared in *Prairie Schooner* and is reprinted by permission of the author. Copyright © 2005 by Judith Cofer. "Siempre" is reprinted by permission of the author. Copyright © 2005 by Judith Cofer. "Lessons of the Past" is from *Silent Dancing*, copyright © 1990 by Judith Cofer. Reprinted by permission of Arte Publico Press.

Billy Collins: "Consolation" and "Workshop" are from *The Art of Drowning*, by Billy Collins, copyright © 1995. Reprinted by permission of the University of Pittsburgh Press. "Taking Off Emily Dickinson's

Design and Production

Cover and text design by Kathy Boykowycz

Set in Stone Serif fonts,
designed in 1987 by Sumner Stone

Printed by Thomson-Shore of Dexter, Michigan,
on Natures Natural, a 50% recycled paper